Praise for *Enhanc* *Practices Guide for Innovations in* *Community Colleges*

"The sustaining power of community colleges as disruptive innovation is fostered by the ever-evolving 'Islands of Innovation' that continue to emerge throughout the community college landscape. This book provides thoughtful insights and practical ideas and reinforces the 1969 writings of B. Lamar Johnson, known as the father of community colleges, that innovation occurs throughout the college."—**Rufus Glasper**, PhD, president and CEO, League for Innovation in the Community College; Chancellor Emeritus, Maricopa Community College

"The 2020 pandemic was a catalytic event forcing community colleges to accelerate innovation on campuses across the nation. The authors provide a robust sample of effective practices appropriate for the challenges and opportunities facing colleges today. This book serves not only hope, but models, tools, and approaches anchored in empirical evidence and amplified with voices and experiences of students, faculty, staff, and administrators from across the country. Written for 'practice-ready' leaders, the authors cover topics from supporting minoritized students, building sociocultural capital, assessing student learning outcomes, evaluating technology to support student retention, and professional development for faculty and staff. The post-pandemic world and the national activism around racial equity calls for modernizing the community college mission to prepare students for greater citizenship in their communities and beyond. The authors touch upon these and other topics relevant for other populations traditionally served by community colleges—the economically disadvantaged, first generation, and adult students. In sum, Enhancing Performance is a powerful collection of examples of collaborations that empower leaders within their institutions to experiment and steward in innovative ways, and in service of their students and communities."—**Yves Salomon-Fernández**, PhD, president, Greenfield Community College (Massachusetts)

"A very helpful read. This series of well-curated short essays provides a broad and representative survey of the critical contemporary issues and challenges facing community colleges, drawn from the experiences of institutions from across the nation. Ideas are fresh and innovative, from design thinking in building effective student services to a beliefs-based approach to achieving student success outcomes. They represent some of the best thinking of the emerging generation of leaders who will continue to make community colleges the most relevant institutions of higher education needed to tackle the nation's most significant challenges. This book is an important contribution to the literature, as is Ferris State's contribution to the development of community college leaders as reflected here."—**Don Doucette**, chancellor, Eastern Iowa Community Colleges; previous Associate Director of the League for Innovation in the Community College

"While many books for aspiring community college leaders focus on theory, *Enhancing Performance* delivers the practical, real-world knowledge needed to succeed in a higher education landscape being transformed by rapid economic, technological, and demographic change. The skilled practitioners who authored this important text have drawn on their experience as change agents to produce essential reading for those seeking to enhance their expertise in academic and student affairs, finance, information technology, and compliance and risk management."—**Lee D. Lambert**, JD, chancellor, Pima Community College (Arizona)

"By sharing practitioner-focused strategies for innovation at the community college, this book provides a framework for leaders to ground good decisions and to lead change. The evidence-based approaches described in this book comprise a field guide for future leaders who aspire to make sustainable, student-centered innovation at their institutions." —**Jo Blondin**, PhD, president, Clark State Community College (Ohio)

"This book, informed and influenced by higher education practitioners, provides an engaged higher education graduate student or an emerging or seasoned community college leader with insights on how to ensure success for the students of today who choose to change their lives, destinies, and family trees at a community college. The relevant and real-world student and organizational success examples presented in this book provide the reader or researcher with demonstrated evidence on what currently works in this ever-changing landscape of higher education, especially within Democracy's College, the modern-day Ellis Island of higher education—community colleges."—**John J. "Ski" Sygielski**, MBA, EdD, president and CEO, HACC, Central Pennsylvania's Community College (Pennsylvania)

"Having worked with the DCCL program for several years I find *Enhancing Performance: A Best Practices Guide for Innovations in Community Colleges* to be reflective of the high quality and attention to detail seen in the Ferris State University faculty and staff. What a great professional development opportunity for aspiring leaders in community colleges!"—**Bill Pink**, PhD, president, Grand Rapids Community College (Michigan)

"*Enhancing Performance: A Best Practices Guide for Innovations in Community Colleges* stands as a testament to the positive and long-lasting impact of Ferris State University's Doctorate in Community College Leadership Program. The book takes a comprehensive look at the key issues facing community colleges today. It is an important read for community college leaders committed to action and to making a difference."—**Laurie Chesley**, PhD, president, Central Oregon Community College (Oregon)

Enhancing Performance

Enhancing Performance

A Best Practices Guide for Innovations in Community Colleges

Edited by
Sandra J. Balkema
Roberta C. Teahen

With Cheryl M. Hagen, Margaret Lee, and Bruce Moses

AMERICAN ASSOCIATION OF COMMUNITY COLLEGES

ROWMAN & LITTLEFIELD
Lanham • Boulder • New York • London

Published by Rowman & Littlefield
An imprint of The Rowman & Littlefield Publishing Group, Inc.
4501 Forbes Boulevard, Suite 200, Lanham, Maryland 20706
www.rowman.com

6 Tinworth Street, London SE11 5AL, United Kingdom

British Library Cataloguing in Publication Information Available

Library of Congress Cataloging-in-Publication Data

Names: Balkema, Sandra J., 1954– editor. | Teahen, Roberta C., 1945– editor.
Title: Enhancing performance : a best practices guide for innovations in community colleges / edited
    by Sandra J. Balkema, Roberta C. Teahen ; with Cheryl M. Hagen, Margaret Lee, Bruce Moses.
Description: Lanham : Rowman & Littlefield, [2021] | Includes bibliographical references. | Sum-
    mary: "This collection of essays from community college leaders across the country addresses
    the challenges facing today's community colleges and provides practical, successful solutions
    their institutions have implemented. Topics include creating agile institutions, engaging students
    and faculty in learning, and responding to changing needs."—Provided by publisher.
Identifiers: LCCN 2020055345 (print) | LCCN 2020055346 (ebook) | ISBN 9781475858327 (cloth) |
    ISBN 9781475858334 (paperback) | ISBN 9781475858341 (epub)
Subjects: LCSH: Community colleges—United States—Administration. | Educational innovations—
    United States.
Classification: LCC LB2328 .E54 2021 (print) | LCC LB2328 (ebook) | DDC 378.1/5430973—dc23
LC record available at https://lccn.loc.gov/2020055345
LC ebook record available at https://lccn.loc.gov/2020055346

Contents

Introduction

Leadership Matters!

Roberta C. Teahen

NEW LEADERS NEEDED

Many have written about the impending challenge of finding sufficient, well-qualified leaders for America's community colleges (Smith, 2017; Aspen Institute, 2017). In raising this leadership concern, the authors typically refer to senior-level positions, especially presidents. According to the American Association of Community Colleges (AACC; 2018a), "In 2016, more than 50% of the presidents of colleges that award associate degrees reported that they anticipated stepping down within the next five years."

As the essays that follow will reveal, much of the vital leadership for our colleges will be found below the level of president or vice president, and colleges would benefit from ensuring that talented leadership exists throughout the organization. Indeed, it has become increasingly evident in these times of the pandemic, economic uncertainties, and civil unrest provoked by systemic racism that the real "mission" work is achieved at the front lines of our communities and enterprises. This introduction reviews some approaches to developing both next-generation and every-level leaders to realize what Kouzes and Posner (2019) referred to as "enabling others to act" (p. 10).

PREPARING NEW LEADERS FOR MISSION/VISION ACHIEVEMENT

If leaders want to champion innovation, an entrepreneurial culture, and an enhanced learning environment for all, leadership development and empowerment must permeate the organization. AACC addressed this shift in emphasis from top leaders to leaders at all levels with its publication of the third edition of its *AACC Competencies for Community College Leaders*, where they acknowledge the goal "to prepare leaders capable of spearheading change at all levels within the institution" (AACC, 2018b, p. 2). The AACC document describes the essential roles that faculty, mid-level managers, senior leaders, and presidents will play in functional areas such as advocacy and mobilizing/motivating others.

New models of leadership are necessary to achieve our highest purposes; enable our colleges to nurture graduates who will be competent, ethical, collaborative, and civically engaged; continue the work of creating a more just society; and lead transformational efforts that increasingly rely on teamwork and technology. More diverse leaders are also needed. The Aspen Institute (2017) noted that there are "inadequate systems for preparing diverse and nontraditional candidates for the presidency." While progress has been made in the proportion of senior leaders who are female or non-White, they are still underrepresented when considering the composition of student enrollments of our colleges. Developing more leaders within the organization heightens the likelihood that more diverse candidates will be prepared for subsequent senior-level positions.

Kouzes and Posner (2019) observed that "inspiring a shared vision" is one of the five practices of exemplary leadership. Just having a vision, however, is not enough. They wrote: "One of *the* most important practices of leadership is giving life and work a sense of meaning and purpose by offering an exciting vision of the future that could be better than what exists at the moment" (Kouzes & Posner, 2019, p. 48).

Achieving desired missions and visions requires broad-based engagement and leadership at all levels of the organization. One important task of leaders is development of others, yet the complexities of keeping colleges operating each day often preclude an intentional approach to developing next-generation leaders. On this significance, Gallup (2018) reported, "Cultures that win bring together highly talented individuals and provide them with the support they need to do what they do best, to grow and to develop."

A LEADERSHIP DOCTORATE TO MEET TODAY'S NEEDS

Doctoral programs contribute to leadership development in two ways: First, higher-level leadership roles often require completion of a doctorate degree; and second, a systems perspective is essential for higher-level leaders. The doctorate in community college leadership (DCCL) at Ferris State University was created to address the development of practice-ready leaders. The 10th anniversary of this program was the impetus for this book, providing a means for us to share the history of our program, our philosophies, and our faculty, advisors, and graduates' innovations.

A study funded by the Kellogg Foundation through a grant to the AACC, *Breaking Tradition: New Community College Leadership Programs* (Amey, 2006), summarized the new approaches to doctoral education for programs that were developed after 2000. Among the features of the programs highlighted were cohort models, structured curricula, accessible delivery, and research support. While the *Breaking Tradition* work may not have directly informed development of the Ferris program, many of these features are embedded, such as the cohort model, accessible delivery, and research support.

DCCL's development team relied heavily on interviews with sitting community college presidents, predominantly from Michigan, in 2008 to 2009. Drs. Robert L. Ewigleben and J. William Wenrich, both former Ferris State University presidents and recognized community college presidents and leaders, were the champions for the program. Dr. Ewigleben and his daughter, Lynne Ewigleben Hernandez, conducted the needs assessment and advocated for the program to Dr. David Eisler, president of Ferris.

The first cohort, enrolling 27 Michigan-based students, began in June 2010. The original DCCL mission, significantly influenced by long-time National Advisory Board member Dr. Gunder Myran (who is also president emeritus of Washtenaw Community College), served the program by maintaining the centrality of sound leadership decision-making: "DCCL empowers graduates to advance community colleges toward excellence and community responsiveness through exemplary leadership" (Ferris State University, n.d.).

MAKING AN IMPACT

Since the admission of the first cohort, Ferris DCCL has produced the following, as examples of its impact:

- Through May 2020, 197 students (current and prospective college leaders) have completed the program.
- An additional 122 current and prospective community college leaders are enrolled as of June 2020.
- By 2023, DCCL will have more than 320 graduates, who are sure to create a "tipping point" in the program's influence in the United States.
- As of 2020, DCCL graduates or students work in 26 states and more than 100 colleges.
- Over 65% of our students/completers are women, reflecting the growing significance of women in college leadership roles.

- Over our 10-year history, 35% of our students have been ethnically diverse; this is especially important given the diversity of community college students and the great need for representative leadership teams.
- The most recent cohorts reflect even greater diversity, with Cohorts 10, Texas 2, and Cohort 11 enrolling over 50% ethnically diverse students.
- Annual surveys of DCCL graduates indicate that more than two-thirds have taken on additional responsibilities or changed jobs during their time in the program.

These statistics and other indicators of program success foretell the impact these leaders will have in serving our communities and enhancing colleges' capabilities to nurture students' success and realize college missions. With their practice-oriented education, DCCL completers are both poised and prepared to contribute to mission achievement and advancement.

HOW DOCTORAL PROGRAMS DEVELOP LEADERS

Doctoral programs focused on community college leadership are one key way leaders of tomorrow will be developed. A survey of community college leaders in California by McNair (2009) found that in addition to doctoral studies, on-the-job training, mentoring, and professional development activities are contributors to leaders' development.

DCCL is distinguished by its practitioner focus, its practitioner faculty, and its emphasis on real-world problems—including those of the student enrollees' colleges. While many doctoral programs take a more theoretical approach and have academic scholars/teachers—many (or most) of whom have no experience in a community college—DCCL relies on the expertise and experience of presidents and other senior-level leaders. Since 2010, programs have come and gone, changed or morphed—the landscape is ever-changing. However, DCCL remains steadfast in its emphasis on an applied focus.

Prior to program launch, Ferris invited community college leaders from across the nation to serve as a National Advisory Board. In addition to Drs. Ewigleben and Wenrich, early members included current and former presidents, Drs. Don Burns, Joyce Elsner, James Jacobs, Ann Mulder, David Ponitz, Laura Meeks, and others over the years. Current membership includes president emeritus of Oakton Community College, Margaret (Peg) Lee; William Serrata, new chair of the AACC; and Johnson County Community College president Andy Bowne. A full list is available on our website (https://www.ferris.edu/ccleadership). Membership continues to evolve to ensure the currency of the board's guidance. This National Advisory Board has played a crucial role in keeping the program relevant and connected, as they routinely contribute ideas about the attributes leaders should possess, the roles successful leaders must fulfill, and the values leaders must embrace. The advisory board considered the type of leaders they envisioned, using the six-word story approach; here are two of many examples of what the program strives to produce:

- "Innovative, global, resourceful, student-focused, transformative."
- "Creative, courageous leader. Committed to community" (DCCL, 2011).

CREATING CULTURES FOR EMPOWERMENT, EQUITY, AND EXCELLENCE

Leaders are most effective in environments that support their leadership and growth. Thus, leadership development does not operate in isolation but must also be considered within the context of where individuals will function. This is where leadership philosophies and practices are significant. Organizations (i.e., senior and mid-level leadership) must be receptive to empowering others to act, encouraging initiative, practicing inclusion, and committing to promoting the excellence and equity that most college missions envision. While leadership philosophies are a guide in creating such cultures, including concepts like shared or authentic leadership, fundamentally the culture will be influenced by how leaders behave and how followers respond.

SHARED LEADERSHIP MODELS

In describing shared leadership, Kezar and Holcombe (2017) observed that conditions "include team empowerment, supportive vertical or hierarchical leaders, autonomy, shared purpose or goal, external coaching, accountability structures, interdependence, fairness of rewards, and shared cognition" (p. v). The authors also observe that leadership is not based on position or authority (Kezar & Holcombe, 2017).

Central to considering the concept of shared leadership is what it can do for the organization. Shared leadership produces increased satisfaction among team members (Robert, 2013); stronger group cohesion (Bergman et al., 2012); increased confidence among individuals and groups (Hooker & Csikszentmihalyi, 2003, as cited in Kezar & Holcombe, 2017); and increased trust among team members (Drescher et al., 2014, as cited in Kezar & Holcombe, 2017). Importantly, Kezar and Holcombe (2017) reported that shared leadership produces increased effectiveness (p. 8).

BEHAVIORS OF SHARED LEADERSHIP LEADERS

Having a shared purpose is one critical ingredient for successful organiza-tions. Listening to and conversing with others are essential behaviors of leaders who will thrive in a shared leadership environment. Senior leaders must relinquish some of their perceived power if the environment is to em-brace leaders as followers and followers as leaders. Relinquishing may be one indication of humility, a trait reflective of the best leaders, according to Collins (2001/2005). As leaders acknowledge that they may not have all of the answers or maybe even all of the questions, they may discover that there are others in the organization with the proper expertise for varied challenges.

A WIDELY EMBRACED AND PROVEN APPROACH

Messages from Kouzes and Posner's (2019) book *Leadership in Higher Edu-cation* have provided evidence on practices compatible with an empowering, effective, and/or shared leadership organization. Their extensive research produced these "practices of exemplary leadership" (pp. 3–4):

1. Model the way;
2. Inspire a shared vision;
3. Challenge the process;
4. Enable others to act; and
5. Encourage the heart.

Incorporating these general ideas into one's leadership approach is sure to be beneficial in enabling more innovative and more productive cultures. In elaborating on the practice of "challenge the process," Kouzes and Posner (2019) wrote:

> When we look at leaders, we see that their work is associated with adversity, uncertainty, hardship, disruption, transformation, transition, recovery, and new beginnings. Sometimes the changes are small and sometimes they are large, but they are all about awakening new possibilities. Leaders don't always have to change history, but they do have to make a change in "business as usual." (p. 69)

In the following chapters, readers will learn of the ways DCCL leaders—faculty and graduates—are contributing to their colleges' missions through inventive approaches, utilization of data to inform interventions, and continu-ous improvement in pursuit of excellence. Examples exist for changing "business as usual" and "awakening new possibilities." One can reasonably speculate that these innovations occur in empowering environments.

Leadership—at all levels—matters!

REFERENCES

American Association of Community Colleges. (2018a, April). *Executive leadership transitions at community colleges*. https://www.aacc.nche.edu/2018/04/30/executive-leadership-transitioning-at-community-colleges.

American Association of Community Colleges. (2018b, November). *AACC competencies for community college leaders* (3rd ed.). https://www.aacc.nche.edu/wp-content/uploads/2018/11/AACC-2018-Competencies_111618_5.1.pdf.

Amey, M. (2006). *Breaking tradition: New community college leadership programs meet 21st-century needs*. A leading forward report. American Association of Community Colleges.

Aspen Institute Task Force on the Future of the College Presidency. (2017, August). *Renewal and progress: Strengthening higher education leadership in a time of rapid change*. https://assets.aspeninstitute.org/content/uploads/2017/05/Renewal_and_Progress_CEP-05122017.pdf?_ga=2.153212856.1273522607.1594593025-572878142.1594593025.

Bergman, J. Z., Rentsch, J. R., Small, E. E., Davenport, S. W., & Bergman, S. M. (2012, January). The shared leadership process in decision-making teams. *The Journal of Social Psychology, 152*(1), 17–42.

Collins, J. (2005, July–August). Level 5 leadership: The triumph of humility and fierce resolve. *Harvard Business Review*, 67–76. (Original work published 2001).

DCCL Program, National Advisory Board. (2011, April 11). National Advisory Board Meeting Minutes. Ferris State University.

Ferris State University. (n.d.). *Extended and international operations*. Retrieved January 11, 2021, from https://www.ferris.edu/HTMLS/administration/academicaffairs/extendedinternational/index.htm.

Kezar, A., & Holcombe, E. (2017). *Shared leadership in higher education: Important lessons from research and practice*. American Council on Education.

Kouzes, J., & Posner, B. (2019). *Leadership in higher education: Practices that make a difference*. Berrett-Koehler Publishers.

McNair, D. (2009). Preparing community college leaders: The AACC core competencies for effective leadership & doctoral education. *Community College Journal of Research and Practice, 34*(1–2), 199–217.

Robert, L. (2013). *A multi-level analysis of the impact of shared leadership in diverse virtual teams* [Proceedings of the 2013 Conference on Computer Supported Cooperative Work]. ACM Press.

Smith, A. (2017, May). *The future of the college presidency*. Inside Higher Education. https://www.insidehighered.com/news/2017/05/15/report-envisions-future-college-presidency.

Part I

Creating Agile Institutions

Successful institutional change requires keeping students and their learning front and center and empowering change agents from across the institutions.

"Innovation and the 21st-Century Community College" opens a new approach to problem-solving, shifting the emphasis on finding the one best answer to identifying a range of better possible solutions. Iterative, human-centered processes enable change management and nurture a culture of collaborative leadership.

"The Power of Connection" focuses on the impact of a human-centered approach to increasing persistence, a critical factor in student success. The Faculty Persistence Project has created a roadmap and strategies to create high-quality relationships with students. When students feel cared for, engaged, and connected, they are much more likely to persist in the pursuit and completion of their educational goals.

"Strategic Enrollment Management: SEM and the Art of Enrollment Maintenance" analogizes solving the enrollment-management challenge to Robert Pirsig's 1974 novel, *Zen and the Art of Motorcycle Maintenance*. Innovation comes from fresh perspectives from leaders in the middle of the organization who understand enrollment as a continuum of the student experience. Echoing the premise advanced in "Innovation and the 21st Century," the SEM team operates with the conviction that there is no one single answer: one size does not fit all, and successful strategies require "fluid measures" to remain relevant.

"Could Your Campus Be Safer?" tells one institution's story of building a system and network for timely and comprehensive communications concerning a range of potentially critical incidents. In addition to responding to a number of reporting requirements, the *SC Aware* system has improved the campus climate and makes everyone campus feel more connected and engaged. Data-based and data-driven, the building and use of the *SC Aware* system has been successful, not because of the statistics amassed, but rather because the culture and climate of trust and accountability where every person on the campus community feels connected and committed to protecting the safety and wellbeing of all.

Chapter One

Innovation and the 21st-Century Community College

Paige M. Niehaus

ALL ABOARD

I sometimes compare implementing change at a large, multi-campus institution to an attempt to stop a speeding train and change the destination after the train has left the station. It is not easy, and there are many moving parts that work against the effort. Wayne County Community College District (WCCCD) in Detroit, Michigan, is an urban, multi-campus district that serves over 60,000 students. Implementing change and moving an institution of this size into a different, new direction can, similarly, be very challenging.

In 2015, WCCCD chancellor Curtis Ivery and senior consultant to the chancellor Dr. Gunder Myran had a vision: to create a design center with a student-centered focus that would assist the chancellor in implementing institution-wide change and, thus, redirect the speeding train. This would require innovation.

Community colleges are faced with rapidly changing critical issues, requiring an innovative and creative approach to problem solving. While the mission of community colleges has remained consistent for over 100 years, the needs of students and the community have changed significantly. Today's community college student is more likely to be part time (63%), female (56%) and/or a minority (54% of credit-seeking students), and hold a job (62% full-time students, 72% part-time) (American Association of Community Colleges [AACC], 2020). Community colleges must be diligent about aligning products and services to meet the specific needs of these current students. Our focus needs to shift from relying on students being college ready to our institutions being student-ready colleges. So how can we be innovative in meeting the needs of our students and be a student-ready college addressing the rapidly changing critical issues?

HOW CAN WE BE INNOVATIVE?

Human-Centered Approach: Design Thinking

Community college leaders are, therefore, focusing on being human-centered, or student-centered, as they adapt to the changing demographics and student needs. At the core of being human-centered is concentrating on human welfare and keeping human needs as the focus of planning and strategic thinking. One human-centered approach to problem-solving is known as design thinking. It is a creative approach to problem-solving that starts with a person—or user—seeking a solution, and ends with new, innovative solutions that are designed to fulfill their needs.

Design thinking can be traced back to the work of Thomas Edison. As he invented, Edison envisioned how people would want to use his inventions and considered people's needs and preferences. His approach to problem-solving, coupled with a human-centered design, is an early example of design thinking. Edison's innovation was "powered by a thorough understanding, through direct observation, of what people want and need in their lives and what they like or dislike about the way particular products are made, packaged, marketed, sold, and supported" (Brown, 2008, p. 1). One of the first published books on the theory of design thinking was titled *The Universal Traveler: A Soft-Systems Guide to Creativity, Problem-Solving, and the Process of Reaching Goals* (1973) by Don Koberg and Jim Bagnall. *The Universal Traveler* has been described as a "quirky guide to the design process that was created long before 'design thinking' became a buzzword among business-oriented designers" (Lupton, 2009). Koberg and Bagnall outlined the creative process steps in problem-solving that are the foundation for present-day design thinking.

Design thinking differentiates from traditional problem-solving in that it begins with empathy for and understanding of the user. Where traditional problem-solving seeks to find the one "best" answer in an orderly, linear fashion, the design thinking process is an interactive, risk-taking process that uses iterative experimentation to identify a "better" answer. Design thinking, then, is a very human-centered process, whereas traditional problem-solving may be described as a more standardized process that operates from a fixed viewpoint or perspective.

Design thinking models vary, and there is not one definitive model to use. Stanford University houses a design thinking institute, the Hasso Plattner Institute of Design at Stanford, commonly known as the d.school. The d.school incorporates modes or components of design thinking: empathize, define, ideate, prototype, and test. These modes are iterative, not linear, with the exception that *empathize* is the first mode in the process.

Regardless of the design thinking model, the design thinking process is consistent with beginning with the users and with the designer seeking to understand their needs. Empathy is the foundation of human-centered design and can be accomplished through observation, engagement, and immersion with the user. The designer, stepping into the shoes of the user, provides a valuable method for understanding and obtaining information. The user is involved iteratively throughout the redesign process to ensure the process is meeting their needs.

In design thinking, the *define* mode requires the designer to develop a point of view, or actionable problem statement, based on the understanding of the user and their environment. The point of view "is a unique design vision that is framed by your specific users" (Doorley et al., 2018, p. 5). It is important to connect with the user iteratively to ensure you are accurately defining their needs.

Ideation, or wide-range brainstorming, drives innovation. It is in this space that designers should practice "flaring," or going wide open, with concepts and outcomes versus tunnel vision, or maintaining a defined focus. Ideation mode is where the outcomes from the empathize mode are utilized in a divergent thinking process.

Typically, most people seek solutions through a convergent, or business, thinking process. Think of a group convening in a location such as an office or conference room to come up with the best solution to a problem or issue. For example, a male colleague shared with me that he was meeting with other male colleagues to identify continuing education programming for teenage girls. Using convergent thinking, many of their solutions will reflect the point of reference of older males, and not necessarily that of the wants and needs of a teenage girl. Unlike convergent approaches, divergent thinking uses the information collected about the users and their environment during the empathize mode to generate a larger number of ideas for problem-solving, ranging from the most obvious, first idea to the random, crazy idea. Divergent thinking is the exploration phase and captures all that is known about the user: their environment, wants, and needs—imagine, lots and lots of sticky notes.

Designers review, discuss, and categorize the ideas and information to converge and formulate a possible solution. Innovation occurs at the intersection of three areas of focus:

1. *Desirability*—the needs, wants, and desires of the users
2. *Feasibility*—the resources available to meet those needs, wants, and desires
3. *Viability*—the alignment with our mission, vision, and values

DIVERGENT   CONVERGENT

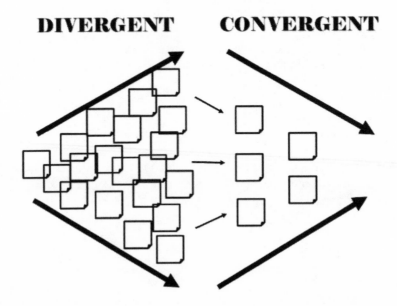

Figure 1.1.   Divergent Versus Convergent Thinking. *Author created (Paige M. Niehaus)*

Think of an architect and a customer who is a homeowner. The homeowner may desire the newest, most sought-after items for their home. The architect must empathize with the homeowner to understand their desires and then assess if those desires are feasible. Can the customer afford the items? Likewise, are the items viable? Can the items physically be incorporated into the design? It is the point where desirability, feasibility, and viability meet where innovation occurs. How will the architect meet the desires of the homeowner, remain within their budget, and be appropriate to the construction of the design?

The *prototype* mode is when the designer can apply or implement the ideas and information into a creative, physical solution to experience or test. By creating a physical solution, such as an object, visual program plan, role playing, and so on, designers and users can actively engage and interact with the solution process. Typically, a designer or design team may have more than one prototype.

Testing the prototype is an interative process that circles back to the previous design thinking modes. Remember: Design thinking is not linear, with the exception that it begins with empathy. The *test* mode provides an opportunity to build empathy by allowing the user to experience the prototype solution and provide real-time feedback and insights. For example, if a

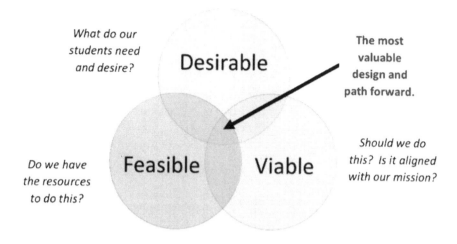

Figure 1.2. **Three Lenses of Innovation.** *Author created (Paige Niehaus)*

design team developed a new process for curriculum review, the physical solution may be a wall full of post-it notes that walks the user through the process. Through the test mode, a designer may learn more about the user and have greater insights to make adjustments or to start over if needed. This mode is also a time for the designer to revisit their point of view, or actionable problem statement, to ensure they understand the needs of the user and framed the problem correctly.

HOW ARE COMMUNITY COLLEGES BEING INNOVATIVE?

Design Thinking in Higher Education

Education Design Lab ("the Lab") is a non-profit founded by Kathleen deLaski that focuses on applied human-centered design and the principles of design thinking for institutions of higher education. Since 2014, the Lab has worked with over 100 institutions and facilitated over 15 design challenges.

In 2017, "the Lab" launched the Seamless Transfer Pathways Design Challenge to address how community colleges and 4-year universities could increase both transfer and baccalaureate attainment rates. Based on dismal data from the NCES and National Student Clearinghouse indicating that only 25% of community college students transfer to 4-year institutions within 5 years, the Lab set out to increase the overall transfer and graduation rates by 30% over 6 years (Education Design Lab, 2019, pp. 2–3). To do so, the Lab selected four teams from community colleges and universities expressing interest in participating. Of the 100 institutions that applied, the following teams were invited to participate in the design challenge: (1) Miami Dade College and Florida International University; (2) Township High School District 211, Harper College, and Northern Illinois University; (3) Collin College and University of North Texas; and (4) Northern Virginia Community College and George Mason University (Education Design Lab, 2019, p. 3). Each team embraced a student-centered approach to solve the issue of low transfer and graduation rates: "Ultimately, human-centered design can help institutions identify and utilize their existing strengths to meet the needs of the market and the students they serve" (deLaski, 2019, p. 18).

As with any design thinking process, it is necessary to begin with empathy and understand the needs of the user, in this case the student. The teams began with collecting and sharing aggregate data from each of their institutions to create a big picture of a student's journey from community college to 4-year institutions. The Lab convened the teams to review the aggregate, "big" data. Doing so allowed the teams to define the issues by seeing the leaks in the pipeline from community college to 4-year institution and opened an opportunity for redesign. Next, the teams gathered information, "small" data, to better understand the students' needs, behaviors, and motivations using journey maps, empathy maps, observation, and interviews with the students, administrators, and faculty.

The ideation for this challenge involved the use of a gallery walk where information and data were visibly displayed in a room, allowing participants to walk through and view the collective information. Each team hosted, at one of their institutions, a gallery walk displaying all the "small" data and invited over 100 stakeholders—including students from the partner institutions—to draw insights and shape themes. The Lab reconvened the teams to better define the design opportunities and discovered that seven themes emerged across all the partner campuses, with *belonging* and *trust* being umbrella themes. Five other most compelling design opportunity areas included (1) flexible modalities to consume information; (2) personalize and engage with a purpose; (3) primary relationships matter; (4) think beyond pathways; and (5) early career exposure is essential (Education Design Lab, 2019, p. 7). Each team identified the themes that became their primary drivers.

Prototypes, or concepts for this design challenge, were developed by each of the four teams. The primary driver for the team from Illinois, which consisted of Township High School District 211, Harper College, and Northern Illinois University, was number 3 ("primary relationships matter") coupled with number 4 ("think beyond pathways"). Initial prototypes were developed and tested with faculty, students, and administrators against the 30% increase in attainment goals. The Illinois team brought four prototypes to a joint 2018 design session with the other teams and facilitated by the Lab. The four prototypes were (1) business marketing pathways, (2) social hub, (3) what you need to know, and (4) low-cost bachelor's degree (Education Design Lab, 2019, p. 8).

With a focus on a low-cost bachelor's degree within 3 years of earning a high school diploma, the Illinois team planned to launch their pilot program, Degree in Three, for testing in fall 2019. As a next step, because the design thinking process is not linear but iterative, the Illinois team will evaluate their prototype pilot program and consider circling back to various design thinking steps in order to revise and refine their prototype to keep in line with the goal of increasing the attainment rate by 30% and meeting the needs of their students.

Lakeland Community College in Kirtland, Ohio, used design thinking to make changes to its first-year experience (FYE) courses that were first launched in 2015 (Amster, 2020). Using the five design thinking steps outlined earlier, Lakeland's FYE advisory committee interviewed and held focus groups with faculty and students to understand their experience. The advisory committee learned that neither group liked the required textbook and that the course curriculum deviated among the faculty. The advisory committee then defined the needs of the students and faculty to introduce a new textbook and develop curricular consistency for the FYE courses.

During the ideation phase, the advisory committee brainstormed innovative ways to address the defined needs. The team decided to replace the textbook with open educational resources (OER) and create an FYE instructor resource site through the Blackboard LMS. Prototyping of the FYE instructor resource site and use of OER was scheduled for summer 2019. Full-time and part-time faculty were asked to test the site and provide feedback prior to being launched for FYE faculty. Based on this feedback, the FYE advisory committee made various changes to the site to make it more user-friendly. Student evaluations at the end of the semester provided feedback on the transition from the textbook to OER.

Design Centers

In recent years, community colleges and 4-year institutions have joined this national focus on becoming more student- or learner-centered. Higher education institutions are making room for design centers on their campuses and are increasingly using design thinking as an innovative approach to solving issues.

As mentioned earlier, WCCCD's Design Center was developed to facilitate, support, and advocate redesign and improvement projects that expedite the achievement of WCCCD's mission, vision, and strategic goals. The Design Center embraces a human-centered approach and design thinking process to innovatively implement redesign projects and plan for WCCCD's future. The Design Center of WCCCD's new transformational initiative, Pathways to the Future IV, will engage students, faculty, and staff in an equity-driven redesign of the total student experience at WCCCD in an effort to increase student retention, persistence, and completion.

Montgomery College in Maryland developed the SparkLab, which is designed to spark collaboration and innovation. Faculty gather to create, invent, share ideas, learn, inspire problem-solving, innovate, and engage in serious play in support of student success, institutional success, and professional development (*Innovation*, 2020).

The IDEA Lab at Red Rocks Community College in Colorado brings together students and faculty to explore, innovate, and create. Part design studio, part makerspace, it is an environment that facilitates peer-to-peer learning and rapid prototyping. Skills gained in the IDEA Lab include design thinking; rapid prototyping such as 3D printing, CNC, and laser cutting; robotics and electronics; data analysis; and multimedia and storytelling (*Idea Lab*, 2020).

Colorado State University opened the Nancy Richardson Design Center, an innovative hub for design thinking, design leadership, and entrepreneurship. Curricular opportunities include a new undergraduate certificate program in design thinking (*Welcome to the Nancy Richardson Design Center*, 2020).

Professional Development

Valencia College in Orlando, Florida, was searching for a training program that would address creative thinking and problem-solving skills for their faculty, staff, and administration in light of the rapidly changing critical challenges faced by community colleges. Finding nothing readily available that complemented their collaborative culture, Valencia developed its own program, Prototype: An Exploration of Collaboration by Design. Known simply as Prototype, this robust program grew from a leadership initiative and explores areas such as creative problem-solving, design thinking, collaboration, change management, and systems thinking.

The framework for Prototype includes seven full-day sessions focused on creative thinking and collaboration, an overnight retreat held offsite, and two half-day sessions focusing on change management and creative and collaborative leadership. Valencia College's Prototype is the catalyst for the paradigm shift from quick decision-making to creatively thinking and exploring options in the mindsets of the over 80 faculty, staff, and administrators who have been Prototype participants in the past 5 years.

> [Prototype] is designed for participants not only to explore new ideas, but also to reflect on their own preferences, examine their blind spots, build empathy

for the experiences of others, and deliberately stretch beyond their comfort zones in order to authentically collaborate toward innovative solutions. (Bosley et al., 2020)

Curriculum

Applying design thinking and creative problem-solving, both user experience (UX) research and user interface (UI) design curricula are growing academic fields. The University of Michigan, the University of California Berkley Extension, Austin Community College, and Normandale Community College are examples of higher education institutions offering programs, degrees, bootcamps, and certifications in UX/UI areas. The UX/UI curriculum educates students on user-centered design, design thinking, and the ability to build compelling user experiences.

CONCLUSION

Community colleges need to be nimble, flexible, adaptable, and especially innovative in responding to the ever-changing demographics and needs of our students and move toward becoming student-ready institutions. We need to be able to stop the speeding train and change direction when necessary. The importance of understanding student needs is not a radical idea for education; in fact, most educators would claim we've been doing that for centuries. In many cases, though, education's focus seems to have moved away from meeting the needs of students who walk through their doors to focusing instead on diminishing budgets and shrinking pools of future students. Putting the students front and center of an empathetic, creative thinking approach may help us become the student-centered institutions our future needs.

REFERENCES

American Association of Community Colleges. (2020). *AACC fast facts 2019*. https://www.aacc.nche.edu/wp-content/uploads/2019/05/AACC2019FactSheet_rev_combo.jpg.

Amster, R. (2020, June). *Innovation: Using design thinking to enhance the first-year student experience course at Lakeland Community College*. League for Innovation in the Community College. https://www.league.org/learning-abstracts/using-design-thinking-enhance-first-year-student-experience-course-lakeland.

Bosley, A., McKnight, C., & Tagye, K. (2020). Prototype: Enhancing creative and collaborative leadership. League for Innovation in the Community College. *Leadership Abstracts, 33*, 2. https://www.league.org/node/21908.

Brown, T. (2008). Design thinking. *Harvard Business Review, 86*(6), 84.

deLaski, K. (2019). *The learner revolution: How colleges can thrive in a new skills and competencies marketplace*. Education Design Lab. https://eddesignlab.org/learnerrevolution.

Doorley, S., Holcomb, S., Klebahn, P., Segovia, K., & Utley, J. (2018). *Design thinking bootleg*. d.school at Stanford University. https://dschool.stanford.edu/resources/design-thinking-bootleg.

Education Design Lab. (2019). *Seamless transfer pathways: Student-centered solutions to improve transfer student success*. https://eddesignlab.org/stp/.

Idea Lab. (2020, February). Red Rocks Community College. https://www.rrcc.edu/idea-lab.

Innovation. (2020, February). Montgomery College. https://www.montgomerycollege.edu/offices/elite/innovation.html.

Koberg, D., & Bagnall, J. (1973). *The universal traveler: A soft-systems guide to creativity, problem-solving, and the process of reaching goals*. Kaufmann.

Lupton, E. (2009). Before design thinking. *Print Magazine*. https://www.printmag.com/article/before-design-thinking.

Welcome to the Nancy Richardson Design Center. (2020, February). https://design.chhs.colostate.edu.

Chapter Two

The Power of Connection

Joianne L. Smith and Ruth Williams

STUDENTS' NEED FOR CONNECTION

Oakton Community College (OCC), a medium-sized (4,700 FTE) public 2-year, high-transfer, associate-degree-granting institution in northern Illinois, has a history of providing access to a high-quality education. In 2013, Oakton Community College joined Achieving the Dream (AtD), recognizing the importance of providing *access through the lens of success.*

Through participation with AtD, Oakton established a culture of evidence—examining data on student success and identifying areas of concern that would allow for the development of targeted interventions. Our analysis demonstrated a clear problem with persistence. Oakton students were not persisting from term to term, and the persistence from fall to fall was even more dismal. In 2015, the fall-to-fall persistence rates of Oakton new students was 45%, significantly below the 54% persistence rates of higher performing peers who participated in the National Community College Benchmarking Project and the national average for 2-year public institutions of higher education.

This persistence rate translated to Oakton losing five students a day, and when the data was disaggregated by race/ethnicity, glaring equity gaps emerged, with the fall-to-fall persistence rates for Black students even more significant. During the kick-off to the 2015–2016 academic year, President Smith made a call to action. She challenged every college employee to employ behaviors that would keep just *one more student a day* enrolled at the college. This "all for one" call to action was designed to keep more students enrolled and on track to meet their educational and personal goals. Faculty, staff, and administrators designed opportunities for inescapable engagement with students, recognizing the importance of connection and belonging in a student's decision to remain enrolled at the college.

An extensive body of literature recognizes the importance of a sense of belonging, engagement, and connection on students' academic success. The most important place for creating opportunities for engagement, student connections, and sense of belonging is in the classroom. Community colleges are primarily commuter schools that serve diverse student populations. Most of these students attend school part time and have challenging external schedules and obligations (Quaye & Harper, 2015). The extent to which a student engages in effective educational practices in and out of the classroom is dependent on the opportunities created by the institution and the extent to which students participate in them (Kinzie et al., 2008). The classroom may be the only opportunity to engage many community college students academically, cognitively, and relationally (Alicea et al., 2016; Barnett, 2011; Liu & Liu, 1999; McClenney & Marti, 2006). Community college faculty invest 90% of their time in teaching and learning. As a result, students' success is not dependent solely on students' abilities and work ethic. Faculty contribute significantly to students' success (Micari & Pazos, 2012).

At the suggestion of the executive director of the Institute for Evidence-Based Change (and Oakton's AtD data coach), Oakton initiated a project to engage faculty more intentionally in student success. Oakton faculty used Chickering and Gamson's (1987) *Principles of Good Teaching and Learning for Undergraduate Education* to develop a persistence initiative, referred to as the Faculty Persistence Project.

CREATING INTENTIONAL OPPORTUNITIES FOR CONNECTION

The Faculty Persistence Project was implemented in fall 2016 and creates intentional opportunities for participating faculty to communicate high expectations and provide prompt feedback to students. Most importantly, deliberate student-faculty interactions are incorporated into the students' academic experience. Decades of research have demonstrated a connection between frequent and substantive formal and informal student-faculty interactions to improved student success indicators and outcomes, including student retention, sense of belonging, academic motivation, satisfaction with the institution, persistence, goal attainment, and completion.

The results of Oakton's faculty efforts have consistently shown that students enrolled in the Faculty Persistence Project sections persist at higher rates than their peers in nonparticipating sections. This effect is even more pronounced for students of color. The Faculty Persistence Project efforts have changed the teaching and learning environment at Oakton. By the fall of 2019, Oakton Community College's fall-to-fall persistence rate for new students increased to 51.4%, and Black students' new student persistence increased to 42% (from 33% in 2015).

WHY DOES PERSISTENCE MATTER?

Although retention, persistence, and completion rates have gradually increased at 2-year public institutions since 2009, there is still significant room for improvement. The average fall-to-fall persistence rate for the fall 2015 cohort of students attending the same 2-year public institution was 49.1% (National Student Clearinghouse Research Center, 2017). Part-time community college students persisted at a rate of 44.2% at their starting institution. When student success outcomes remain low and stagnant, student debt increases, the quality of a college education is questioned, and most importantly, students fail to achieve their goal of obtaining a meaningful career that provides life-sustaining wages. Community colleges are often the pathway to the "American Dream" for first-generation students, low-income students, and students of color. When students fail to persist and complete, these dreams aren't realized, leading to continued economic hardship for students and their families.

Students don't persist at college for a wide range of well-established reasons, including finances, poor academic performance, social integration, transition to a new environment, quality relationships with faculty and institutional fit, and academic goals that did not include completion. Racially and ethnically diverse students at Predominantly White Institutions (PWIs) face additional challenges that influence their decision to stay or leave college. They encounter barriers such as social isolation, alienation, discrimination, and exclusion that negatively impact persistence.

Achieving early success indicators and educational goals are a gauge of a student's academic and social integration into the college environment and the commitment of the institution to the student's development and well-being. Students who engage with the institution, evident through the quality of their effort and involvement in formal and informal educational experiences and activities, will begin to evolve and become academically and socially integrated into the college environment (Pace, 1998; Astin, 1984). The first year of college is a critical and decisive time for college students.

Students want to be successful in college, and they set high personal expectations. However, when students transition to college, they often face challenges that can make their integration into the college environment difficult. It is during this time that students are making the decision to stay or leave. During the first year, the relationships students establish with faculty, peers, staff, administrators, and the institution will influence their sense of belonging and engagement and certainty in the institution (Lay-Hwa Bowden, 2013). These relationships will impact student development (Tinto, 2012), and positive relationships will increase motivation, which in turn will influence students' integration and satisfaction with the institution (Chambliss & Takacs, 2014). Colleges can assist students' integration by creating comfortable learning environments and implementing supportive policies and practices.

Faculty play a pivotal role in student engagement by creating a learning environment that is conducive to an increased sense of belonging for students. Faculty can create this type of environment by demonstrating that they care about and value their students, model respect, set clear expectations, incorporate active and collaborative learning, and facilitate productive and healthy discussions (Gayle et al., 2013; Wilson & Gore, 2013). The extent to which faculty create an engaging classroom environment can influence student-faculty interactions outside of the classroom (Tinto, 2012). For community college students, the environment faculty create in and out of the classroom and the relationships faculty form with students are important to their transition to college, their sense of belonging, and their success. Extensive research has demonstrated the connections between frequent, substantive student-faculty interactions to positive student outcomes, including retention, persistence, academic performance, completion, and personal, social, and academic development.

Oakton's Faculty Persistence Project, a faculty-led and institutionally supported project, is one such educational practice that creates deliberate opportunities for students and faculty to interact and create connections between faculty and students that establish a sense of belonging and motivation for students to persist on their educational path.

HOW CAN INSTITUTIONS INCREASE PERSISTENCE?

In response to the national focus on student engagement, persistence, and retention, Oakton formed a Student Success Working Group in 2010. The Student Success Working Group (SSWG) developed a success plan that focused on building a culture committed to student success. Although Oakton was not yet a member of AtD, the SSWG used a number of AtD approaches, including the formation of a cross-institutional team, the use of data to make informed decisions about how to enhance student success, and studying and replicating student success interventions from other colleges. In its student success plan, the SSWG also adopted a number of student success indicators comparable to those outlined by AtD, including successful course completion, successful progress through course sequences, term-to-term retention, completion of a credential, and successful transfer to a 4-year college or university.

Data revealed that work within three priority areas—placement, developmental education, and persistence—had the potential to significantly impact the success of all students. Though the SSWG laid the foundation for an institutional student success focus, it struggled to cultivate broad-based engagement around student success, to bring student success interventions to scale, and to impact the success of a significant number of Oakton students.

As a result, the college's senior leadership team sought a new model that would align with the student success strategic goal outlined in the 2013–2017 strategic plan, *Connecting What Matters*. The determination was made that participation in AtD would provide external expertise and prompt the college to make courageous, transformative decisions. Additionally, the senior leadership team surmised that participation in a national movement might catalyze change at Oakton if faculty and staff were aware of student success interventions taking place at other institutions across the country.

In 2015, the college also experienced a leadership transition and the new president determined that persistence would become the college's "wildly important goal," as persistence serves as both a leading and lagging indicator for student success outcomes. Term-to-term retention is a leading indicator for year-to-year persistence (lagging indicator). The college's fall-to-fall persistence rate was the lowest among its peer institutions, and several projects were developed to positively impact the college's persistence rates. Establishing a mandatory new student orientation program (a high-impact cocurricular practice) and the Faculty Persistence Project (a high-impact pedagogical practice) were the two primary projects undertaken to improve persistence.

THE ROLE OF FACULTY IN INCREASING PERSISTENCE

One student success intervention brought to Oakton's attention resulting from joining AtD was the Drop Rate Improvement Program (DRIP) at Odessa College, in Odessa, Texas. Odessa's program, and Chickering and Gamson's (1987) *Seven Principles of Good Practice for Undergraduate Education*, provided the framework for Oakton's Faculty Persistence Project. Odessa's program was developed in response to low course success rates and high course withdrawal rates. The goal of Odessa's program is to decrease withdrawal rates by intentionally creating opportunities for faculty and students to interact, thereby leading to increased course retention, success rates, and credential completion (Kistner & Henderson, 2014). Odessa faculty who had the highest course withdrawal rates committed to making personal connections with students in one-on-one meetings at the beginning of the academic term; providing consistent feedback throughout the course; facilitating a get-to-know-you activity on the first day of class and using students' names in the first week of class; monitoring students' attitudes and performance and engaging students when necessary; and allowing for flexibility when the need arose (Williams & Wood, 2017). As a result of Odessa's program, course withdrawal rates decreased, and course success rates and credential completions increased.

Although Oakton data revealed relatively high rates of course completion, students were not continuing their enrollment in courses for subsequent semesters. Oakton's Faculty Persistence Project adapted Odessa's DRIP to address concerns about student retention and persistence. The Faculty Persistence Project provides a framework for specific classroom activities that foster connections between faculty and students.

Faculty Interventions

Faculty members who volunteer for the project agree to incorporate four activities based on best practices of highly effective classrooms. These activities, incorporated within the first three weeks, include:

- learn the names of students as quickly as possible and create community in the classroom by having students learn the names of peers;
- schedule a 15-minute conference with each student;
- present class requirements clearly and set high academic standards; and
- make an appropriate assignment as early as possible to give students early feedback.

Participating faculty also agreed to make an effort to incorporate the following activities into their class for the remainder of the semester: acquainting students with resources and opportunities at Oakton, attending at least one cocurricular event with students, contacting students who are struggling in class and offering them help, talking with students about completing an associate degree or certificate, and participating in an assessment of the overall project.

Early Evidence

The Humanities and Philosophy Department piloted the Faculty Persistence Project in the spring of 2016, and qualitative data from both faculty and students was overwhelmingly positive, with students reporting feeling more supported and cared for by their faculty, and faculty reporting a deeper understanding of students and their needs as well as reporting a more engaging classroom dynamic with more students actively participating in classroom discussions.

In the fall of 2016, faculty across the college were invited to participate. In the fall 2016 semester, 132 faculty participated, impacting over 2,388 students and 25% of Oakton course sections. The evidence of the importance and tremendous impact of faculty connection can be found in the data. Data indicate that students who were enrolled in a course section that participated in the initiative had a 17% higher fall-to-spring retention rate. The impact on students of color was especially noteworthy (see figure 2.1).

While all project activities are beneficial, the one-on-one conference has been described as creating a transformational classroom experience by facilitating high-quality student/teacher relationships early in the semester. These relationships are the cornerstone of the project's success and have changed the culture of teaching and learning at Oakton. During the one-on-one conferences, faculty take the time to get to know students, rather than focusing on questions related to the syllabus or course work. Participating faculty are given a series of open-ended questions to consider in order to facilitate those conversations. Faculty learn about students' career goals, learning styles, and barriers to success. From faculty/student conversations, faculty learned of students' difficulties in obtaining textbooks, their challenges with public transportation, and conflicts with work schedules—personal information that helped faculty develop a deeper and more holistic understanding of their students.

As faculty were asked to engage more directly in student success initiatives impacting their students and classroom learning environments, more

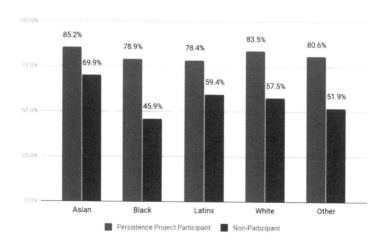

Figure 2.1. A Comparison of the Fall 2016 to Spring 2017 Retention Rates of the Faculty Persistence Project Participants With Non-Participants by Race/Ethnicity. *Author created (J. Smith and R. Williams)*

professional development opportunities for faculty on persistence, retention, and/or completion were offered and integrated into existing seminars.

In fall 2016, student success formed an explicit component of the full-time new faculty seminar and the teaching credential seminar offered annually. These opportunities concentrate on classroom persistence and retention as they relate to engagement and learning. Student Success Team members and other faculty success experts share updates and data and provide training during joint division meetings and professional development orientation, weeks prior to the start of fall and spring semesters. Recent workshop sessions during orientation week included:

- "The Next Steps in Implementing the Faculty Persistence Project: Changing the Culture at OCC";
- "Exploring Modes of Student Success"; and
- "Promoting Student Success While Maintaining Responsible Academics: Where Are the Boundaries?"

These professional development opportunities reinforce the college's value of high-quality teaching and learning experiences.

THE IMPACT OF THE FACULTY PERSISTENCE PROJECT

The Faculty Persistence Project has continued since 2016 with about 130 faculty (full and part time) participating each term and approximately one-third of new students enrolled in at least one persistence project course in their first term. To understand the program's impact, the college has tracked both leading (term-to-term retention or persistence) and lagging (fall-to-fall persistence) indicators, and surveyed students and faculty participants each term to better understand their experiences.

Persistence Rates

Consistent from 2016 to 2017, Oakton students who are in the Faculty Persistence Project sections persist from term to term and fall to fall at higher rates than their peers who are not in a course affiliated with the project. Fall-to-spring persistence for students in the Faculty Persistence Project remains 17 percentage points higher overall, with the largest differences for Black students (see figures 2.1 and 2.2). The fall 2018 to fall 2019 persistence rates for all new students was 51.4%. For students who were in a persistence project course, the fall-to-fall persistence rate was 65.7%—a 14% percentage point difference. The impact for students of color was even more significant. For Black students, the overall persistence rate from fall 2018 to fall 2019 was 42.2%. For Black students in a participating course, the persistence rate was

60.7% (see figure 2.2). These trends have been consistent since the inception of the program. The latest data from fall 2019 to spring 2020 demonstrate the same trend (see figure 2.3).

Students who are in Faculty Persistence Project sections have also been surveyed each term since the beginning of the project, and they report strong connections to faculty and a strong sense of belonging in the class and at Oakton. Based on survey results from fall 2018, spring 2019, and fall 2019, over 90% of students agreed or strongly agreed that their instructor knows their name, values interacting with them, cares about their presence and perspective in class, and cares about their success. Further, 81% said the instructor communicated that they could succeed in college, and 73% said the instructor communicated that they belong at Oakton.

National Survey Results

The results from national surveys also show that Oakton students are reporting higher levels of engagement in and out of the classroom. The college conducted the Survey of Entering Student Engagement (SENSE) in 2014 and 2019. SENSE collects data about institutional practices and student behaviors in the first weeks of college to help colleges understand practices and procedures to improve student success and retention of new students. In the 2019 SENSE results, three key areas where students reported higher levels of engagement were in early connections, engaged learning, and academic and social support networks (see figure 2.4). These benchmarks include a number of survey items that are associated with Faculty Persistence Project practices,

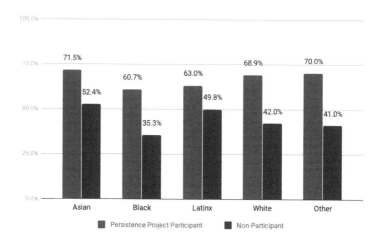

Figure 2.2. Fall 2018 to Fall 2019 New Student Persistence Rates by Race/Ethnicity. *Author created (J. Smith and R. Williams)*

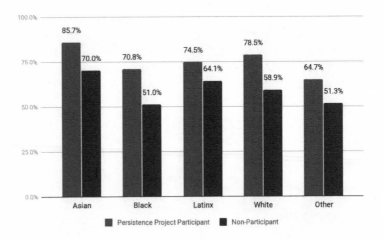

Figure 2.3.   A Comparison of the Fall 2019 to Spring 2020 Retention Rates of the Faculty Persistence Project Participants With Non-Participants by Race/Ethnicity. *Author created (J. Smith and R. Williams)*

such as discussing an assignment or grade with an instructor, having an instructor learn their name, learning the names of other students in their class, and receiving prompt written or oral feedback on their performance. In 2019, the college saw gains in the engaged learning benchmark, outperforming the average score of the national sample as well as the average of other AtD institutions.

The Community College Survey of Student Engagement (CCSSE) was conducted in 2015 and 2018. During this time, there were gains in all benchmark areas, including the measure of student-faculty interaction. This benchmark measures the degree to which career goals, course content and assessments, and academic performance were discussed between students and faculty. Student-faculty interaction was also the area that saw the largest gains and where Oakton students report the highest scores relative to the national peers. These gains were all realized since the implementation of the Faculty Persistence Project (see figure 2.5).

Faculty Gains

The Faculty Persistence Project not only has improved outcomes for students but also has had positive impacts on faculty participants. One faculty member shared, "The gift of these deeper connections with my students is a payment that cannot be measured, knowing what a difference it has made not just in their lives, but my own." Another faculty member stated, "The relationships I have formed have been transformative." The power of the connec-

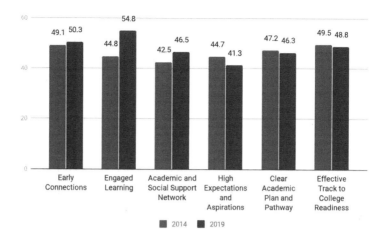

Figure 2.4.   A Comparison of 2014 and 2019 Oakton Survey of Entering New Student Engagement (SENSE) Benchmarks. *Author created (J. Smith and R. Williams)*

tion between faculty and students changes the teaching and learning environment for both faculty and students. Students want to be known and feel like they belong. The Faculty Persistence Project at Oakton offers a roadmap for faculty to develop a relationship that is meaningful, connecting each student to a faculty member and the college.

HOW TO SCALE AND SUSTAIN CONNECTIONS

Oakton recognizes the value and impact the Faculty Persistence Project has on students, student outcomes, and faculty. The Faculty Persistence Project initiative team continues to strategize ways to scale up the initiative, provide relevant and timely professional development, and provide resources for students and faculty. When the project was initiated, many faculty were attempting to implement all the project requirements in every class, including the one-to-one student conferences. As a result, some faculty were conducting 75 to 125 student conferences in the first 3 weeks of classes. In many cases, this was not sustainable term after term. Faculty participants are now asked to commit one class to the project, with the goal of all faculty implementing the project, so all students are engaged in this valuable experience. However, the project continues to be voluntary on the part of the faculty, so scaling up beyond the average of 130 faculty a term remains a challenge. Oakton continues to work with the faculty leadership to identify ways to engage more faculty with the project.

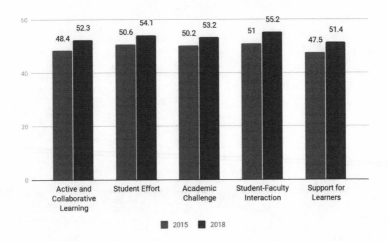

Figure 2.5. **A Comparison of 2015 and 2018 Oakton Community College Survey of Student Engagement (CCSSE) Benchmarks.** *Author created (J. Smith and R. Williams)*

Adjunct faculty have also been active participants in the Faculty Persistence Project and make up over half of the participating faculty. Participating adjunct faculty conduct the one-to-one conferences with students within and outside of their required weekly office hours (50% of office hours can be used for these meetings) and in shared adjunct faculty office spaces. To respect the unique nature of these conferences, the college identified available private office spaces that adjunct faculty could reserve to conduct their one-to-one conferences. The college worked with the Adjunct Faculty Association to include Faculty Persistence Project participation as an institutional service for continued teaching eligibility and to provide a stipend for the additional office hours adjunct faculty were offering. Continual engagement of adjunct faculty with the project is necessary to impact as many students as possible and the college will continue to collaborate with adjunct faculty leadership to identify ways to do this.

Responding to Student and Faculty Needs

As faculty engaged in deeper connections with students, some students revealed very personal information, such as domestic violence, sexual assault and harassment, mental health issues, and serious financial hardship including food and housing insecurity. These concerns led to increased awareness of faculty about issues of equity as well as a need for additional resources for both students and faculty.

Through Oakton's Educational Foundation, a Student Success Fund administered through the Office of Student Affairs provides emergency funding to students in need. Faculty participants were provided with information and a streamlined process to refer students in financial need to access this fund. Referrals for mental health support were also facilitated through the Office of Student Affairs. Although employees complete Title IX and Mandated Reporter training, and faculty and staff are aware of resources and services for students, faculty were not necessarily trained on how to manage these types of conversations, including when to refer them to trained staff. As a result, some faculty were also experiencing empathy fatigue, stress, and anxiety.

The Faculty Persistence Project initiative team brought these concerns to the Faculty Professional Development Team, resulting in a 6-week Mental Health Literacy Credential offered by the college's counseling staff that includes topics such as trauma-informed teaching, professors as first responders, dialectical behavioral therapy basics, responding to students' concerns, and student support services. The Faculty Professional Development team also collaborated with other areas of the college to offer workshops on Title IX processes at Oakton. The annual faculty retreat in 2019–2020 focused on self-care and work-life balance. The project faculty participant surveys continue to offer insight into faculty professional development needs.

A COMMITMENT TO CONNECTION

Oakton's commitment to student success has led to a holistic redesign of the student experience. The Faculty Persistence Project is the cornerstone of that student success effort. Relationships matter and the Faculty Persistence Project creates a roadmap and strategies to help create high-quality relationships. When students feel cared for and like they belong, they are more likely to persist and complete their educational goals. Further, a 2014 Purdue-Gallup study showed that the quality of students' relationships at college predicted long-term outcomes such as engagement in work and overall well-being (Ray & Marken, 2014). The impact of high-quality relationships during a student's college experience can quite literally change a student's life—to one of connectedness and purpose, creating a life that matters.

REFERENCES

Alicea, S., Suarez-Orozco, C., Singh, S., Darbes, T., & Abrica, E. J. (2016). Observing classroom engagement in community college: A systematic approach. *Educational Evaluation and Policy Analysis, 38*(4), 757–782.

Astin, A. W. (1984). Student involvement: A developmental theory for higher education. *Journal of College Student Personnel, 24*(5), 207–308.

Barnett, E. A. (2011). Validation experiences and persistence among community college students. *The Review of Higher Education, 34*(2), 193–230.

Chambliss, D. F., & Takacs, C. G. (2014). *How college works.* Harvard University Press.

Chickering, A. W., & Gamson, Z. F. (1987). Seven principles for good practice in undergraduate education. *AAHE Bulletin, 39*(7), 3–7. http://www.aahea.org/articles/sevenprinciples 1987.htm.

Gayle, B., Cortez, D., & Preiss, R. (2013). Safe spaces, difficult dialogues, and critical thinking. *International Journal for the Scholarship of Teaching and Learning, 7*(2). https://doi.org/10.20429/ijsotl.2013.070205.

Kinzie, J., Gonyea, R., Shoup, R., & Kuh, G. D. (2008). Promoting persistence and success of underrepresented students: Lessons for teaching and learning. *New Directions for Teaching and Learning, 115*, 21–38.

Kistner, N. A. & Henderson, E. E. (2014). The drop rate improvement program at Odessa College. Achieving the Dream.

Lay-Hwa Bowden, J. (2013). What's in a relationship?: Affective commitment, bonding and the tertiary first-year experience—a student faculty perspective. *Asia Pacific Journal of Marketing and Logistics, 25*(3), 428–451.

Liu, E., & Liu, R. (1999). An application of Tinto's model at a commuter campus. *Education, 119*(3), 537–542.

McClenney, K. M., & Marti, C. N. (2006). Exploring relationships between student engagement and student outcomes in community colleges: Report on validation research. Working Paper. Community College Survey of Student Engagement.

Micari, M., & Pazos, P. (2012). Connecting to the professor: Impact of the student-faculty relationship in a highly challenging course. *College Teaching, 60*(2), 41–47.

National Student Clearinghouse Research Center. (2017). *Persistence and retention—2017.* https://nscresearchcenter.org/wp-content/uploads/ SnapshotReport28a.pdf.

Pace, C. R. (1998). Recollections and reflections. In J. C. Smart (ed.), *Higher education: Handbook of theory and research* (Vol. 13, pp. 1–34). Agathon.

Quaye, S. J., & Harper, S. R. (2015). *Student engagement in higher education: Theoretical perspectives and practical approaches for diverse populations.* Routledge.

Ray, J., & Marken, S. (2014, May 6). Life in college matters for life after college. *Economy.*

Tinto, V. (2012). *Completing college rethinking institutional action.* University of Chicago Press.

Williams, G., & Wood, D. (2017). Leading and lagging indicators in action: Odessa College. In B. Phillips & J. E. Horowitz (Eds.), *Creating a data-informed culture in community colleges: A new model for educators.* Harvard Education Press.

Wilson, S., & Gore, J. (2013). An attachment model of university connectedness. *The Journal of Experimental Education, 81*(2), 178–198. https://doi.org/10.1080/00220973.2012.699902.

Chapter Three

Strategic Enrollment Management

SEM and the Art of Enrollment Maintenance

Daniel Herbst

THE TRIP BEGINS

In *Zen and the Art of Motorcycle Maintenance: An Inquiry Into Values* (1974) Robert Pirsig used a long motorcycle ride with his son as an allegory to explain how people interact with technology and systems. He described how people react to things that do not go as planned, and how quality and passion must be recognized as a vital component when working on a complex system such as a motorcycle. A smooth ride can be disrupted by the smallest unforeseen changes in air temperature or the failure of an engine belt. Similarly, community colleges can experience the same bumpy road when dealing with the myriad of factors related to enrollment management.

In July 2018, Henry Ford College (HFC) hired a new president who was young, intelligent, passionate about education, and completely new to the community college system. The president held meetings with various constituents at the college, including Board of Trustee members, and came away with the idea that enrollment decline was going to continue, which, if not abated, could lead to reductions in workforce. The information proved to be correct, as colleges in Michigan saw reductions of 10% or more for several years and HFC experienced eight straight semesters of enrollment decline. HFC lost approximately 8,000 of its 18,000 students from 2011 through 2018, with an additional predicted 3% enrollment decline for 2018–2019.

Discussions moved from enrollment declines to possible layoffs, and from the president's office to all areas of campus—and then led to the development of a new model of strategic enrollment management at HFC.

STRATEGIC ENROLLMENT MANAGEMENT (SEM)

SEM and the Art of Enrollment Maintenance is a description of how Henry Ford College addressed the complex, yet common, problem of enrollment and the ways HFC rethought its ride on the journey to find enrollment stability. As with many community colleges, HFC had made several attempts at implementing SEM plans over the previous 13 years. The efforts were unable to prevent an enrollment decline, and the college culture had come to believe that enrollment decline was inevitable.

It became obvious that a new approach was needed: a new SEM model to reverse multi-semester declines. Key to our success was teamwork and a "can do" mindset.

SETTING THE STAGE

HFC has an 80-plus-year history in Dearborn, Michigan, and is located within walking distance of auto tycoon Henry Ford's Fair Lane Estate. With its meager beginning in the basement of Fordson High School in 1938, HFC has grown to serve over 17,000 students annually on its 75-acre campuses (Henry Ford College, n.d.).

HFC faces some unique challenges regarding its location, district size, and funding sources. It is the smallest community college district in Michigan and receives less than 15% of its funding from property taxes. With only four high schools in the district, HFC recruits more than 67% of the students from outside the district's boundaries. The budget at HFC is heavily dependent on enrollment in order to keep operating, since tuition and fees make up 52% of the annual revenue, state appropriations comprise 27%, and property taxes contribute approximately 14% to the operational budget. Obviously, fluctuations in enrollment impact the budget and lead to tough decisions.

THE SEM TEAM

In 2018, HFC identified the need for a cohesive institutional approach to managing enrollment long term, and the Strategic Enrollment Management Team was created. Previously, HFC attempted to address important issues by convening large committees representing every possible contingency, including enrollment planning and projections. The early efforts in enrollment management also tended to focus entirely on recruitment and enrollment. This team needed to be different and take a new approach.

First, the team needed strong, representative leadership. The dean of the School of Liberal Arts and the executive director of Enrollment Services, both strong leaders who had demonstrated ability to work across divisional barriers, were selected as co-chairs.

Next, HFC chose to have a small, active, core of faculty and staff to serve on the SEM Steering Team. The result was a team of 10: seven faculty and three staff and mid-level administrators. The primary goal of the Steering Team was to provide continuing strategic guidance for and coordination of the entire scope of enrollment activities at HFC. Its mission: to provide strategic vision to ensure enrollment and financial sustainability and focus strongly on student success, an aspect of enrollment not previously emphasized in enrollment initiatives.

The SEM Team was designed to be a data-informed decision-making committee that would accumulate available data to prompt decision-making around enrollment. The Strategic Enrollment Management Plan, goals, and objectives would continue to evolve as the core team moved forward (Claybourne et al., 2020).

MAKING SEM PART OF THE COLLEGE CULTURE

For HFC to develop an efficient SEM process, the Steering Team needed to recognize the effect of the campus culture and engage the entire college community. HFC's president led the way, emphasizing the importance of SEM during his state-of-the-college speech, in campus-wide emails, and in conversations with individuals and groups on campus. He stressed the need for collaboration over departmental isolation, where the college could find a common ground and allow innovations to come from fresh voices.

As change agents preach, for change to take hold, the culture of the institution must embrace change as something it truly wants and needs. Those who understood the importance of SEM to the health of the college realized the college's self-dialogue needed to change. Phrases such as "What is in it for me?" needed to be replaced with "What is best for students?" and "What am I willing to do about it?" A culture where "no" was a common response to change needed to be replaced with "find a way to say yes."

THE TEAM APPROACH TO CHANGE

To support the change in the campus's dialogue, it was important that all Steering Team members were using the same basic concepts and speaking the same language when discussing SEM. Each team member received a copy of Sigler's *SEM Core Concepts: Building Blocks for Institutional and Student Success* (2017), which provided a baseline for early discussions and started the team on the same path. An early section in the text, describing what SEM is not, provided a focal point: SEM is *not* something that quickly solves all enrollment ills, an enhanced admissions and marketing operations (without faculty involvement), an administrative function separate from the academic mission of the institution, or a waste of valuable institutional resources (Sigler, 2017).

The Steering Team would provide ongoing coordination, support, and guidance at the strategic level. The SEM Team's initial goal was to conceptualize enrollment as a continuum of student experience: from recruitment to enrollment to retention through completion of an academic credential, with primary emphasis on retention and student success.

The initial membership of the core team, drawing from Student Services, Academic Affairs, Marketing and Communications, and Institutional Research, reflected the broader charge of the team. Holly Diamond, executive director of Enrollment Services and co-chair of the SEM Steering Team, believes that the team's success started with its membership: The right influencers were at the table to make a positive impact on enrollment by introducing efficiencies within the enrollment process.

In addition to gathering—and listening to—perspectives of stakeholders across the institution, the SEM Team was also committed to transparency by publicly posting meeting agendas and minutes, subcommittee reports, membership rosters, and various other information. SEM created opportunities for other stakeholders on the campus to directly connect with the SEM Team and make suggestions through an electronic feedback form.

What made this model different from other attempts was the deliberate use of subteams. SEM subteams offered opportunities to involve many more stakeholders in analyzing enrollment challenges, operationalizing strategic priorities, and quickly addressing specific problems. Each subteam included a Steering Team member, who acted as the liaison between the subteam and the Steering Team, and subteam members, who were recruited from all areas of the college.

Each subteam also had a specific mission, deliverables, and time frame. These subteams were formed around key issues or initiatives recommended either by core SEM Team members or by other stakeholders within the college community. The duration of the subteam existence varied based on their charge and tasks, from a few months to projects lasting a year or more. Some teams tended to be more tactical, such as the subteam that redesigned the seven-step enrollment process. Some subteams, such as Adult Education, were invested in higher-level data analysis and provided the data supporting specific initiatives or recommendations.

WHAT A RIDE

By 2019, SEM had begun to make positive inroads at the college and contributed to two straight semesters with enrollment increases. The success of SEM at HFC came from the top-down encouragement, middle-management coordination, and the bottom-up planning and development. The 2019 fall semester had the first increase of enrollment in eight semesters, and 2020's winter semester indicated an increase of more than 3% over the previous year (the COVID-19 pandemic, of course, affected these numbers).

In the 2019–2020 school year, 50 members of the campus community served on one or more SEM subteams. Subteam accomplishments included a new personalized enrollment process and a communication system that notified over 1,200 graduation-eligible students of their status and contacted 3,100 students who were nine credits or fewer away from graduating.

A BROAD TEAM CHARGE

A phrase adopted by the SEM Team is "one size does not fit all," implying that looking for one way to address the myriad of issues involved in enrollment management no longer works in 2020's community colleges. The SEM Team addressed the vital issues that affect student enrollment and success, from the uncertain economy and the decreased numbers of high school graduates, to the need to develop realistic goals and use data to support all decisions. The team also broadened its view, recognizing that retention and recruitment are equally important and that the value of each marketing and recruitment initiative must be tracked and measured. The team focused on a range of solutions by developing appropriate financial aid/scholarships for students and putting clearer value on investment for students, community, industry, and the state.

To measure its success, the Steering Team established 10 key performance goals:

1. improve data-informed decision-making;
2. create a dashboard to monitor enrollment;
3. identify resources to promote increased retention, student success, and graduation;
4. target new student enrollment;
5. establish student retention benchmarks;
6. address student concerns regarding diversity, equity, and inclusion;
7. maintain affordability for all students;
8. evaluate market positions;
9. examine student outcomes; and

10. provide for the financial stability of the college.

These indicators will be fluid measures and will be adjusted as internal and external forces indicate.

A current effort of the SEM Team is to develop a model to determine the optimal enrollment point (OEP) for HFC. The OEP can be described as the number of students who can be served at the highest level by the current college infrastructure and potential markets for growth. This project is ongoing and has stimulated many innovative approaches for developing an accurate, predictive matrix.

THE ROAD GOES ON

Many colleges cannot expect to see enrollment increases for up to 3 years after implementation of a new SEM (Sigler, 2017). HFC's enrollment increases happened 1 year after the initial creation of the SEM Steering Team. These early successes inspired the college and provided motivation for tackling current and future challenges.

The college now faces difficult organizational issues when addressing enrollment management and maintaining steady, but controlled, growth. The first is to get the college community to recognize the need for continual strategic shifts. Sticking with the old and familiar, although no longer successful, is often more attractive than pursuing the sometimes-painful unfamiliar options. For example, continuing to fund the SEM structure and initiatives comes with a risk, and without a guarantee of a return on the financial investment.

Often linked to a comfort with what's known and what's worked in the past is a fear of change and a lack of motivation to accept change. Breaking the barriers that resist change can be difficult, emotionally draining, and time-consuming—because they are often intrinsically tied to the college's culture.

The final issue, and perhaps the most insidious, is that of internal politics. The real challenge with internal politics is the hidden power that is not represented on a college's organizational chart (Kim & Mauborgne, 2015). Individuals with this power may agree publicly about a change strategy in a meeting and then kill it dead with a hallway conversation 1 hour later. To address these issues and bring them into the open, change agents—teams such as the SEM Steering Team—must be conscious of the college's culture and where institutional power lies, both on an organizational chart and in the minds of the rank and file within an organization.

APPLYING THE SEM TEAM MODEL

Since the advent of the SEM Steering Team model, HFC applied the framework to other projects as well. In the aftermath of the initial wave of COVID-19 pandemic, the president appointed two vice presidents to address the legal, health, and pedagogical challenges the colleges will face in order to safely bring students and staff back to campus. The vice presidents applied the organizational concepts developed by the SEM Team: the small central core team supported by four subteams with specific missions, timelines, and deadlines. Each subteam is responsible for one of four topics: (1) safety and health, (2) workplace integration, (3) communication, or (4) academics. The core team, also known as the "Return to Campus Team," created over 80 pages of documents and recommendations in just over 3 weeks through the work of the four subteams and created a six-phase plan for safely reopening the college.

The SEM model, while it appears simple in design, provides a complex, efficient model for addressing tasks. Central to the model is the belief that positive change is possible, even in the most challenging of times. Enrollment management has something in common with quantum physics, motorcycle maintenance, and, perhaps, a bit of Zen.

REFERENCES

Claybourne, C., Diamond, H., Ernst, J., & the SEM Core Team. (2020). *Enrollment is everybody's business!* Henry Ford College. https://www.hfcc.edu/sites/hfcmain/files/hfc-sem-plan-public.pdf.

Henry Ford College. (n.d.). Henry Ford College history. Retrieved January 14, 2021, from https://www.hfcc.edu/history.

Kim, W. C., & Mauborgne, R. (2015). *Blue ocean strategy: How to create uncontested market space and make the competition irrelevant.* Harvard Business School.

Pirsig, R. M. (1974). *Zen and the art of motorcycle maintenance: An inquiry into values.* William Morrow and Company.

Sigler, W. (2017). *SEM core concepts: Building blocks for institutional and student success.* American Association of Collegiate Registrars and Admissions Officers.

Chapter Four

Could Your Campus Be Safer?

Comprehensive Support and Safety Strategies That Work

Cheryl M. Hagen

HOW IT BEGAN

It was a radio report of a shooting on our campus that actually started School-craft College on a path to improve its campus safety operations. Early on that lovely morning during spring break, the campus was quieter than usual since faculty and students were away and staff were the only ones at work. The first clue that something was amiss that morning was the sound of helicopters circling over the campus, and then a trickle of phone calls from panicky relatives asking about their loved ones. Apparently, a local radio station had been broadcasting that there was a shooting on campus, but no one seemed to know anything about it. As the reports filtered in and other radio stations began broadcasting the story, the response quickly escalated from a sense of concern and urgency to an atmosphere of chaos. Was it true that there was a gunman on campus? Should staff shelter in place? Should they leave? Should the cabinet assemble for an emergency meeting? What should staff be told? What should be communicated to the media?

Within a few hours, the story was unraveled and proven to be false. Once everyone calmed down, the president wisely decided to call a team together to debrief—to look at what had happened and how we had responded, with an eye toward improvements across the board.

In the years since that spring break event, Schoolcraft has built a sophisti-cated and comprehensive system that enables college personnel to be far more aware and informed than in the past. At the heart of the system is a reporting mechanism that collects information on every campus incident, making each member of the campus community a valuable force multiplier for those whose job it is to keep the campus safe, keep the students enrolled, and solve minor problems before they become major problems.

One of the greatest benefits from this college-wide system is its ability to deliver reliable and accurate data—to track response times, to compile required reports, and to drive improvement. Because of this efficient system, Schoolcraft is able to quickly and accurately ascertain, for example, the most prevalent student complaint, the number of students with suicidal ideation, the time it takes to resolve campus crime reports, and data for the annual Clery report, all with just a few clicks.

Within the last decade, college administrators' need to know what is happening on campus has grown exponentially. The days of "circling the wagons" and keeping unpleasant incidents under wraps are long gone. Changes to federal regulations and reporting requirements, the need to serve students holistically, and the importance of student satisfaction and retention are all critical factors that make it imperative for leaders to be aware of incidents on campus. Surfacing possible threats or serious mental illness are crucial, of course, but it is also advantageous to be aware of opportunities to positively impact the student experience.

Establishing an accessible method for everyone in the campus community to file reports, creating a culture of reporting, and using data to drive improvement are all crucial steps. "We can't expect students, or even faculty and staff for that matter, to keep up with exactly what office has what functionality," asserted Dr. Martin Heator, dean of students at Schoolcraft College. "All everyone needs to know is that *SC Aware* is easily available on our website, and it handles everything" (M. Heater, personal communication, February 12, 2020).

NEED TO KNOW: FEDERAL REGULATIONS AND ACCOUNTABILITY

> According to the Department of Education, key provisions of the new rule, which has the force of law, include . . . [requiring] schools to offer clear, accessible options for any person to report sexual harassment. —M. Zalaznick (2020)

In the last decade or so, the trend toward making higher education more accountable has really gained traction. Not only is there a focus on completion rates and increasing costs, but also cultural shifts and public awareness of issues on college campuses have brought campus safety into sharp focus. One of the primary causal factors of the damaging, traumatic, and highly publicized debacles at Penn State and Michigan State was the old, unspoken higher education practice of maintaining a shroud of secrecy (Lombardi, 2009).

As the public became aware of the horrific stories of administrators seemingly more concerned about the reputation of their college and football program than they were about the welfare of children and young athletes, people began asking a lot of questions. Conversations began chipping away at the culture of silence shrouding sexual misconduct in the college setting, and survivors began to come forward with their stories. Campus safety, particularly in regard to sexual misconduct, became a signature issue of the Obama administration (Harris & Kelderman, 2017). At this juncture, colleges are now expected to be "open books," and be transparent about any incidents of sexual misconduct. Schools are legally required to respond to sexual harassment and violence because they are forms of gender-based discrimination.

In addition to reporting sexual misconduct, colleges are required under the Clery Act to report incidents that may be threats to health and safety. Institutions are required to issue a "timely warning" about any immediate perceived threats in order to share that information with the campus community so that students can take appropriate protective measures. College police forces must categorize campus crimes that occur on campus, as well as those that occur in college-sponsored events off campus. "The process of counting and publishing crime statistics has created an increasing amount of work for college police forces," observed Lee Gardner (2015, p. 6). Reports of crimes, including a daily log, are a part of the requirement of every institution's Annual Security Report, also known as the Clery report (Gardner, 2015).

It must be noted that the details and parameters of federal reporting do change (e.g., the Clery Handbook has been revised four times, and the Department of Education recently released new guidelines on Title IX). New expectations rarely result in fewer reporting requirements; however, it is much more likely that the opposite will occur.

The expectation of creating a campus climate that is safe and secure becomes particularly challenging when one considers that many, if not most, community colleges enroll registered sex offenders, convicted felons on parole, and prisoners on work release as part of the open admissions mission. Combine this with the growth in dual enrollment, continuing education programs, the presence of a childcare center, and summer programs with numerous children on campus, and the expectation of a safe, secure environment becomes risky indeed.

NEED TO KNOW: PREVENTING CAMPUS VIOLENCE

Hartnell College in Salinas, California, recently averted a probable tragedy when someone reported to the police that a student was talking about shooting up the institution. In that case, police and mental-health professionals worked together to evaluate the student and found him to be a credible threat to campus safety, with both the means and the desire to cause harm. They subsequently detained him and placed him under psychiatric care (Sulkowski, 2016).

Although college campuses remain, statistically, among the safest of communities, the random nature of campus violence contributes to a sense of powerlessness among faculty and staff. What can ease anxieties, however, is a structure that is designed to flag potentially violent behavior and assess the level of threat. As Dr. Brian Van Brunt stated in his book, *Ending Campus Violence*, "The only way we can understand and assess the potential threat is to understand the context of the behavior" (2012, p. 6). A well-trained, collaborative behavior intervention team (BIT) is essential for community college campuses. The team should include "an even mix of those staff and faculty members who are directly connected to the 'campus pulse' along with those who have the ability and authority to make decisions" (Van Brunt, 2012, p. 54).

Any BIT, however, is only as effective as the information being funneled to it. In terms of preventing campus violence, research by the Secret Service, FBI, and Department of Education shows that often someone is aware that a person is planning an attack before it occurs (Sulkowski, 2016): "If all threats of violence were taken seriously and reported, preventing attacks on campuses would be much more possible" (p. 1).

Faculty at Schoolcraft are encouraged to report everything from the student who just seems "off," to more apparent troubling behaviors. For example, thanks to an alert faculty member and the *SC Aware* system, the college was notified about a student who was infatuated with Eric Harris and Dylan Klebold, the students responsible for the 1999 Columbine High School shooting. Because this kind of "hero worship" is definitely a red flag, local authorities as well as the FBI became involved, and the student received the professional help that was needed. As Van Brunt (2012) pointed out, "The need to break the code of silence that surrounds potentially dangerous behavior must be reinforced" (p. 58). Once faculty, staff, and students understand that this kind of reporting can literally make the campus a safer place, they are much more willing to come forward and speak up. Indeed, Cornell (2010) stated, "If the institution is able to help people who are upset, angry, depressed, or troubled in some way, many problems can be addressed before they rise to the level of a threat" (p. 221).

NEED TO KNOW: STUDENT SATISFACTION

"I have had an awesome experience at Schoolcraft. Advisors are so encouraging, the teachers approachable, and students are very welcoming. I am an older student and Schoolcraft experience has been rewarding. Each teacher has been exceptional," a student commented on a 2016 campus climate survey in response to the question: "If you were in charge of Schoolcraft, what would you to do improve the campus climate?"

Most long-term higher education administrators recall the "students as customers" trend that started back in the 1990s. Rather than the centuries-old tradition of instructor-learner as a relationship with a significant power differential, an increasing focus on students and student success led to changes in the student/professor dynamic. Morrow (1994) documented this trend and cautioned that higher education as a commodity would lead to "a heightened sense of entitlement among student and a corresponding rise in student incivility" (Heator, 2018, p. 1).

One issue is that some of today's students seem to regard education as a transaction rather than a transformational experience. With very little prompting, faculty can share stories of students who insist that because they came to class every day, they deserve a passing grade, whether or not they have demonstrated mastery of the material. Many faculty also complain of rude and disrespectful behavior toward them, often surrounding the issuing of final grades. Student discipline cases have accelerated rapidly in the past 20 years. One beleaguered dean of students had lunch with his predecessor and lamented all the time spent on student discipline cases. The retiree sighed and said, "Yes, we had to deal with at least five cases a year when I was dean." The current dean brought his predecessor up to date: five cases per *day* was not unusual now.

Awareness of campus issues due to classroom behaviors is just one source of concern. Another critical factor is what is being posted on the ubiquitous social media channels. Social media can be a great service to everyone in the campus community, but the use of this outlet can spark a host of other issues. Students who use social media to express their frustrations with the institution or with particular faculty or staff members can have a negative impact (Heator, 2018). These negative effects include damage to the instructor-student relationship, instructor self-efficacy, and instructor job satisfaction (Frisby et al., 2015). In addition, other students may be dissuaded from taking particular classes or instructors (Mukherjee et al., 2009).

Clearly, negative social media posts can ultimately harm the institution's reputation. Research has shown that students often do not complain to the institution; instead, they complain to others both on and off campus (Su & Bao, 2001). When the institution isn't given the opportunity to remedy the student's complaint, the potential exists that many other students are also dissatisfied, and some may simply walk away.

Student complaint reports at Schoolcraft can range from the mundane (losing money in a vending machine) to the routine (financial aid staff was rude to me) to the urgent (my professor shows up smelling like alcohol). If students have an internal outlet for filing instructional complaints, and this outlet is monitored, responded to, and serves to actually solve the problem, students are more likely to use that tool than to go on social media to vent. Not only should the college make it easy for students to complain, they should welcome those complaints. "By staying with the organization and voicing their concerns," Heator (2018) observed, "they buy the organization time to fix the problem before large numbers of others exit the organization without complaining."

NEED TO KNOW: STUDENTS WITH MENTAL HEALTH ISSUES

> Today I was alarmed to receive a private text that said she feels she is not doing well at all, very depressed and having suicidal thoughts. I immediately reached out to notify my administrator and am filing this report for immediate action. —*SC Aware* report, Winter 2020 semester

Mental health issues are pervasive among the college student population in general (Gallagher, 2015), and community college students may be even more vulnerable due to characteristics, such as being first-generation students and/or single parents, and having low socioeconomic backgrounds (Kalkbrenner et al., 2019). The number of students coming to community colleges with mental health issues is increasing, perhaps due to "better access to services during K–12 and increasing support and encouragement for students to reach further toward their goals" (Van Brunt, 2012, p. 221). Despite the fact that mental health is a significant contributing factor to overall student success and wellbeing, few community colleges have the resources to cope with the rising number of students who need help (Blackburn, 2019). At most community colleges with counseling services, counselors are also responsible for tasks such as student advising and career counseling.

Numerous mental health issues can prevent college students from performing at their full capacity: "Examples include suicidal behavior, off-topic questions related to a personality disorder or Autism, manic behavior, delusions and hallucinations, eating disorders and substance abuse" (Van Brunt & Lewis, 2014, p. 110). All of these are complex and debilitating issues that have the potential to disrupt the educational environment. While faculty and staff may do their best to respond to students with these challenges, it is unrealistic to assume that they have the time and expertise to offer in-depth assistance.

These students need to be connected with the services of mental health counseling resources either on or off campus. Some may believe that students provided with a referral to a counseling center will seek out the help they need, but this is not always the case. Success is more likely if notification goes to a counselor, who then reaches out to the student. Faculty at Schoolcraft are encouraged to report any behavior that seems out of character for a particular student. Counseling staff have found that a casual check-in with that student or a friendly outreach may be exactly what is needed at the time.

A SOLUTION: A CENTRALIZED REPORTING SYSTEM

In 2011, the vice presidents of academics, student affairs, and finance at Schoolcraft College teamed up to implement an online reporting system known as Maxient. Originally, the software was intended for use as a student discipline tool and tracking system. It soon became apparent, however, that this tool could be more useful and powerful if used to track other kinds of campus issues as well.

At the time, complaints at Schoolcraft were handled by a variety of departments. Student complaints about instructors, for example, went directly to the appropriate dean. It was possible (and in some cases, very likely) that some overloaded administrators' offices had stacks of complaints that were never dealt with at all. Facilities concerns went to someone in that department. Complaints sparked by possible violations of the Americans with Disability Act (ADA) were directed to the vice president and chief financial officer. Cases of cheating or plagiarism were handled by the respective faculty member, with no tracking. In essence, complaints were discouraged because most students (as well as many faculty and staff) had no idea where to report.

A guiding principle of the work in centralizing the reporting system was to make it easy for everyone to file a report. The software enables the reporter to select from the following categories: Instructional concerns or academic matters, concerning behavior or misconduct, request a late drop, withdrawal ("W" grade) or retake, customer service concerns or issues, or website or technology accessibility concern. (Note: During the COVID-19 crisis, an additional form was created for students to request assistance if they were impacted by the virus.) Each category then brings up a customized form to be completed by the reporter. The reporting software was branded as *SC Aware*. By centralizing reporting, complaints and concerns can be standardized in terms of the response, dispensation, and resolution. Because the software is date-driven, it is possible to see the length of the turnaround time for specific issues.

CULTURE OF REPORTING

No reporting system can be called effective unless it is being used. And no reporting system will be used if there is not a clear understanding about what happens after a report is filed, how confidentiality is protected, and any possible implications for the reporter.

Once the software was installed and set up, training sessions for faculty and staff began almost immediately. At one early training session, a faculty member asked about a student whose journal writing was becoming increasingly more dark and violent. Should she report him? The facilitator of the session was surprised to hear this question because the answer was so obvious. She quickly realized, however, that beneath this question were other questions: Who would receive the report? How would it be handled? What could happen to the student? Would the student know that she was the one who reported him?

It became clear that before faculty and staff were going to report incidents, they had to understand the process and trust that their reports would be handled with confidentiality and care. The training sessions were modified to include a clear step-by-step demonstration of how reports were triaged, routed, and monitored.

The training sessions also included information and lively discussion on why people may fail to report. Common barriers that keep people from reporting threats of violence include:

- not trusting authority figures;
- worrying about being perceived as a "snitch";
- being afraid of being personally targeted by a perpetrator;
- worrying that the person being reported will get in serious trouble; and
- expecting that college administrators will not take the threat seriously.

Students are informed about the *SC Aware* system as part of orientation, in their "Student Success" class, and from faculty and staff. When the system was first established, a decision had to be made about whether or not to allow anonymous reports. The concern was that reports filed anonymously could take up a tremendous amount of time and resources, but there was the potential for no closure because additional questions could not be asked, and follow-up would be impossible. The decision was made to allow anonymous reports but to inform the reporting party that anonymous reports may not receive the same level of follow-up. The result, after 9 years with the system, is that only a handful of anonymous reports have ever been received.

KEY COMPONENTS OF THE SYSTEM

For faculty and staff, *SC Aware* is publicized through the college website as well as at numerous training sessions. Emphasis is placed on the fact that anyone can file a complaint. Concerns that are raised via other channels are funneled to *SC Aware* by faculty or staff members. For example, staff may advise or suggest to a student that they file a report, but that staff member will also file in case the student fails to do so. This is particularly important when the incident is a sensitive or urgent one. Although this results in duplicate reports about a particular incident, it can sometimes prove useful during the investigatory period, since each report comes from a unique perspective. Concerns about the safety or wellbeing of instructors or students are acted upon immediately, regardless of whether an *SC Aware* report is filed or not.

Triage

The *SC Aware* form available on the website captures important information including the specific nature of the concern and what resolution is being sought. A single triage person sees every case and routes it to a case manager for follow-up. An automatic email is generated to the reporting party so that they know the report has been received and is being acted upon. The Student Relations office, which manages the system, also monitors the time that it takes to resolve cases. This is helpful for staffing purposes, for reporting, and for ensuring that no report "falls through the cracks."

Setup of the system can be time-consuming, since routing rules must be cognizant of confidentiality and sensitive to the workloads of those receiving reports. (For example, some senior administrators at first requested a copy of every report, but soon realized that it may not be a good use of their time to view every police report of a traffic incident or every instructor complaint.) Since the system is web-based, it is available 24/7, so administrators do receive reports of incidents in real time. More than once in recent memory, the immediacy of the reporting mechanism has enabled the college to respond to emergency situations in a timely manner.

CARE Team

Schoolcraft's Campus Awareness Response and Education (CARE) team receives and discusses discipline cases and cases involving students of concern. Soon after the team was founded, it received excellent training from Dr. Van Brunt, senior vice president for professional program development with the National Center for Higher Education Risk Management. The training included an extremely helpful video of what a behavioral intervention team team meeting should look like. Essentially, the team makes sure that all the information about a student comes to the table, and that he or she is on everyone's radar. If necessary, the team reaches out to the faculty and enlists their assistance and cooperation. Without disclosing any details, a member of the team may simply ask an instructor to keep a special eye on a student and to notify the team immediately if faculty see any change in behavior, or anything that is of concern.

Two members of the campus police force sit on the CARE team, and their participation is critical. Other members include representatives from the dean of students, associate deans of student relations, human resources, risk management, and counseling, and one of the academic deans.

The system's structure, then, is a triage person who reviews each case, case managers who handle routine cases that may be resolved fairly quickly and easily, and a CARE team that meets weekly to review and find resolution for more serious or complicated cases. Occasionally the CARE team's operations surface the need for a new or revised institutional policy or procedure; it is helpful to have all of the essential people at the table in order to draft a proposed change.

Intelligence Operations Center

As on many campuses, Schoolcraft's security includes cameras in key areas across campus. The college has a campus police force that includes technicians who monitor cameras on campus as well as keep an eye on social media for any negative information about the college that might be posted. One major benefit of this approach is that if students express frustration with some aspect of the college, the technicians will complete an *SC Aware* report, enabling someone from the college to reach out to that student with assistance. Students who get that phone call from the college learn two things: (1) The college cares about them, and (2) everything posted on social media is public information.

Data From *SC AWARE*

Table 4.1 below lists and defines the categories and demonstrates almost 100% growth in cases over the past 5 years for the academic and student services areas. As trust in the system and its administration has grown, the CARE team has met weekly to discuss cases and "connect the dots."

Complaints from students give the institution a chance to make things right, and hopefully retain the student; for, as Barlow and Møller (2008) pointed out, "A complaint is a gift." Another example of how the system's data can be used is to identify the most common instructional complaints from the student population, in hopes of finding remedies. Table 4.2 shows the fall-to-winter retention of students who were assisted with a student complaint or issue. It was apparent that clarity in expectations on instructor syllabi would be a positive action that could be taken. Additional and deeper insights were found when student satisfaction survey instruments were compared with *SC Aware* reports.

Table 4.1. *SC Aware* **Reports (Academic and Student Services) Fall 2015 vs. Fall 2019**

Categories	Definition	2015 Fall Term	2019 Fall Term
Instructional Concerns/Matters (grade, instructor complaints)	Student complains about a course and/or their instructor; student challenges the instructor's grading.	98	157
Students in Need of Assistance (ombudsman-style support)	Student in need of crisis intervention and/or emotional and mental health support.	24	11
Behavioral Concerns (counseling support, not conduct case)	Student accused of plagiarism or cheating.	51	78
Conduct: Academic Integrity (plagiarism, cheating)	Includes reports of conduct that violate the college's Title IX policy.	13	36
Conduct: Sexual Harassment, Misconduct	Includes violations of the Student Code of Conduct that don't fall into the sexual harassment/ sexual misconduct category or the discrimination category.	10	26
Conduct: Other Cases (various conduct code violations)	Reports of students violating the college's policy against discipline and harassment.	27	39
Customer Service Concerns	Complaints about services provided by employees and offices.	15	41
Request for Late W, Refund	Students who experience life circumstances that interfere with their ability to pass or complete a course request a late W grade, refund, or retake credit.	184	415
Discrimination	Cases where students need support and assistance that don't fall into one of the other categories.	N/A	2
Total		**422**	**805**

The college conducted a campus climate survey for students in 2016 and 2018. The results of both of those surveys demonstrated high satisfaction levels with the campus's safety.

Table 4.2.   Persistence Rate of Students Assisted by *SC Aware*

Case Type	# Helped Fall 2019	# Enrolled Winter 2020	Persistence Rate (%)
Extenuating circumstances	269	131	49
Instructional complaints	89	60	67
Concerning behavior	57	36	63
Customer service complaint	27	13	48
Ombuds support	7	4	47
Totals	**449**	**244**	**54.8%**

CONCLUSION

Because of its comprehensive scope, the *SC Aware* system at Schoolcraft helps with compliance reporting, takes a proactive approach to preventing campus violence, increases student satisfaction, and promptly raises awareness in order to address student mental health challenges. But perhaps its most important overall function is that it improves the campus climate and makes everyone on campus feel more connected and engaged.

Even a perfunctory look at the reports filed through *SC Aware* reveals the usefulness and value of this tool. Faculty have a place to turn when they have a student who is behaving in a disruptive, difficult, or disturbing manner. Students have an outlet to express concern over customer service issues, fellow students who seem depressed or discouraged, or policies that they perceive as unfair. Staff monitoring social media can alert those in service areas to frustrated and vocal students who need assistance. All of the above are actual reports that have been filed, and cases that have been successfully handled.

The benefits of having a centralized reporting system include removing barriers to complaining and providing a mechanism for timely intervention and resolution. The data can shed light on critical issues that need to be addressed, and reports can be viewed in conjunction with other data (e.g., student satisfaction survey results) to give additional insights.

One of the stories that illustrates the effectiveness of the system took place a few years ago and involved a student who was writing and behaving erratically in class. The *SC Aware* system received two separate reports from faculty and one from a group of concerned students, so the student was brought in for a conference. A threat assessment tool was used to determine that the student was a danger to himself, and his parents were notified. (In situations where health and safety are at risk, FERPA does not have priority.) Unbeknownst to the parents, the student had ceased taking his medication and was on the verge of a psychotic break. He was hospitalized, medications were adjusted, and he was able to return to finish the semester. The parents expressed great appreciation for the college's network of support, believing that it truly prevented something unfortunate from occurring.

Research reported by Michael Sulkowski (2016) discussed how ensuring a healthy climate is the core of effective violence prevention on college campuses. Essentially, people's willingness to report increases when they feel connected to the campus community, have confidence in college administrators, and trust campus police officers. If every person on the campus community feels engaged and connected, they will work to protect each other's safety and well-being.

Working to create a campus culture of trust and accountability—one that promotes individual investment in the good of the community and the safety of all faculty, staff, students, and visitors—can only benefit all stakeholders. We're all in this together.

REFERENCES

Barlow, J., & Møller, C. (2008). *A complaint is a gift: Recovering customer loyalty when things go wrong* (2nd ed.). Berrett-Koehler.

Blackburn, S. (2019, November 4). How higher ed is struggling to provide mental health services. *University Business.* https://universitybusiness.com/college-mental-health-mental-health-among-college-students.

Cornell, D. (2010). Threat assessment in college settings. *Change, 42*(1), 8–15.

Frisby, B. N., Goodboy, A. K., & Buckner, M. M. (2015). Students' instructional dissent and relationships with faculty members' burnout, commitment, satisfaction and efficacy. *Communication Education, 64*(1), 65–82. doi:10.1080/03634523.2014.978794.

Gallagher, R. P. (2015). National Survey of College Counseling Centers 2014. http://dd-scholarship.pitt.edu/28178/1/survey.2014.pdf.

Gardner, L. (2015, March 9). 25 years later, has Clery made campuses safer? *Chronicle of Higher Education.* http://www.chronicle.com/article/25-Years-Later-HasClery/228305.

Harris, A., & Kelderman, E. (2017, September 7). Citing Obama-Era failures, DeVos will replace landmark directive on sexual assault. *Chronicle of Higher Education.* https://www.chronicle.com/article/Citing-Obama-Era-Failures/241117.

Heator, M. (2018). *College students and the rhetorical dissent goal: Associations between dissent goal, dissent target, and perceptions of instructor power* [Unpublished doctoral dissertation]. Eastern Michigan University.

Kalkbrenner, M. T., Brown, E. M., Carlisle, K. L., & Carlisle, R. M. (2019, October). Utility of The REDFLAGS Model for supporting community college student mental health: Implications for counselors. *Journal of Counseling and Development, 97*(4), 417–426.

Lombardi, K. (2009, December 1). *Sexual assault on campus shrouded in secrecy.* The Center for Public Integrity. https://publicintegrity.org/education/sexual-assault-oncampus-shrouded-in-secrecy.

Morrow, W. (1994). Entitlement and achievement in education. *Studies in Philosophy and Education, 13*, 33–47.

Mukherjee, A., Pinto, M. B., & Malhotra, N. (2009). Power perceptions and modes of complaining in higher education. *The Service Industries Journal, 29*(11), 1615–1633.

Su, C., & Bao, Y. (2001). Student complaint behavior based on power perception. *Services Marketing Quarterly, 22*(3), 45.

Sulkowski, M. (2016, January 28). Averting tragedy before it occurs. *Inside Higher Ed*. https://www.insidehighered.com/views/2016/01/28/encouraging-students-reportthreats-violence-essay.

Van Brunt, B. (2012). *Ending campus violence: New approaches to prevention*. Routledge.

Van Brunt, B., & Lewis, W. S. (2014). *A faculty guide to addressing disruptive and dangerous behavior*. Routledge.

Zalaznick, M. (2020, May 6). How revised Title IX alters colleges' sex assault response. *University Business*. https://universitybusiness.com/title-ix-campus-sexual-assault-harassment-misconduct-trump-betsy-devos.

Part II

Meeting Students' Needs

As the world becomes ever more complex, so have the needs of students. Responding to these increasingly complex needs demands a new array of interventions focused on the students and requiring collaboration at every level of the institution.

"Fearless Leaders: Improving Student Persistence Through Advising Transformation" presents an innovative and disruptive commitment to reengineer the relationship of institutional advising and counseling to improve student persistence and success. Built on the premise that relationships matter, the investment in the case-management model demonstrates the value of connectedness and belonging as critical factors for students.

"Institutional Responsiveness to African American Male College Students (AAMCS): Are Minority Male Initiatives Working?" discusses the challenges and barriers to the AAMCS population and proposes strategies used to support the success of these often-underrepresented and -underserved students.

"Cracking the Barriers for African American and Latinx Students in STEM Education" focuses on approaches to attract and retain students from underrepresented groups, especially Latinx and African American minorities.

"College Students in Poverty: Examples of Collaborative Efforts and Interventions" outlines the challenges that food and housing insecurity present to student persistence and success.

Chapter Five

Fearless Leaders

Improving Student Persistence Through Advising Transformation

Kris Hoffhines

A NEED FOR ADVISING REFORM

The role of academic advisors in retaining community college students has been widely studied and has a long history of supporting student success in higher education (Cook, 2009). Throughout this history, academic advising models have evolved from being mostly prescriptive in nature, to taking a more developmental approach, with a keen focus on the importance of the relationship between advisor and student. In his seminal article, "Academic Advising: A Cornerstone of Student Retention," Crocket (1978) recognized the critical link between retention and academic advising and suggested that the frequency and quality of the advising relationship are important factors to consider when strengthening an advising program. It may not be enough to meet once a semester with a student, but rather, "dynamic advising programs are characterized by frequent high-quality contacts between adviser and advisee" (Crocket, 1978, p. 33).

Strengthening advising programs so that advisors are able to form meaningful relationships with students has become more important than ever, as the United States has fallen to a rank of 16th in the world for community college completion rates (American Association of Community Colleges [AACC], 2012). Low retention and graduation data for American community colleges in recent years has brought much attention to how best to support student success in higher education. In 2017, Harper College, a large community college located in the suburbs of Chicago, undertook a major transformation of their advising program with the intention of strengthening the relationship between the advisor and student by using a case management model. Our hope was that persistence and completion rates would increase if students felt more connected to our campus community and knew they had one person they could go to when faced with challenges.

As important as advising reform is to the success of community college students, it also involves major disruption to advising programs that, for most colleges, have been in place for many years. As we begin our fourth year of case management advising at Harper College, we can provide both qualitative and quantitative data that illustrate the power of a meaningful relationship between advisor and student. However, the undertaking of advising transformation at our college was fraught with disruption as well as innovation. The disruption that was necessary to overhaul our advising model was felt at all levels of our department and required fearlessness and fortitude of department leaders in order to navigate this journey successfully.

RELATIONSHIPS ARE CRITICAL TO RETENTION

Some academic advising models have been shown to be more effective than others when it comes to developing a relationship between advisor and student. Case management is a form of proactive advising that assigns students to one advisor who provides support in educational planning, goal setting, and career exploration, allowing for a stronger relationship between service provider and student. A case manager serves as a "human link between the client and the community system" (Adams et al., 2014, p. 448) and works to coordinate services based on individual needs.

We knew that case management potentially could lead to higher completion rates by allowing us to nurture that connection between advisor and student. The use of case management as a proactive academic advising strategy has taken a strong foothold recently at colleges that are participating in Achieving the Dream's iPASS initiative. For example, when South Texas College implemented the case management approach in their academic advising program in 2005, they assigned all new students to one of 21 certified case managers from the advising and counseling center (Excelencia in Education, n.d.).

The importance of a relationship with a critical person at the college—specifically an academic advisor—to student persistence and completion is supported by theories of marginality, mattering, and validation (Schlossberg, 1989; Rendon, 1994) that suggest that if students feel that they matter to a significant person at the college, they will be more likely to feel motivated to be involved in the campus community. Furthermore, increasing student involvement in the campus community has been shown to lead to increased student success and a decrease in college dropout (Astin, 1975, 1977, 1984; Tinto, 1975; Spady, 1970; Bean & Metzner, 1985). Based on these theories, transforming our college's advising program to case management had great potential for students to feel more connected to the campus community and increasing the likelihood that they would persist and complete. Our goal was to put a structure in place that would foster that connection and lead to students recognizing that they matter to Harper College.

IMPLEMENTING CASE MANAGEMENT

Until 2017, the primary service providers of academic advising at Harper College were tenured faculty counselors who held a master's degree in counseling or student personnel and worked under a 9-month faculty contract, with an option to work during school breaks for overload pay. Students in need of academic advising and support typically would meet with the counselor of their choice, with most students electing to schedule an appointment with a different counselor every time they needed advising, based on schedule availability and timing. This structure made it difficult for students to develop a lasting relationship with one counselor, resulting in students "counselor hopping" to get their advising needs met.

With the implementation of case management, 12-month professional academic advisors were hired. At first their role was to supplement the advising function in the new model alongside the faculty counselors, but eventually they were to become the sole service providers of academic advising. Initially, both advisors and counselors provided advising to students based on their academic standing at the college. Students in good academic standing were assigned to advisors, and students with academic caution, warning, and probation status were assigned to counselors. We used this approach believing that students at serious academic risk would benefit from counseling support.

However, as the new model evolved in the first year of implementation, we quickly realized that the academic standing of our students could be very fluid in nature. It became increasingly difficult to reassign students from advisors to counselors, and then back again, if the student's academic standing fluctuated. This approach also undermined the philosophy of case management and the nature of relationship-building between student and service provider.

To maintain the case management model, we made the decision to assign all students, including academically at-risk students, to an academic advisor. While advisors continue to refer students to counselors for non-academic reasons as needed, counselors moved out of the academic advising role completely. The college's counseling program, in fact, used this role transition to complete a redesign; the program now focuses solely on personal, career, and educational counseling. This shift away from academic advising has allowed counselors to focus on more extensive programming to assist students with life challenges.

For the academic advisors, the shift in advising workload to include the academically at-risk students also brought challenges. At first, the advisors struggled when they began receiving higher-risk students on their caseloads. Many felt ill-equipped to assist students in serious academic trouble. Our efforts focused on training advisors to understand the differences between academic and non-academic concerns and to provide strategies for supporting students in the higher-risk categories.

ARE WE THERE YET?

While the transition to case management advising offered great potential for more personalized, effective support to students, it also required a significant disruption to the "standard" service delivery methods and business processes that had been in place since the beginnings of Harper College in 1967. Four years into the transformation, we continue to ask ourselves, "Are we done yet?" We have finally come to the conclusion that the work of disruptive innovation is an ongoing process, requiring constant evaluation and quality improvements, and that we will likely never really be finished. Innovative disruption "is less a single event than a process that plays out over time, sometimes quickly and completely, but other times slowly and incompletely" (Wessel & Christensen, 2012, p. 4). Between 2017 and 2020, the following changes were implemented in support of case-managed advising and in the name of innovation for a more holistic approach to student success:

- promotion of two current staff to the level of associate dean: associate dean of advising services and associate dean of student success initiatives;
- addition of 25 professional academic advising staff positions;
- implementation of advising technologies, including expanded use of an early alert platform, creation of an "advisor dashboard," and increased use of an analytics platform;
- creation of case management guiding principles and expectations;
- conversion of 10 student development "specialist" positions to professional advising staff, resulting in a total of 35 academic advisors who work 12 months;
- separation of the function of academic advising from faculty counselors to professional advisors;
- creation of two lead academic advisor job descriptions and positions intended to provide necessary support of a large advising team;

- development of a comprehensive training program and ongoing professional development opportunities for newly hired advisors and current advisors;
- redesign of the Counseling Services department that included a "counseling model reboot" and formation of a more robust career, personal, and academic counseling team;
- remodeling and repurposing of existing office space previously used by other student services to create an Advising Services Center; and
- redesign and implementation of the college's Standards of Academic Progress model—to align with case management and to provide more proactive support of students who are on academic probation.

These changes were a heavy lift for our department and supported the initial implementation of the new advising model. However, the work to improve our model continues as we evaluate the impacts on both students and staff.

EVALUATION IS KEY

The two-pronged structural revision within the department represented a significant amount of change. First, we faced onboarding, training, and managing a large new advising staff. At the same time, we were transitioning our counselors away from their long-held role in academic advising. In the midst of experiencing the resulting effects of major change, we faced the challenges of new program implementation.

Expectations were high for the new case management model, from faculty, staff, executive leadership, and most of all students who would rely heavily on their assigned advisor for support. Would students value the relationship with their advisor enough to reach out for support when needed? Would case-managed students persist at higher rates than non-case-managed students? Evaluating the impact of the new advising program would be critical in order to demonstrate that the financial and human resources invested in this transformation were worthwhile.

Historically, evaluating the effectiveness of advising programs has not been a common occurrence in higher education institutions. Grites (1979) was among the first to call for a more organized approach to evaluating the quality of academic advising programs and suggested that "before an advising program can hope to improve, its current efforts and efficiencies must be clearly understood" (p. 35). When a college makes the effort to evaluate and revise its advising program, student retention has been shown to increase. In a national survey of 944 colleges and universities, administrators reported that ineffective academic advising programs were the primary cause of student attrition at their institution, and improving the advising program was the most common retention strategy utilized to increase retention and persistence (Beal & Noel, 1980).

Focus Group Sessions

To evaluate the impact of the case management advising model, we used both qualitative and quantitative measures. In 2018, just one year after the implementation of the new model, we conducted focus group sessions with three stakeholder groups: students, advisors, and counselors. The students were asked about the value of having assigned advisors and the impact of having an assigned advisor to their success in college. Advisors and counselors were asked about the effect of the case management model on their ability to develop relationships with students and the challenges of working in the new advising model.

Results: Student Focus Groups

Themes from the student focus groups included the following:

- Theme 1: It's easier to develop a personal relationship when you're assigned to one person. This personal relationship allows students to open up about challenges they may face in college, allowing the advisor to provide relevant support.
- Theme 2: Navigating the college system is easier when you have one person to whom you can go for help, any time you need it.
- Theme 3: Having a relationship with one advisor allows the advisor to know the student better, and to provide advising that is relevant, based on each student's individual situation.
- Theme 4: Being assigned to one person had an impact on campus involvement.
- Theme 5: Being assigned to one advisor or counselor leads to feeling more confident in ability to succeed.

It was clear from the student responses that they value having a relationship with one person for academic advising purposes and that this relationship can lead to feeling more confident in their ability to succeed in college. As one student summarized:

> I think it feels very warm and comforting to know that you have someone who's involved in your education other than a parent, a guardian, or yourself. So, to be having someone like that at school also makes you want to expand that kind of feeling into other places. You're like "oh, I'm comfortable here, I might as well join a club; I'm comfortable here, I can talk more in class." Like it definitely has an effect I've noticed.

Students also value the educational plan to completion that is provided within the context of case management advising. Another student reported:

> I think for me, especially, it kind of goes back, again, to having that framework of knowing what grades I need to stay ahead and be ready to leave in two years is what really helped me. Seeing in Degree Works, I use it all the time. I know my future, I know what classes I'm looking to take, I know what grades I need to get into the classes.

Overall, the five student focus group responses illustrated clearly that students feel that being assigned to one person for academic advising is beneficial to them in several ways. The case management model fosters a relationship that allows students to get to know their advisor on a deeper level, helps them to navigate the campus resources more easily, encourages campus involvement, and leads to increased feelings of confidence to succeed.

The themes that emerged from the student focus groups align with the literature of Ender et al. (1982), who was one of the first to suggest that the inclusion of student development theory in the academic advising process was critical because it introduced the concept of building a caring human relationship between the advisor and student. Frost (1991) also suggested that the relationship between the advisor and student could play a profound role in the student persisting to complete their academic goals. Furthermore, Varney (2013) presented the idea that a proactive case management advising model, such as the one implemented at Harper College, "involves institutional contact with students such that personnel and students develop a caring relationship that leads to increased academic motivation and persistence" (p. 137).

Results: Advisors' Focus Groups

Similarly, the themes from the advisors' focus group session included the following:

- Theme 1: Being assigned to one person can be both beneficial and limiting for students.
- Theme 2: The case management technology currently being utilized is complicated.
- Theme 3: There is pressure to build relationships with students quickly.
- Theme 4: It's too soon to measure the impact of the model on student success.

The counselors' sessions elicited these themes:

- Theme 1: Academic advising is valued more than counseling.
- Theme 2: There is a lack of trust between counselors and department administrators.
- Theme 3: It's too soon to measure the impact of the model on student success.
- Theme 4: Case management provides a valuable framework/system for supporting students.
- Theme 5: The case management model is too prescriptive.

Interestingly, the themes from the advisor and counselor focus groups tended to be more evaluative of the case management advising model itself, rather than on the impact of the model on the student's relationship with their assigned advisor and how this relationship impacted the student's academic success. While this focus may have been more a reaction to the changes the groups were experiencing, collecting these perceptions was important and essential as part of the evaluation process. Because the focus group sessions were held early in the implementation process—within the first year of the model's implementation—staff members were experiencing varying levels of reactions to the disruption. Although both advisors and counselors saw value in the case management model, both groups also expressed concerns that the case management technology might lead to overly complicated and prescriptive advising results, potentially serving as an impediment to the relationship-building process.

Counselors expressed perceptions that the function of counseling was being devalued in the case management model, and that there was a lack of trust between themselves and leadership in the department. These perceptions, clearly the result of the disruptions caused by the implementation of the new advising model, the introduction of 12-month academic advisors, and the substantial changes in the counselor's role, reflected the difficulties the faculty counselors were experiencing during the transition. One participant summarized the group's feelings:

> But the case management model currently is very focused on the academic advising piece, and so it was pushing some of the personal counseling, maybe some of the career counseling to the side because of this focus on the plan, on the academic piece. So, as practitioners we really had to refocus what was important to the student and then pick up the rest of the administration piece later.

Aside from the evaluative commentary on the case management model in general, both advisors and counselors acknowledged the value of assigning each student to one person. However, they also identified a significant new stressor: there was a perceived pressure to build relationships with their assigned caseloads too quickly, perhaps within the first appointment with a student. One respondent expressed concern that building a relationship quickly with students will become more difficult as caseload sizes grow.

Caseloads are a recognized concern in advising and especially in case management programs. According to Robins (2013), the National Survey of Academic Advising conducted by NACADA in 2011 suggested that the average caseload size for advisors working in 2-year institutions is 441. Robins (2013) continued, stressing that colleges must define the ideal caseload size for their advising program based on student needs, advising delivery modes, and other advisor responsibilities. As Harper College moves forward with the case management model, we will need to be cognizant of these issues and stay within national averages for caseload sizes in order to provide an appropriate level of support.

Interestingly, both advisors and counselors felt that building an educational plan to completion during the first advising appointment could disrupt the rapport-building process with students and can feel overwhelming to them. The process of building a plan to completion in the college's degree audit platform was introduced as a new expectation as part of case management. One advisor noted:

> I think they also want us to build their plan to completion relatively soon in the first appointment, which I don't think is . . . the best use of time because if you're trying to build a relationship, you're trying to get familiar with the student's goals and what they're trying to achieve. . . .
>
> So no, I'm not doing that for that student. No way. I'm going to do this semester and next semester, and we're going to call it a day, because that's where the student's at. Because if I overwhelm you, guess what? You're not going to come back and see me. You're going to think I'm nuts, right? And you're going to walk away and have a bad taste in your mouth.

What the Data Revealed

We also evaluated the new approach using institutional student success data. Fall-to-spring persistence rates for case-managed students indicated that in the first years of case-managed advising at Harper College, students who met with their assigned advisor/counselor persisted at higher rates than students who did not.

Specifically, students who were *not* assigned to an advisor or counselor during the 2016–2017 academic year, the year prior to the implementation of the case management model, persisted at lower rates (83%) than students who were assigned to one advisor/counselor in 2017 as part of case management (86%). Fall-to-spring persistence rates have remained strong for the first 3 years of the program: In 2017–2018, students who met with their advisor persisted at 92%, compared to 70% for students who did not meet with their advisor. In 2018–2019, persistence rates were 84% for students who met with their advisor, 67% for those who did not. In 2019–2020, case-managed students reflected an 86% persistence rate; those who did not, persisted at only 57%.

Overall, these early data on the impact of case management advising at Harper College illustrate that students perceive a value in developing a relationship with one advisor, and persistence improves for students who meet with an assigned academic advisor for educational planning and support in comparison to students who don't meet their advisor.

HOW CAN WE CONTINUE TO IMPROVE?

As the Harper College Advising Services department looks ahead to the next 3 to 5 years, we must consider ways to strengthen our case management advising model. First, we will continue to apply change management strategies to support the advising and counseling staff as they continue to navigate the evolving advising model. Effective change leadership and continuous trust-building between leadership and staff, as well as among the advising and counseling team, will allow for continuous innovation and improvements to the model.

Increasing Student-Advisor Meetings

We are also considering strategies to increase the rate that students meet with their assigned advisor. Although the overall number of students who met with an advisor increased 22% from fall 2018 to fall 2019, only 60% of all case-managed students met with their assigned advisor in fall 2019. We are currently recommending mandated advisor meetings within the first semester of enrollment; the recommendation is being vetted through the college's shared governance system for approval.

Collecting Assessment Data

Ongoing qualitative and quantitative evaluation will be necessary to support the value of case management for student success. The cornerstone of case management—a strong relationship between student and assigned advisor—is key to the success of the model. National data support the value of this relationship in increasing persistence and completion rates. To avoid larger caseload sizes that could affect advisors' ability to proactively support students, our data, too, must support this connection and allow us to maintain appropriate caseload sizes of no more than 350 to 400 students.

Refining Technology Supports

Continuing to refine the technology used to support case management will allow advisors to provide more seamless supports to students as they work with them on educational planning. Too many platforms may cause confusion and unnecessarily complicate the model. Providing training for a large staff of advisors that supports their ability to balance the need to build relationships with their students while meeting case management expectations will be crucial.

Rebuilding Trust

Increasing opportunities for collaboration and trust-building between counselors and advisors will also be critical as the model continues to evolve. The transition to case management advising and the replacement of the long-standing traditional approach to academic advising on Harper's campus resulted in significant disruption to the counseling staff and caused a chasm between advisors and counselors. Improving the relationship between counselors and advisors will improve the ability of both groups to provide a holistic approach to supporting student success.

Focusing on Additional At-Risk Groups

When we initially redesigned our advising model, our focus was on providing effective academic advising for all students. Our strategies focused on providing the important personal contacts that are the foundation of case management advising. However, while the case management advising model is designed to support persistence and completion of all Harper College students, we recognize that various subgroups within this population may benefit from additional supports that the case management model can also provide. As we fine-tune the model, we hope to include more intentional strategies that will chip away at our achievement gaps in the White, African American, and Latinx student populations.

CONCLUSION

In order for community colleges to effectively increase retention and completion rates, we must continue to refine and improve a long-recognized key element to student success: academic advising. The more proactive advising model that takes an intrusive approach and develops one-on-one relationships has shown a positive impact at Harper College. The importance of a relationship with an academic advisor to student persistence and completion is supported not only by theories of marginality, mattering, and validation

(Schlossberg, 1989; Rendon, 1994) but also by our own institutional data. Transforming and strengthening advising programs will provide community colleges with a tool for increasing retention and completion rates and, more importantly, will better serve our students who come to our colleges with aspirations for success.

REFERENCES

Adams, S. D., Hazelwood, S., & Hayden, B. (2014). Student affairs case management: Merging social work theory with student affairs practice. *Journal of Student Affairs Research and Practice, 51*(4), 446–458.

American Association of Community Colleges. (2012). *Reclaiming the American dream, a report from the 21st-Century Commission on the Future of Community Colleges.* American Association of Community Colleges. http://www.aacc.nche.edu/21stCenturyReport.

Astin, A. W. (1975). *Preventing students from dropping out.* Jossey-Bass.

Astin, A. W. (1977). *Four critical years.* Jossey-Bass.

Astin, A. W. (1984). Student involvement: A developmental theory for higher education. *Journal of College Student Personnel, 25*(4), 297–308.

Beal, P. E., & Noel, L. (1980). *What works in student retention.* American College Testing Program.

Bean, J. P., & Metzner, B. S. (1985). A conceptual model of nontraditional undergraduate student attrition. *Review of Educational Research, 55*(4), 485–540.

Cook, S. (2009). Important events in the development of academic advising in the United States. *NACADA Journal, 29*(2), 18–40.

Crocket, D. S. (1978). Academic advising: A cornerstone of student retention. *New Directions for Student Services, 1978*(3), 29–35.

Ender, S. C., Winston, R. B., & Miller, T. K. (1982). Academic advising as student development. *New Directions for Student Services, 1982*(17), 3–18.

Excelencia in Education. (n.d.). *The case management approach to academic advising program.* Retrieved January 15, 2021, from http://www.edexcelencia.org/program/case-management-approach-academic-advising-program.

Frost, S. H. (1991). *Academic advising for student success: A system of shared responsibility.* School of Education and Human Development, the George Washington University.

Grites, T. J. (1979). Academic advising: Getting us through the eighties. AAHE-ERIC/Higher Education Research Reports No. 7. ERIC database, ED178023.

Rendon, L. I. (1994). Validating culturally diverse students: Toward a new model of learning and student development. *Innovative Higher Education, 19*(1), 33–51.

Robins, R. (2013). *Advisor load.* NACADA Clearinghouse. http://www.nacada.ksu.edu/Resources/ Clearinghouse/View-Articles/Advisor-Load.aspx.

Schlossberg, N. K. (1989). Marginality and mattering: Key issues in building community. *New Directions for Student Services, 1989*(48), 5–15.

Spady, W. G. (1970). Dropouts from higher education: An interdisciplinary review and synthesis. *Interchange, 1*(1), 64–85.

Tinto, V. (1975). Dropout from higher education: A theoretical synthesis of recent research. *Review of Educational Research, 45*(1), 89–125.

Varney, J. (2013). Proactive advising. In J. Drake, P. Jordan, & M. Miller (Eds.), *Academic advising approaches: Strategies that teach students to make the most of college* (pp. 137–154). Josey Bass.

Wessel, M., & Christensen, C. M. (2012). Surviving disruption. *Harvard Business Review, 90*(12), 56–64.

Chapter Six

Institutional Responsiveness to African American Male College Students (AAMCS)

Are Minority Male Initiatives Working?

Michael A. Couch II and Tina L. Hummons

HOW ARE AAMCS DOING IN 2020?

Historically, educational responsiveness to African American Male College Students (AAMCS), as well as completion, retention, and graduation rates have been low. The United States has historically been "less supportive of African Americans in society and educational institutions, particularly with regards to educational attainment" (Palmer et al., 2010, p. 107). Educational reforms over the past few decades that have resulted in increased achievement failed to close massive gaps in both enrollment and achievement of AAMCS (Shuford, 2009). Data reported by the U.S. Census Bureau for the 2014–2015 academic year showed that 34% of African American men between the ages of 18 and 24 enrolled in higher education. This figure is compared to almost 39% of White male counterparts (U.S. Department of Education, 2010). Furthermore, the U.S. Department of Education, Integrated Postsecondary Data System Completion Survey (2015) reported that participation rates for African American men who attended community colleges were only half the rate for African American females.

During the 1980s and 1990s, there was a considerable increase in AAMCS attending higher-education institutions; however, they continue to fall behind White and female counterparts in college participation, retention, persistence, and degree completion (Noguera, 2003; "Black Student College

Graduation Rates," 2020). Researchers have found that in contrast to other major demographic groups, AAMCS have the lowest educational outcomes in the United States (Palmer et al., 2010). Specifically, AAMCS have the highest attrition rates and lowest completion rates among all ethnic groups and genders.

Perhaps most alarming is that AAMCS educational outcomes continue to plummet after years of attention and intervention. Some researchers have predicted that if the current trend of low graduation and enrollment continues, AAMCS may not be participating in higher education at all by the year 2070 (Cross & Slater, 2000). While this prediction is dire, it may be useful as a motivator for renewed attention and focus on strategies that have demonstrated success. We must reconsider and refocus successful strategies so that policymakers, educators, and administrators can reverse these trends in AAMCS' educational attainment (Palmer et al., 2010).

HOW HAVE COMMUNITY COLLEGES RESPONDED?

Responding to this population and providing appropriate academic supports have presented challenges for higher education institutions, especially community colleges. AAMCS' have a unique set of needs, and support for this population looks different.

Historically, community colleges have been the preferred higher education settings for AAMCS (Harper, 2012; Harper & Wood, 2016). However, data has shown that AAMCS have the lowest degree attainment of all other demographic groups within community colleges. Research (O'Keeffe, 2013) also has indicated that this demographic group faces complex barriers to academic success, including prior educational experiences, feelings of rejection and disconnection, a lack of belonging in the learning environment, low teacher expectations, and the competing responsibilities of employment and family with school. These barriers have proven to be critical in African American male students' ability to persist in college to achieve degree attainment (Jones, 2014; Simmons, 2013; Wood et al., 2015).

Community colleges responded to the needs of these students and developed specific initiatives addressing these barriers in the early 2000s. In 2003, the Lumina Foundation for Education launched a bold, multiyear, national initiative called Achieving the Dream: Community Colleges Count, to help students stay in school and succeed. The initiative was focused particularly on students who faced the most barriers to success, including low-income students and students of color. Another initiative called My Brother's Keeper provided programming targeted to help shift the educational experiences of these students. In 2010, the American Association of Community Colleges (AACC) launched a minority male initiative (MMI) database to catalog programs, interventions, and initiatives designed to enhance the success of men of color in community colleges (Christian, 2010). In 2014, the Center for Community College Student Engagement reported on community college efforts in their report *Aspirations to Achievement: Men of Color and Community Colleges.*

During this same time period, community colleges also focused on increasing their efforts to recruit and retain young men of color (Hampton, 2002; College Board, 2010). Improving retention and completion rates of AAMCS is a fundamental task of community colleges, extending from college leadership to faculty, staff, and other stakeholders, but also including community members and policymakers.

Early programs that sought to expand college enrollment for at-risk and underrepresented populations—such as Young Scholars, Upward Bound, and Brother to Brother—have supported thousands of students but, because of their programmatic thrust, could not recruit participants from, or address needs of, a specific demographic. Other programs, including post-secondary enrollment options (PSEO) and Talent Search, had limited success but often didn't receive sufficient institutional support or resources to have a significant effect. Thus, these programs' success with the AAMCS population is not clear. As attrition and degree completion rates continue to be well below other groups and show few signs of improvement, community colleges' role in resolving this problem has become even more critical to the success of AAMCS. Community colleges must identify and implement strategies and successful program ideas that show the most promise for shifting the narrative for these men.

WHAT DO AAMCS THINK ABOUT CURRENT SUPPORT PROGRAMS?

One research study, conducted in 2018, focused on AAMCS currently enrolled at Sinclair Community College (Ohio). A focus group session with 14 students who participated in the institution's African American Male Initiative (AAMI) identified strengths and weaknesses of the current programming and issues that the students felt the college needed to address.

Effect of Pre-College Educational Experiences

The focus group conversations revealed that the students' pre-college experiences had considerable influence on their hesitations about enrolling in college, while poor academic progress, lack of faculty support, and the absence of positive role models were prevalent in their early lives.

The students identified their educational challenges to be rooted in a lack of belief in themselves, noncaring faculty members, lack of educator confidence in them as students, and lack of self-initiative. The participants acknowledged that these educational challenges grew from the negative opinions of AAMCS they experienced from the broader society and that these opinions affected their confidence and belief in their ability to succeed. Another significant theme that arose in the focus group sessions was the impact of microaggressions on their educational success.

Research indicates that microaggressions have a large influence on the psyche and can cause physical, emotional, and spiritual distress. These subtle aggressive behaviors can prompt feelings of anger, hostility, and/or distress for recipients (Sue, 2010). In the United States, microaggressions have root in the socially constructed categories of race and attitudes of superiority and inferiority (Solózarno et al., 2000). Attitudes and beliefs that are grounded in these constructs are reflected in low expectations held by teachers, family members, or society members; "innocent" comments about a person of color's educational attainment; or preconceptions about a person of color's ability to succeed (Solózarno et al., 2000).

For African American college students, the widely held perception of many of their White counterparts is at the root of the microaggressions they face in their classroom. In many White students' minds, African American students are accepted into college only because of affirmative action quotas. This belief, which stems from a long history of misrepresentation of the true meaning of affirmative action, can affect faculty expectations as well as student-to-student interactions (Solózarno et al., 2000).

Influences of the AAMI Program

The students who participated in the focus group sessions reported that they initially felt isolated and frequently misunderstood by both faculty and peers in the college setting. The participants also reported that disengagement, inappropriate behavior, and lack of academic stamina were results of negative interactions with peers and teachers; however, once they joined the AAMI, they gained a feeling of belonging when they connected with an AAMI counselor or found support or connection to another faculty or staff member. Even after participants experienced educational challenges and obstacles, they mustered the resolve to seek out support and positive reinforcement from faculty and peers within AAMI and then strove toward the goal of persisting with their education. Participants reported that disengagement was often the result of negative interactions with peers and teachers, but that their interactions with AAMI were significant in overcoming these barriers. The students' comments suggested that self-confidence was the biggest obstacle.

Campus Climate

In terms of the campus climate, the focus group participants reported that they had seen positive changes in terms of campus diversity and efforts to provide support. They noted that the campus environment had definitely changed over the last few years. With increased enrollment of AAMCS, the environment seemed to shift quickly. The students noted, however, that cultural differences were still evident. As one student observed, when faculty and staff see a group of AAMCS, their reaction is telling: "They kind of stare . . . not say a hostile environment, but it makes you really think about the environment you're in. It is like I am welcome, but I still feel like an outlier in a school that is supposed to be a safe haven" for educational diversity and inclusion.

Advice for the College

To close the focus group conversations, participants were asked to provide advice and suggestions for the institution that would help them and other AAMCS succeed. The participants provided a number of recommendations for both entering AAMCS and increased institutional responsiveness in the future. The 14 students who participated in the study recommended that, even with budgetary constraints at the institution, the AAMI program warranted continued support. They noted the importance of broader campus support for the program, recognizing that campus and community involvement can ensure longstanding sustainability of the program.

An increased effort to diversify the campus with African American administrators, staff, and faculty members was a second recommendation they offered. A third recommendation was for the campus to increase focus on student support services available to all learners, with recognition of the specific needs that some African American male college students may require. A final recommendation supported their earlier comments about the importance of acceptance and positive reinforcement from the institution as a whole; they stressed the importance of institutional acceptance of their value and their abilities to succeed in their educational pursuits.

WHAT CAN WE LEARN FROM THESE STUDENTS?

This study illustrated clearly that our institutional responsiveness to AAMCS, especially through the AAMI, is emergent. The program has been successful in facilitating AAMCS by providing role models, avenues for institutional culture change, group identity and mentorship, and awareness of the extensive student support services that are available for AAMCS. Participating in these focus groups also provided the students with opportunities to reflect on their educational paths: to describe individuals who influenced them; to identify the signs of a changing culture; to value the positive impacts of AAMI; and to acknowledge the obstacles and challenges they face.

The focus groups reinforced the value of programs like AAMI and similar mentorship programs. Student organizations specifically designed to support and aid in the retention of African American males, such as the Student African American Brotherhood and the AAMI, are highlighted in the literature as being impactful in terms of enabling persistence and degree completion for Black male college students (Brooms, 2016). These organizations allow students to be supported by adults who come from the same culture and who are successful professionals. As the men in this study reported, the programs also provide peer-mentoring opportunities, which foster institutional commitment, camaraderie, and support.

HOW CAN OTHER INSTITUTIONS ADAPT THESE PROGRAMS?

Nationally Recognized Programs

On a national level, there are large-scale programs that institutions can model or adapt to fit their institutional structure and student needs. These programs include the African American Male Initiative Program and the Student African American Brotherhood, located at more than 100 colleges and universities. These programs focus on creating a sense of belonging and connectedness. As Brooms (2018) wrote, "By establishing meaningful interactions and connections on campus and building up Black male students, these programs can enhance Black male students' sense of belonging and sociocultural capital" (p. 150). Here are a few examples—from our institutional experiences—of community colleges that have incorporated similar programming.

Ivy Tech Community College (Indiana)

In response to the research related to causes of low AAMCS achievement and enrollment, the Ivy Tech Community College system is developing the African American male strategic enrollment plan for central Indiana based on best practices and approaches on successful college enrollment, retention, and completion efforts. The goal is to create a roadmap for making significant and immediate progress for AAMCS at the college. As a statewide system, Ivy Tech currently offers a mixture of programs on the campuses. These include AAMI, My Brother's Keeper, and an Indianapolis program named Ivy Men of Merit. Through the system's strategic enrollment plan, Ivy Tech hopes to identify best practices from these programs, identify new ideas from other areas, and build a comprehensive program that will help the AAMCS population become successful.

Grand Rapids Community College (Michigan)

At Grand Rapids Community College, the Brother-2-Brother (B2B) Network puts equity at the core of its program. Participants are led through evidence-based pillars of success that redress historical and systemic inequities that male and male-identified students encounter in academic environments. The goal of the B2B Program is to tap into and enhance students' cultural capital; strengthen their academic acumen; foster leadership development; and support personal development. All students, not only AAMCS, are welcome to enroll in B2B.

At the foundation of many of these community college efforts is a framework that has provided a construct for addressing educational inequities. Dr. Joan Holmes (2016) presented a "Theory of Black Student College Success" in her book *African American/Black Student Populations: Cutting-Edge Models for Best Practice.* Her model incorporated years of best practices in enhancing retention and completion and mentoring programs focused on AAMCS. In her model she talked about the four pillars of academic success for Black college students:

1. Create a culture of academic achievement.
2. Understand ethnic/cultural differences.
3. Expose students to new environments and opportunities.
4. Provide adequate resources, including mentoring opportunities.

Within each pillar, Holmes identified key approaches that have shown positive outcomes; these features have been incorporated into many campus programming efforts and continue to drive successful change. Strategies such as intentional and intrusive academic advising and planning; a cohort model for support; a focus on the student life cycle; peer and faculty mentorship; and exposure to campus allies, community support services, and a wide range of opportunities for campus involvement help to create programming to support these men.

PROGRAMMING THAT WORKS

Many best practices designed to support student success for all students have shown promise when designed or focused to address needs of specific populations. The practices highlighted here are just a few that many campuses are currently using to support AAMCS. While these practices have been successful in improving outcomes for all students, they can be adopted to address specific needs of AAMCS.

Mentoring Programs

Mentoring programs have been implemented in higher education in an effort to close the achievement gap between minority populations and the general student population by assisting students with their adjustment to college, academic performance, and persistence decisions (Fowler & Muckert, 2004; Hicks, 2005; Salinitri, 2005).

The success of programs closing the achievement gap by recruiting and retaining minority students has also been prevalent in the literature (Campbell & Campbell, 1997; Canton & James, 1997; Salinitri, 2005). Brawer (1996) suggested that minority retention is improved when peer mentoring is utilized in order to develop social support networks among new students.

AAMCS often have difficulty with a variety of identity, self-esteem, and even racial battle fatigue issues while attending college (Smith et al., 2007). Smith and colleagues (2007) suggested that racial battle fatigue is often demonstrated through frustration, anger, exhaustion, physical avoidance, and emotional withdrawal among AAMCS at Predominately White Institutions (PWIs). In an attempt to address these issues, an increasing amount of research has been examining the impact of mentoring relationships on a person's identity and self-esteem (Bonner & Bailey, 2006).

While mentoring has been consistently associated with increased retention in the literature (Harper, 2012), a related finding is the importance of the connection between students and their faculty members. Research has shown that African American students, and males in particular, benefit from having African American instructors in the classrooms. The importance of having an educational culture and environment that reflects a student's own is critical for student success; however, research also suggests that it is sometimes difficult for African American faculty members to support African American students because minority faculty often experience the same challenges as the students, such as insufficient mentoring and professional development opportunities (Sedlacek et al., 2007).

Focused Support Services

Walsh and colleagues (2009) theorized that students failed to stay in school and to matriculate and graduate not because of lack of mentors or professors who look like them, but rather because of a lack of effective and appropriate student support services. According to the researchers, students reported that they "preferred" support mechanisms for academic and educational issues including academic tutors, peer instructional support in their courses, pastoral care, career services, and financial advice (p. 405). Walsh et al. (2009) emphasized that the one concept universities and colleges must understand is that supporting student success is the key element that will affect retention.

Evidence has also indicated that institutions that help AAMCS become a part of the college community increase student retention. As Tinto (1993) argued, "A central factor in students' success is integration with their institution" (p. 88). Tinto (1993) suggested that students must get involved in campus interactions outside of the classroom.

Guided Advising: Sinclair Community College's MAP

Instead of leaving AAMCS on their own to navigate an often unclear and convoluted process of registration and course sequencing, one promising intervention strategy to increase retention for all students is the Guided Pathways model. According to Jenkins and Cho (2014), the *Guided Pathways to Success Model* relies on three distinct features: (1) explicit roadmaps to reach student outcome goals; (2) on-ramping that includes redesigned intake, advising, and academic remediation; and (3) advising opportunities at regular points throughout students' programs to provide progress-monitoring, feedback, and interventions or supports if needed. All of these program features are essential for AAMCS' success.

In 2014, the associate provost and director of academic advising at Sinclair Community College (Ohio) created an academic pathway and redesigned the curriculum to increase relevancy through implementing My Academic Plan (MAP). The technology allows students, faculty, and staff to more clearly lay out requirements leading to completion. While this technology promises to be enormously beneficial for all students, it also provides a much-needed advising component for the institution's AAMCS.

Intrusive Advising

Similar to the advising model offered by Guided Pathways programs, intrusive advising is a one-on-one, supportive relationship between the advisor and advisee. Advisors see advisees as individuals, needing more than just information about registration and college policies. The intrusive advising approach focuses on increasing academic success through proactive academic interventions that assist students struggling both academically and personally (Levinstein, 2018). Intrusive advising is also focused on increasing students' use of campus resources and creating awareness of how to seek assistance.

According to Donaldson and colleagues (2016), intrusive advising is a proactive approach to advising, building relationships with students by anticipating their needs and connecting them with resources and support at the beginning of their academic careers. A key component of the intrusive advising model includes mandatory appointments set throughout the semester to help with the entire student experience. With mandatory appointments, the program creates another layer of support and accountability for AAMCS.

College Student Success Courses

Research has indicated that integrating college student success courses during the student's first year of enrollment is an effective practice to improve student retention (Cho & Karp, 2013). Furthermore, Derby's (2007) study of 3,538 students at a Midwestern, rural community college found graduation rates for student success course participants were 72 times higher than non-participants. Because one of the goals of these courses is to increase students' involvement in the institution and integration into the college culture, the courses can address this key need for AAMCS' success. The courses can direct students to the various services offered at the college; facilitate their adjustment to the college environment; and give them the tools they need to be successful at the institution.

Early Alert Systems

As noted earlier, AAMCS often experience a lack of self-confidence and a belief in their own abilities to succeed in the educational environment. Frustrations in the classroom or with their academic work can build and erode their confidence. To address these problems for all students, many colleges are incorporating early alert systems. These systems allow educators to systematically monitor student performance and intervene when academic challenges arise. Patterns of marginal course engagement—such as missing assignments, arriving to class late, or receiving low grades—can predict when a student is facing challenges and on a negative path.

Using an early alert system, the college can identify and meet the needs of students who demonstrate concerning patterns by referring them to academic advisors and counselors. These staff provide appropriate referrals to support services that can lead to enhanced course performance. The goal of an early alert system is to intervene with a wide range of support services—including childcare, tutoring, financial aid, and career advising—in order to address the underlying problem while there is still time to change the trajectory of a student's success.

WHAT'S NEXT?

While each of these programming features may address a barrier that keeps AAMCS from succeeding in their educational endeavors, simply offering the programs isn't enough. Institutions must create well-informed, well-re-sourced strategies for improvement. In years past, colleges and universities have haphazardly created stand-alone, piecemeal programs with no strategic plan or measurable objectives. Harper (2014) noted that such "efforts . . . launched in stand-alone and fragmented ways . . . had not emerged from substantive, collaborative conversations and planning" with colleges/university administrators or key stakeholders (p. 142).

Until community college institutions are ready to have cultural dialogue and embrace the opportunity to eliminate the disparities, we cannot continue to serve AAMCS with the tools we currently have in place. The opportunity gap separating minority males from other student groups must be addressed and resolved.

Community colleges have the perfect opportunity to lead this work. To be faithful to the mission of open-access institutions, we must create positive educational experiences and wrap-around support from entry to graduation. In order to improve outcomes for Black male college students, institutions have to begin with thoughtful, campus-wide plans for improvement. By developing targeted programs with specific practices, we believe the opportunity gaps will close and we will see the retention and completion rates for African American males begin to trend in a positive direction.

REFERENCES

Black student college graduation rates remain low, but modest progress begins to show. (2020, July). *Journal of Blacks in Higher Education.* https://www.jbhe.com/features/ 50_blackstudent_gradrates.html.

Bonner II, F. A., & Bailey, K. (2006). Assessing the academic climate for African American men. In M. Cuyjet (Ed.), *African American men in college* (pp. 24–46). Jossey-Bass.

Brawer, F. B. (1996). *Retention-attrition in the nineties.* Office of Educational Research and Improvement. ERIC Document Reproduction Service No. ED393510.

Brooms, R. D. (2016). Building us up: Supporting black male college students in a Black male initiative program. *Critical Sociology, 44*(1), 141–155. http://journals.sagepub.com/ doi/abs/ 10.1177/0896920516658940.

Brooms, R. D. (2018). Exploring black male initiative programs: Potential and possibilities for supporting Black male success in college. *Journal of Negro Education, 87*(1), 59–72. https:/ /doi.org/10.7709/jnegroeducation.87.1.0059.

Campbell, T. A., & Campbell, D. E. (1997). Faculty/student mentor program: Effects on academic performance and retention. *Research in Higher Education, 38*(6), 727–742. doi: 10.1023/A:1024911904627.

Canton, M. E., & James, D. P. (1997). Models in mentoring through faculty development. In H. T. Frierson (Ed.), *Diversity in higher education: Mentoring and diversity in higher education* (pp. 77–92). JAI Press.

Center for Community College Student Engagement. (2014). *Aspirations to achievement: Men of color and community colleges.* Center for Community College Student Engagement.

Cho, S. W., & Karp, M. M. (2013). Student success courses in the community college: Early enrollment and educational outcomes. *Community College Review, 41*(1), 86–103. doi: 0.1177/0091552112472227.

Christian, K. (2010). *AACC launches minority male student success database.* American Association of Community Colleges.

College Board. (2010). *The educational crisis facing young men of color*. The College Board.

Cross, T., & Slater, R. B. (2000). The alarming decline in the academic performance of African American men. *The Journal of Blacks in Higher Education, 27*, 82–87.

Derby, D. C. (2007). Predicting degree completion: Examining the interaction between orientation course participation and ethnic background. *Community College Journal of Research and Practice, 31*(11), 883–894. doi:10.1080/10668920600859350.

Donaldson, P., McKinney, L., Lee, M., & Pino, D. (2016). First-year community college students' perceptions of and attitudes toward intrusive academic advising. *NACADA Journal, 36*(1). http://www.nacadajournal.org/doi/abs/10.12930/NACADA-15-012?code=naaa-site.

Fowler, J., & Muckert, T. (2004). Tiered mentoring: Benefits for first year students, upper level students, and professionals. A paper presented at the Teaching and Learning Forum.

Hampton, P. (2002). *Academic success for African American male community college students* [Unpublished doctoral dissertation]. University of Southern California.

Harper, S. R. (2012). *Black male student success in higher education: A report from the National Black Male College Achievement Study*. University of Pennsylvania, Center for the Study of Race and Equity in Education. https://webapp.usc.edu/web/rossier/publications/231/Harper%20(2012)%20Black%20Male%20Success.pdf.

Harper, S. R. (2014). (Re)Setting the agenda for college men of color: Lessons learned from a 15-year movement to improve Black male student success. In R. A. Williams (Ed.), *Men of color in higher education: New foundations for developing models for success* (pp. 116–143). Stylus.

Harper, S. R., & Wood, J. L. (2016). *Advancing Black male student success from preschool through PhD*. Stylus.

Hicks, T. (2005). Assessing the academic, personal and social experiences of pre-college students. *Journal of College Admission, 186*, 19–24.

Holmes, J. (2016). *African American/Black student populations: Cutting-edge models for best practice*. Stylus.

Jenkins, D., & Cho, S. W. (2014). Get with the program . . . and finish it: Building guided pathways to accelerate student completion. *New Directions for Community Colleges*, (164), 27–35. doi:10.1002/cc.

Jones, J. R. (2014). *College self-efficacy and campus climate perceptions as predictors of academic achievement in African American males at community colleges in the state of Ohio* [Unpublished doctoral dissertation]. University of Toledo.

Levinstein, M. (2018). *A case study of an intrusive advising approach for at-risk, underprepared and traditionally underrepresented college students* [Unpublished doctoral dissertation]. Kent State University.

Noguera, P. (2003). The trouble with Black boys: The role and influence of environmental and cultural factors on the academic performance of African American males. *Urban Education, 38*, 431–459. http://journals.sagepub.com/doi/abs/10.1177/0042085903038004005.

O'Keeffe, P. (2013). A sense of belonging: Improving student retention. *College Student Journal, 47*(4), 605–613. https://pdfs.semanticscholar.org/2fd4/83eb62cf5094f147c9a129470808bc2d07f2.pdf?ga=2.157047359.569918590.15809026511 53788946.1579909978.

Palmer, R. T., Davis, R. J., Moore, J. L., & Hilton, A. A. (2010). A national risk: Increasing college participation and persistence among African American males to stimulate U.S. global competitiveness. *Journal of African American Males in Education, 1*, 106–115.

Salinitri, G. (2005). The effects of formal mentoring on the retention rates for first-year, low achieving students. *Canadian Journal of Education, 28*(4), 853–873. http://files.eric.ed.gov/fulltext/EJ750344.pdf.

Sedlacek, W. E., Benjamin, E., Schlosser, L. Z., & Sheu, H. B. (2007). Mentoring in academia: Considerations for diverse populations. In T. D. Allen & L. T. Eby (Eds.), *The Blackwell handbook of mentoring: A multiple perspectives approach* (pp. 259–280). Blackwell.

Shuford, R. T. (2009). Why affirmative action reminds essential in the age of Obama. *Campbell Law Review, 3*, 503–533. https://heinonline.org/HOL/Page?handle=hein.journals/camplr31&div=22&g_sent=1&casa_token=.

Simmons, L. L. (2013). Factors of persistence for African American men in a student support organization. *Journal of Negro Education,* *82*(1), 62–74. doi:10.7709/jnegroeducation82.1.0062.

Smith, W. A., Allen, R. W., & Danley, L. L. (2007). Assume the position . . . you fit the description: Psychological experiences and racial battle fatigue among African American male college students. *American Behavioral Scientist,* *51*(4), 551–578. http://journals.sagepub.com/doi/abs/10.1177/0002764207307742.

Solózarno, D., Ceja, M., & Yosso, T. (2000). Critical race theory, racial microaggressions, and campus racial climate: The experiences of African American college students. *The Journal of Negro Education, 69*(1/2), 60–73. http://www.jstor.org/stable/2696265.

Sue, D. W. (2010). Micro-aggressive impact on education and teaching: Facilitating difficult dialogues on race in the classroom. In D. W. Sue (Ed.), *Microaggressions in everyday life: Race, gender, and sexual orientation* (pp. 231–254). John Wiley & Sons.

Tinto, V. (1993). *Leaving college: Rethinking the causes and cures of student attrition* (2nd ed.). University of Chicago Press.

U.S. Department of Education, National Center for Education Statistics. (2010). Remedial education at degree-granting postsecondary institutions in fall 2008. NCES 2008-010. Washington, DC. https://nces.ed.gov/surveys/peqis/ publications/2004010/index.asp?sectionID=10.

U.S. Department of Education, National Center for Education Statistics. (2015). The U.S. Department of Education, Integrated Postsecondary Education Data System Completion Survey, 2007-010. Washington, DC. https://nces.ed.gov/pubs2017/ 2017024.pdf.

Walsh, C., Larsen, C., & Parry, D. (2009). Academic tutors at the frontline of student support in a cohort of students succeeding in higher education. *Educational Studies, 35*(4), 405–424. doi:10.1080/03055690902876438.

Wood, J., Newman, C., & Harris, F. (2015). Self-efficacy as a determinant of academic integration: An examination of first-year Black males in the community college. *Western Journal of Black Studies, 39*(1), 3–17. https://education.wsu.edu/wjbs.

Chapter Seven

Cracking the Barriers for African American and Latinx Students in STEM Education

Abdel-Moaty M. Fayek

TALENT GAPS AND BARRIERS

America faces a significant talent gap in the populations pursuing STEM education. Using the often-referenced 1983 educational ultimatum, ours is a "nation at risk," the U.S. Department of Education (2015) reported that few American students major in STEM programs. As a result, the report concluded, the United States will continue to suffer from an inadequate pipeline of skilled STEM teachers and workers.

STEM shortages in the United States have been linked to many causes, from weak science and mathematics education in K–12 to costly programs in higher education. According to the Pew Research Center, "The most commonly cited reason for not pursuing a STEM career was cost and time barriers (27%), such as high expenses required for education or a lack of access to resources and opportunities" (Kennedy et al., 2018).

URMs in STEM Occupations

One of the major contributors to STEM shortages in the Unite States is the lack of underrepresented minorities (URMs) in STEM education and in the workforce, according to Burke and Mattis (2007). Only 2.2% of Hispanics and Latinos, 2.7% of African Americans, and 3.3% of Native Americans and Alaskans pursue STEM careers. With minorities expected to be 57% of the U.S. population by 2060 (U.S. Census Bureau, 2012), educators must start focusing on increasing minorities' participation in STEM careers. The U.S.

Department of Education (2015) reports that while 81% of Asian Americans and 71% of Whites attended high schools that provided a full range of math and science curricula, access to such curricula for African Americans, American Indians, Native Alaskans, and Hispanics is comparably insignificant. The U.S. Department of Education, National Center for Education Statistics (2004) also reported that mathematics classes in high-poverty districts are twice as likely to be taught by faculty with credentials other than mathematics and that science classes are taught by faculty who are three times as likely to have credentials other than science. While all children have an innate interest in science, it is the education system that is not gender- or colorblind that creates a roadblock that has nothing to do with intellect or innate ability (Bayer Corporation, 2012).

Diversity Is Importance to Innovation

Many studies have reinforced the importance of diversity to both innovation and globalization. In the United Kingdom, a study including samples from 7,600 companies concluded that increased cultural diversity was beneficial to innovation and globalization (Nathan & Lee, 2015). Another study, which included development teams from 4,277 companies in Spain, concluded that within 2 years, companies with more women were more likely to introduce new radical innovations into the market (Díaz-García et al., 2014). Other research has provided evidence that diversity is likely to improve the level of creativity, innovation, and quality of STEM products and services (Burke & Mattis, 2007; Perkins et al., 2013).

Higher Education's Role in Changing the STEM Landscape

Because these figures—and the significance of STEM occupations to our country's economic health—are not new or shocking to most of us in higher education, what is mind boggling is why the needle has moved so slowly to change the trends.

Many programs across the country are seeking to encourage students to pursue STEM careers, especially those from URM populations. Some innovative approaches have been designed to help underrepresented minorities break through the roadblocks that prevent them from pursuing STEM careers. The Math Performance Success (MPS) program offered at De Anza Community College (California) is one example. We will learn more about the program as we look into the barriers URMs face in pursuing STEM education.

IDENTIFYING THE ROADBLOCKS

To develop successful programs to increase URMs' desire to pursue STEM careers, we must first attempt to understand the barriers that exist for African American and Latinx students to major in STEM and how a program such as De Anza's MPS program can help to eradicate those barriers.

De Anza College's MPS Program

De Anza College, located in Cupertino, California, is in the heart of the Silicon Valley and the high-tech industry. Established in 1967 by the Foothills-De Anza Community College District, De Anza College serves the community by providing an academically rich, multicultural learning environment that challenges students of all backgrounds to realize their dreams and goals and to be socially responsible leaders in their communities, the nation, and the world.

De Anza's MPS program was initially created as a supportive learning environment for the college's students to remove the obstacle of failure in gateway math courses. The program is led by a skilled team of faculty, counselors, and tutors who work with students to gradually strengthen their math skills through a preset sequence of courses moving from basic skills classes through three levels of algebra, culminating in transferable math skills. The program currently requires students to attend class for 10 hours of instruction per week, and this instructional time is divided equally between whole-class activities and collaborative group work.

Course instructors work closely together to define the method of instruction using a common calendar, similar activities, and common tests. Mentors and tutors are available throughout the class time to assist students who have questions about the material. Counselors and instructors work together to ensure student success and provide immediate help as needed, and an academic counselor is available for each class section. If a student's grade drops below 70% at any point during the course, the student is required to attend tutoring. In addition to in-class tutoring, the program offers group tutoring outside of class. Each week, tutors offer approximately 30 hours of tutoring at various times to accommodate students' class and work schedules. The MPS instructors and counselors meet on a weekly basis to discuss concerns related to students' achievement in the class (De Anza College, n.d.).

Gathering URM Student Voices

In order to identify positive influencers as well as potential barriers that may impact African American and Latinx students in STEM education, this author developed a research study focusing on MPS students' experiences. The study also asked the participants to discuss the effectiveness of the MPS program in helping them reach their educational goals and to share their recommendations for improving the program to better prepare students to pursue STEM careers.

Throughout our nation's history, race has impacted the success of under-represented minorities at all levels of academic institutions. By listening to the voices of students of color, we can better understand their struggles, find ways to address the problems they are facing, and identify what works and doesn't work. Most of the stories shared here help us understand how we can do better to help these students to succeed.

Between 2015 and 2017, 4,747 Latinx and 634 African American students who were either current students or graduates of the MPS program were invited to participate in this study. A total of 415 Latinx and 63 African American students agreed, representing 8.74% and 9.94% of the totals, respectively. As a follow-up to the preliminary survey, a subgroup of 12 Latinx and 14 African American students agreed to interviews to share their stories regarding the barriers and the effectiveness of the MPS program.

Student Responses: Barriers to Choosing STEM Careers

The combined results from both the background survey and the interviews concluded that the most influential factors for these students in selecting a future career in STEM were self-efficacy, pre-college preparation, family support, financial obligation, and the perception of STEM majors (see figure 7.1). While slight differences appeared between the two groups in terms of the level of effect the barrier had on their decision, the similarities were significant. For both groups, self-efficacy and pre-college preparation were identified as major barriers; among the African American students, family support, financial obligations, and their perception of STEM majors were also included as major barriers.

Interesting to note from the results is that most of the major and moderate barriers that the participants noted were either personal or affected by their individual home situations. External influences, such as peer influences, transportation to the college, and the college's support services, were identified as minor barriers by both groups. While family influence on career choices was also rated as a minor barrier by a majority of participants in both groups, several participants noted that the family influence factor was minor because of their lack of understanding of what STEM careers involve in terms of education and training. Imani, who was studying to be a medical doctor, shared:

> I can't ask my parents for answers. You can't. You have to be self-reliant and explaining to them. For example, I have to explain to my mom why I have to

Barrier	Latinx Students	African American Students
Self-Efficacy	Major barrier	Major barrier
Pre-College Preparation	Major	Major
Family Support	Moderate	Major
Financial Obligations	Moderate	Major
Perception of STEM Majors	Moderate	Major
Career Advising	Moderate	Moderate
Parents' Education Level	Moderate	Moderate
Work Schedule	Moderate	Moderate
Mentoring	Moderate	Moderate
Role Model	Moderate	Moderate
First-Generation	Moderate	Minor to Moderate
Family Influence on Career Choices	Minor	Minor
Peer Influence	Minor	Minor
Transportation	Minor	Minor
Student Support Services	Minor	Minor

Figure 7.1.   Barriers Preventing Latinx and African American Students From Majoring in STEM Fields. *Author created (A-M. Fayek)*

> spend the whole day and the whole evening, and sometimes parts of the night, studying at the library to prepare for exams and understand the material.\ . . . She just does not understand why I need that much time because she does not understand the challenges of studying to be a doctor.

IMPACT OF THE MPS PROGRAM

To understand the impact of the MPS program on URMs' success in math and the possibility of pursuing STEM or STEM-related careers, input from participants was collected in seven areas:

1. The effectiveness of the MPS program structure;
2. the MPS impact on strengthening math skills;
3. the effectiveness of having embedded counselors;
4. the impact of the extended class hours;
5. the program influence on pursuing STEM careers;
6. the role of the faculty in student success; and
7. the program influence on pursuing STEM careers.

In all seven areas, the impact was regarded as major.

Based on the results of the study, the program appears to mitigate some of the barriers and successfully prepare a good number of the students in the program to overcome the self-efficacy and the lack of college preparation barriers that they identified. The structure of the program as a learning community provides much of the needed mentoring, role models, positive peer influence, and career advising URMs need to overcome their math phobia and lack of pre-college preparation.

The stories we heard from the African American and Latinx students support the value of the program, and even more significantly, the students found role models and mentors in faculty and counselors.

Felipe was impressed with the program structure and the teaching pedagogies used to cover the material. He shared:

> I think it's really good. I really do enjoy being there, especially that they always give you a progress report every week. I really do like how the counselor is very involved with the students; he wants to make sure everybody is doing what they're supposed to be doing and is willing to talk to the students with whatever they need . . . and I really like how the teachers are very good at teaching the class.

Elijah, who was pursuing a double major in music and computer science, felt it gave him confidence. He stated:

> The MPS program gave me the confidence that even though math is a challenging subject to me and it's kind of one of the foundations for computer science, it gave me the confidence that I needed to continue, because at that time, I didn't know how far I was going and was unsure of my skills.

Although a few of the participants did not like the required longer lecture time due to conflicts with their work schedule, there was a consensus that the extra time was beneficial. Isabel reflected on the extended office hours by saying:

> The extended hours are not only beneficial, but crucial and pivotal to anyone struggling in math. However, that is as long as it should be: two hours a day, every day. I think you tab out after two hours. If there is a plan to shorten the MPS hours, why not take some time off other classes.

Regarding the MPS faculty, Bianca, who was majoring in journalism and women's studies, having failed Statistics twice, joined the MPS program after consulting with a counselor. She commented:

> The MPS faculty are great. Definitely, I think so. I think for the one that I have now—her name is LM—for stats . . . I think it's very easy to contact her. We

used Canvas for the class, so I think it's very easy to contact her through that system.

The imbedded counselors were also found to be effective. Joshua shared, "I feel like they actually help because they sit there and tell you which classes you need to take. If they see you struggling with the material, then they advise you to sign up for individual tutors." Josiah felt they played an important role psychologically, as they help students be focused and calm their anxiety: "They help to not overburden the professor. Having them also reduces frustrations when someone is struggling." Malik considered the MPS counselor as a potential role model. He shared:

> It would have to be the MPS counselor. He's a role model. He sits there and helps you, and he pretty much answers any questions. If he doesn't have an answer right away, he definitely gets back to you quickly.

Makayla indicated that she could easily consider Professor "W" as her role model:

> The way he explained math was a little different [than other professors]. He was a photographer as well. So, he would bring in his pictures and just the way he related it to some of his pictures and stuff it made it easier to understand the mathematical theories. I felt with the MPS Program he took the most time more than anybody, and since it was a long class, he would crack jokes and try to make it fun for everybody.

De Anza College has a strong commitment to the MPS program and is well recognized for its effort to serve URMs and close both the educational and economic equity gaps. However, several of the participants in the MPS program indicated that they were not aware of the program until it was recommended by a friend or one of the instructors, and others reported a lack of familiarity with other aspects of the services. Creating awareness of the available services could help African American and Latinx students succeed in STEM, and this vital communication with students about the services available to them is a challenge that many colleges confront. More targeted efforts by academic counselors and advisors in bringing awareness of the program could significantly improve the service to a larger proportion of the underrepresented population. This research highlighted the need for significant improvement in our communications with and counseling of students. Additionally, discussions on implementing MPS-like programs in other STEM subjects, such as physics, are gaining momentum.

BUILDING A STEM ECOSYSTEM

Although the MPS program continues to show significant success, this success was due to De Anza's effort to engage the various constituencies to collaboratively build an ecosystem with each component being a major player in the students' success. Each of the components of the STEM learning and engagement ecosystem (see figure 7.2) are essential for building an effective MPS-like program to support and improve the participation of underrepresented minorities in STEM careers. The college has taken significant steps to build such an ecosystem and recommends this approach for other community colleges to use as a model for their own programs.

Cross-Institutional Collaboration

If the United States is going to be successful in promoting and increasing STEM occupations, all educational institutions, at all levels, must share the responsibility and work collaboratively. To achieve more comprehensive and notable successes in educating generations of learners to stay globally competitive, elevate the level of innovation, and provide the much-needed STEM workforce to meet the ever-increasing demand, colleges, universities, and K–12 schools must all work together. Institutions must break the culture of silos because the future of our nation's workforce and our economy depend on it. Community colleges have the opportunity to establish exemplary working models by building partnerships with K–12 that can spark the curiosity of young minds and create early interest in pursuing a STEM career through creating a STEM bridge program. One of the students in our study, Pablo, a business communication major, observed:

> I feel if I was introduced to STEM at an earlier stage, I would have developed the passion for STEM from early on. Perhaps introducing different areas to, say, give choices for students to explore different areas would potentially make more people interested.

The most consistent theme that resulted from engaging the participants in this discussion was that they all agreed that some changes to the way math and science are taught in the pre-college setting were needed. All participants also agreed that if such changes were in place, their interest in science would have started at a much earlier age and it would have been stronger and perhaps had an impact on their career choices. Cultivating students' interest in STEM earlier in elementary school and maintaining it through K–12 is a crucial building block in engaging URMs in STEM education.

Colleges can contribute to this early contact by strengthening cross-institutional collaboration, including field trips to the colleges' STEM programs, career days for URMs, STEM summer bridge programs, summer fairs, career

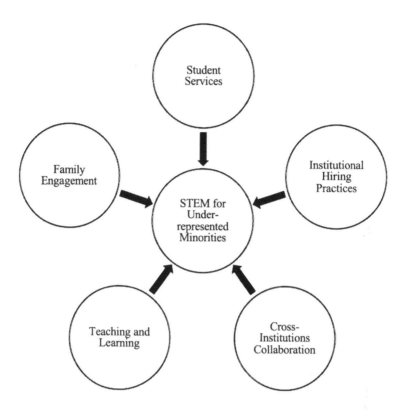

Figure 7.2.   Framework for Building Support Systems for Underrepresented Minorities to Major in STEM. *Author created (A-M. Fayek)*

pathways, expanded dual enrollment opportunities, and opportunities for parents to make them aware of the value of STEM careers.

Partnerships With Business and Industry

Academic institutions at all levels and the various STEM industries need to team together and invest in developing a homegrown STEM workforce. According to Burke and Mattis (2007), the major contributor to STEM shortages in the United States is not only the lack of URMs in STEM educational programs but also the dearth in the workforce. Educational institutions, businesses, and industries must also rethink their partnership approaches to help in increasing the diversity in the STEM workforce through effective partnerships that expose students to STEM careers, mentoring, and internship opportunities.

Institutional Hiring Practices

Higher education institutions have another role to play in changing the future of America's STEM landscape. Actions and policy changes are needed to ensure the success in employment of those ethnic groups. Fairlie and colleagues (2011), who studied over 30,000 students in nearly 21,000 classes, found evidence that the dropout rates, course success rates, and grade performance gaps between White and URM students were narrowed by 20%–50% when the courses were taught by URM instructors.

Several of the participants in our De Anza study shared the fact that going through their educational journey, there were no faculty members of color that they could connect with, specifically in the STEM areas. Some suggested that, had they had such teachers and connections, they may have been motivated and encouraged to pursue STEM careers. The nation's colleges need to step up their efforts to have their faculty be more reflective of their student enrollment demographics. One method to accomplish this is through "grow-your-own" programs where promising faculty and leaders are identified, sometimes as early as in their associate-level coursework, and nurtured through their educational journeys and provided opportunities to gain the work experience they need to serve the college as full-fledged members of the faculty or leadership team.

Student Services

The results of the De Anza study also provided insights into the role of the college's student services in supporting URMs. Student Services departments can play a crucial and important role in creating diversity in the STEM workforce and in guiding URMs to "Think STEM." The stories of the participants in the study reveal that some would have chosen a career in STEM if they had a career advisor. Several were not aware of the availability of some of the student services, including tutoring and counseling. Student Services departments can also work together to identify touchpoints where they can increase focus on STEM while providing essential services for URMs, including recruitment, onboarding/orientation, financial aid advising, and career advising and counseling.

Teaching and Learning

Educational institutions must also change the way the foundational math and science courses are taught to be more effective in engaging students in STEM education (Association for American Universities [AAU], 2012). The AAU recommended a three-layer framework for achieving this change, including pedagogical practices, scaffolding, and cultural change.

Pedagogical Practices

Successful teaching and learning pedagogies are those where faculty and students work in partnership to accomplish a common goal. Such pedagogies should include four elements: (1) articulated learning goals that consider learning at all levels and connect assignments to the learning goals, (2) educational practices that engage students as active participants and use real-world examples while using technology effectively, (3) assessments that are linked to the desired outcomes to assess students' learning, and (4) access to ensure that STEM courses are inclusive of all students and designed to enhance learners' self-efficacy.

Scaffolding

To activate successful support and a sense of community, the AAU recommended (a) providing faculty with professional development opportunities to develop effective teaching approaches and communities of practice, (b) providing faculty with access to resources, (c) collecting data on program performance to assess student retention and equity gaps between various ethnics groups and ensuring the dissemination of data campus-wide, and (d) aligning future facility planning with cutting-edge and modern instructional approaches.

Cultural Change

If higher education is going to contribute to sustainable change, we must be prepared to make changes ourselves. Efforts like these require changes in our institutional cultures and in disciplinary cultures as well. These changes will require (a) ensuring leadership commitment to encourage and support faculty to adopt new evidence-based pedagogies and continually hone and improve their techniques; (b) establishing strong measures for teaching excellence, starting with hiring practices; and (c) aligning incentives with expectations of teaching excellence.

STEM EDUCATION SUPPORTED BY FAMILY ENGAGEMENT

As we saw earlier when we examined the barriers the De Anza study participants identified, the students' parents' education level was a moderate to major influence for Latinx students, and a major influence for African American students. While this barrier is deserving of much more discussion and study, we will simply acknowledge the importance of this final factor: As educators, we must also address the issue of family engagement as both a support and a barrier to minority participation in STEM.

CONCLUSION

Our De Anza research and our conversations with the students in the MPS program have helped us understand the hurdles that our African American and Latinx students have been facing in pursuing STEM careers. We concluded that our first step was to build a STEM ecosystem to provide a platform for the students of color to succeed not only in STEM but also in any major they choose. Our colleges are struggling to close the equity gaps, and we will not be able to make strides without collective efforts through such a supportive ecosystem. America's colleges can, and must, do more to encourage and support minority populations in pursuing STEM careers. Our nation's future depends on it.

REFERENCES

Association for American Universities. (2012). *Framework for systemic change in undergraduate STEM teaching and learning.* https://www.aau.edu/sites/default/files/STEM%20Scholarship/AAU_Framework.pdf.

Bayer Corporation. (2012). *STEM education, science literacy, and the innovation of workforce.* http://www.se.edu/dept/native-american-center/files/2012/04/STEM-Education-Science-Literacy-and-the-Innovation-Workforce-in-America.pdf

Burke, R., & Mattis, M. (2007). *Women and minorities in science, technology, engineering, and mathematics: Upping the numbers.* Edward Elgar.

De Anza College. (n.d.). *Math Performance Success.* Retrieved January 16, 2021, from https://www.deanza.edu/mps.

Díaz-García, C., González-Moreno, A., & Sáez-Martínez, F. (2014). Gender diversity within R&D teams: Its impact on radicalness of innovation. *Innovation, 15*(2), 149–160.

Fairlie, R., Hoffmann, F., & Oreopoulos, P. (2011). *A community college instructor like me: Race and ethnicity interactions in the classroom.* National Bureau of Economic Research. http://www.nber.org/papers/w17381.

Kennedy, B., Hefferon, M., & Funk, C. (2018, January 17). *Half of Americans think young people don't pursue STEM because it is too hard.* Pew Research Center. https://www.pewresearch.org/fact-tank/2018/01/17/half-of-americans-think-young-people-dont-pursue-stem-because-it-is-too-hard.

Nathan, M., & Lee, N. (2015) Cultural diversity, innovation, and entrepreneurship: Firm-level evidence from London. *Economic Geography, 89*(4), 367–394.

Perkins, S., Phillips, K., & Pearce, N. (2013). Ethnic diversity, gender, and national leaders. *Journal of International Affairs, 67*(1), 85–103.

U.S. Census Bureau. (2012). *U.S. Census Bureau projections show a slower growing, older, more diverse nation a half century from now.* http://www.census.gov/newsroom/releases/archives/population/cb12-243.html.

U.S. Department of Education. (2015). *Science, technology, engineering, and math, including computer science.* https://www.ed.gov/stem.

U.S. Department of Education, National Center for Education Statistics. (2004). *The condition of education 2004* [NCES 2004–077]. U.S. Government Printing Office.

Chapter Eight

College Students in Poverty

Examples of Collaborative Efforts and Interventions

Armando Burciaga and Saundra Kay King

A TYPICAL DAY

Imagine a typical day at your college. The main hallway is filled with students hurriedly walking toward their next class. Some are discussing the recent assignments, some are planning a study group for the upcoming exam, and others are sharing their interpretation of a movie they've just seen. As an administrator, instructor, or advisor, you're reminded of how you felt during your early years of college and are gently reminded of the excitement you experienced looking forward to your internship, meeting for a club, or successfully passing your class. What did most of us have to worry about? As a successful student who went on to reach your academic goals, what do you remember worrying about during your time in college? Most of us remember the great times we had in the residence halls where we built strong bonds that led to lifelong friendships and our roommates in the apartments where our friends got together for parties.

Did you worry about finding a place to call home? Or about getting enough money together to buy food? While we certainly had challenges, how do yesterday's challenges compare to those today's students face?

More of our students live in poverty than ever before. College students in poverty are especially vulnerable to withdrawing from college. Cantor (2019) suggested that students from lower socioeconomic areas are less likely to persist, graduate, and transfer to bachelor's degree programs as compared to their counterparts. Students from all levels of higher education, in addition to their rigorous studies, are required to balance their family responsibilities, their employment obligations, and the challenges of meeting their basic needs. In many cases, college staff and faculty from across the institution need constant reminding that the students they serve in their classroom or in their office, or who pass them while walking down the hall, may appear relaxed and focused on their academics; however, many are carefully juggling academics with meeting their basic needs. This balancing act often leads to a struggle between academics and having a place to sleep at night, a home to return to for studying and respite, and food to eat. All detrimental, these struggles consume students' valuable time and effort that should be directed toward their academic studies.

In the recent #RealCollege survey (Goldrick-Rab et al., 2019), more than 50% of the participating students reported experiencing insecurity in food, housing, and even homelessness at some point within the past year. Many of us, whether we are faculty, staff, or administrators, can probably remember a time when we were aware of one of our students facing such a challenge. Unfortunately, the one instance we can recall is likely not the only time that the student, or other students we encountered, dealt with these issues. For many students, these challenges recur and overlap more than once in an academic year. A student may, for example, find themselves without a place to live in the winter, and then again face an uncertain housing situation in summer. Another common combination are students who both endure housing difficulties and lack food resources. Too many of our students are living with one or more of these insecurities. These cycles of basic unmet needs often lead to serious effects including low academic performance, hopelessness, and depression.

Throughout the nation's community colleges, you will find students struggling financially. This struggle is exacerbated when adult students with families of their own find it difficult to meet their family's basic needs for food, shelter, and security. This can lead to tough choices between paying for necessities and paying for books, or tuition, or other academic-related costs. This difficult choice can also lead to students withdrawing or dropping out of college completely to work to meet these basic needs.

For us as educators to offer solutions to these problems, we must first understand how poverty affects our students. We will offer here, as starting points, some of the efforts and interventions that some community colleges have developed to help their students meet their physical needs and achieve their academic goals. We will discuss efforts from our current home states, Colorado and Georgia, as well as other unique approaches for serving such students. While the locations of the interventions are very different, our students' challenges are the same. We hope that these examples will provide insight and motivation to expand conversations and thoughtful approaches within other colleges.

WHAT IS POVERTY, AND HOW DOES IT IMPACT STUDENTS?

Poverty, whether local or on a national level, does not have limits. According to a ranking of all 50 states, Colorado is listed as 14th with an 11.5% poverty rate, while Georgia ranks 46th, with a poverty rate of 16.9%, slightly higher than the national average of 14.6% (Welfare Info, 2020). It is with this statistic in mind that we will address how community colleges are addressing the needs of students while improving student persistence and graduation rates.

One aspect of poverty that community college students deal with is homelessness. Studies have been conducted to identify the existing trends of homelessness. Whether local or regional, the data are a challenge to retrieve, yet very important to better understand the community's needs. Last year's release of the Hope Center's survey report from over 86,000 students at 123 colleges and universities identified that 60% of students had experienced either a food or housing insecurity within the previous year (Association of American Colleges & Universities, 2019). While this is an alarming rate, it is important to get a general understanding of how poverty is determined, by the government, for families and individuals, such as college students.

The U.S. Census Bureau (2019), in their American Community Survey Brief, determined poverty by

> comparing annual income to a set of dollar values (called poverty thresholds) that vary by family size, the number of children, and the age of the householder. If a family's before-tax money income is less than the dollar value of their threshold, then that family and every individual in it are in poverty. For people not living in families, poverty status is determined by comparing the individual's income to his or her poverty threshold. (p. 2)

While *basic needs* and *poverty* are two very different terms when it comes to understanding the many challenges today's college students encounter, they are related and, more importantly, affect college students' ability to complete their academic goals.

Before higher education can address the problem and offer solutions, however, it is important to understand the "how" of the situation—or in other words, just how can community colleges within the higher education system support students living in poverty? How, with "ample" amounts of financial aid, a flexible approach to learning, and a supportive learning community, can community colleges allow homelessness and food insecurities to exist? How can a student's food shortages and homelessness exist when food pantries, dorms, and other college housing options exist at many colleges? Why is there such a high incompletion rate with academic and student support systems in place? While there are many questions that continue to elude community college leaders, we can focus on innovative approaches for addressing the problems and meeting our students' basic needs.

Dr. Russell Lowery-Hart, president of Amarillo College (Texas) provided an example of how college leadership is seeking a better awareness of student needs. To understand the plight of homeless students, Hart spent one weekend during the winter on the streets of Waco, Texas, to experience what homelessness conditions were like. While Amarillo College already provided a student emergency fund, legal aid clinic, and counselors, Hart's experience prompted him to concede that they still were not doing enough (Bombardieri, 2018). His conclusions: successful solutions involve a shared responsibility among all campus employees for helping students succeed. The college must continue to educate the college and the community about the extent of the local problems, and the college must be the center of collaborative college and community resources.

WHAT ARE THE STUDENTS' ISSUES AND NEEDS?

The dream of attending college when one is wishing to earn a degree typically does not include worry about housing, food, and other basic needs and concerns. The challenges of meeting basic needs are not part of the college's marketing slogans: "Start your career here!" or "Build your future."

First-generation college students, though, often struggle with understanding the financial requirements of college. For example, without an "educated" support system, new college students often do not realize that, in addition to paying tuition fees, they will need to travel to the college (transportation costs), eat meals between classes (food costs), and then purchase textbooks and other instructional materials such as computer software—a bill that can easily add up to hundreds of dollars each term. In addition, they'll need funds for a laptop, computer, or tablet, and reliable internet service. While computer labs and wireless access are available on college campuses, they are not always available in the students' households. Many community colleges do not offer on-campus housing, and for students who live in rural areas, or even urban areas without reliable public transportation, transportation to campus can be a real struggle for students living in poverty. Buying, insuring, and maintaining a car costs money, just as it costs money to purchase bus passes.

IS THERE HOPE?

Historically, community colleges have provided the access to education and training that helped people improve their socioeconomic standing and escape poverty. Our job has always included providing opportunity and support. Our communities, too, include organizations and resources to assist community members, including those that assist students through their college journey. Today's challenge is rallying these resources to address the needs of a growing population of students living in poverty.

It Starts With Data

Started in Wisconsin in 2013, the Hope Lab, formerly known as the Wisconsin Hope Lab, has led the basic needs insecurity data collection, helping higher education institutions and community resources understand the extent of the problems. The lab began by assessing institutions within Wisconsin but later expanded to survey colleges nationally to better understand these college student challenges on a national level.

National Organizations

Some of the national organizations that have collaborated to address food insecurity include the College and University Food Bank Alliance (CUFBA), whose members include community colleges and universities across America. CUFBA provides support, training, and resources for campus food banks (College and University Food Bank Alliance, n.d.). Swipe Out Hunger was founded in 2010 in California and currently has over 110 college members across America. Through this program, college students can donate unused meal plan allotments as well as financial donations. Students in need can then either use the "swipes" to purchase food in a campus dining facility or use the funds to purchase items in the campus food pantry (Swipe Out Hunger, n.d.).

What's Happening in Colorado and Georgia?

In our home states of Colorado and Georgia, the efforts to address food and shelter insecurities are gaining steam. Collaborative efforts that include data gathering and sharing of resources are resulting in successful outcomes. The takeaway here is that teamwork from internal and external players is working. The power of collaboration—regardless of how big or small, local or nonlocal—is making a difference to the students at our colleges.

Red Rocks Community College (RRCC), one of 13 community colleges within the Colorado Community College System (CCCS), has recently partnered with a nearby housing shelter, the Action Center. The Action Center has been a community resource in the Denver area that helped area residents meet basic needs; however, funding difficulties forced the shelter to close. When RRCC recently experienced a higher level of anecdotal accounts of students encountering housing insecurities, faculty and staff began exploring student housing opportunities within the community. Community efforts and discussions led to a collaborative effort in funding that enabled the Action

Center to reopen the shelter specifically for Red Rocks Community College students.

An additional location, a family shelter named the Launch Pad, provides housing for approximately 20 RRCC students. While this is a small number, the new housing solution is a financially secure shelter, an innovative housing option that offers college students an environment that supports their education. The housing shelter provides individual rooms for sleeping and studying, as well as community areas for cooking, eating, socializing, and programming. The management staff hosts various evening and weekend programs to promote healthy eating, enhance job-search skills, improve time-management abilities, and provide other academic-supportive programming in collaboration with RRCC. Students are able to reside at the Launch Pad for one semester with the possibility of extending their stay. The goal is for students to use the Launch Pad as a stepping-stone until they can secure long-term housing for themselves.

While this is one example of an innovative solution, RRCC has also taken the steps to include a college-wide approach to improve housing challenges by creating a food and housing insecurity council. The council meets regularly to discuss and support the college's efforts to help students meet their basic needs. Ongoing activities include regular surveys gauging food and housing insecurity levels, improvements to the school's food pantry, and efforts to develop additional community partnerships.

What HOPE Can Be Found in Georgia?

Residents of Georgia who wish to attend college benefit from financial support funded through profits from the state lottery program. The HOPE Grant, HOPE Career Grant, and the Zell Miller Grant provide tuition coverage. Specific to colleges within the Technical College System of Georgia (TCSG), the HOPE Career Grant is aligned to specific workforce needs in Georgia and covers the full cost of tuition for those enrolled in high demand career programs. The Zell Miller Grant provides full tuition for students enrolled in a certificate or diploma program (Georgia Student Finance Commission, 2019).

Because of the system's technical education focus, the TCSG—which is comprised of 22 colleges that offer certificates, diplomas, and degrees—benefits from the Carl D. Perkins Career and Technical Education Act (Perkins Act). The system and colleges receive more than $20 billion dollars through this program. One benefit supported by the Perkins Grant is a special populations coordinator at each of the 22 colleges who works directly with students categorized as being below the poverty level. The program also produces an annual resource guide for each of the colleges, providing information for students for both on campus and community assistance. On-campus assistance includes advising, counseling, and career services; community assistance includes bus schedules and fares, childcare, housing, health, and nutrition.

Several of the colleges provide a food pantry for students. Two examples are North Georgia Technical College and Georgia Northwestern Technical College. North Georgia Technical College is in the Georgia Mountains and has partnered with local farmers to provide a free farmers' market during the summer months. At Georgia Northwestern Technical College, located near the Tennessee state line, the special populations coordinator began a food pantry supported by the college foundation and a local ministry. During fall semester 2019, the coordinator met with 20 to 25 students per week. She has since begun a clothing closet and a successful Free Diaper Day (Georgia Northwestern Technical College, 2020).

While still in infancy stage, the Gretchen K. Corbin Last Mile Fund exists to remove financial barriers that prevent students from continuing and completing their education. The fund is managed by the TCSG foundation, which is working to grow the fund so it can increase funding to students. From July 2018 to July 2019, 199 students received an average of $235 to cover remaining tuition, books, and fee balances. These outstanding bills would have otherwise prevented them from continuing at the institution. Of the 199, 76% continued and 23% earned a credential for that term (J. Fields, personal communication, 2020). In addition, to help students save money and reduce costs, the colleges have moved aggressively toward the use of Open Educational Resources.

OPPORTUNITIES FOR PROFESSIONAL DEVELOPMENT

Community colleges continue to face their own financial challenges as they work to help students succeed and respond to local and national pressures to increase retention and completion rates. As community colleges continue to address their own challenges, they must also empower staff to help students with their academic needs as well as their basic needs. Community colleges, then, must continue to provide professional development opportunities for faculty and staff to broaden awareness and requisite skills. The opportunity to learn gives the opportunity for the campus to work as a whole to deliver valuable and relevant assistance.

Professional development opportunities for faculty and staff exist in many different forms and modalities. The following list describes a few examples of opportunities for college staff, faculty, and administrators to learn about the challenges of poverty and develop collaborative and innovative solutions.

- Institute for Research on Poverty at the University of Wisconsin–Madison: The institute provides resources, training, and events geared toward understanding and educating faculty about poverty. They conduct an annual Teaching Poverty 101 workshop through which instructors develop resources and lessons on poverty and inequality (Institute for Research on Poverty, n.d.).
- The Beegle Poverty Immersion Institute, led by Dr. Donna Beegle, and located in Tigard, Oregon, provides workshops for educators to better understand poverty and tools through which to make a difference (Beegle, n.d.).
- Aha! Process Inc., a Ruby Payne company based out of Highlands, Texas, provides extensive resources and training opportunities framed around her initial work through the "Framework for Understanding Poverty" and "Bridges Out of Poverty" programs (Aha Process, 2020). An example of the professional development opportunities provided by the Aha! Process is described here: https://www.youtube.com/watch?v=hmSFdks-gTM.
- Mercy College (Missouri) conducted a simulation in which students were presented with different scenarios in which they had to deal with being poor. Examples included not enough money to pay rent and possible eviction and stretching pay and food stamps to buy food. Part of the exercise focused on how to ask for help and access resources (Mercy College, 2018).

COMMUNITY COLLEGES ARE COMMUNITY

Students struggling to meet their basic needs are a part of most, if not all, community colleges. Faced with this struggle, their responses may not be conducive to their college success, and they may be forced to drop out and discontinue their education. How can we better assist these students? One way is to better understand poverty and the inability many college students have in meeting their basic needs.

Through our discussion, we have attempted to provide basic information about poverty and the impact it has in our students' lives. There is hope, and examples have been provided that highlight efforts through which colleges, communities, and states are working toward providing funding and services to meet the needs of students. These efforts support the community college mission to provide an opportunity for, and access to, education and training. But, as we have explained, without adequate assistance, some students will find the task difficult, if not impossible.

As communities and colleges implement programs, it is critical that we gather and assess data to determine the efficacy of these efforts. Such an assessment also provides an opportunity to share and replicate best practices.

Many of us have personal stories to share—whether as a community college student living in poverty who has been fortunate to have faculty and staff reach out and help us or, as community college professionals who have helped students secure housing or funds to buy gas, food, or Christmas presents for children. The stories are endless. When we help our students find resources to persist and succeed, our communities also prosper.

WANT TO LEARN MORE?

- College and University Food Bank Alliance: https://cufba.org/about-us
- Aha! Process, Inc., a Ruby Bridges company: https://www.ahaprocess.com
- Conversation Across Barriers: https://www.irp.wisc.edu/training
- Hope and State Aid Programs, Georgia Student Finance Commission: https://www.gafutures.org/hope-state-aid-programs/hope-zell-miller-grants/hope-career-grant/award-amounts
- Institute for Research on Poverty: https://www.irp.wisc.edu/training
- Swipe Out Hunger: https://www.swipehunger.org/aboutus

REFERENCES

Association of American Colleges & Universities. (2019). Majority of college students experience food insecurity, housing insecurity, or homelessness. https://www.aacu.org/aacu-news/newsletter/majority-college-students-experience-food-insecurity-housing-insecurity-or.

Beegle, D. (n.d.). *Communication across barriers*. Retrieved January 19, 2021, from http://www.combarriers.com.

Bombardieri, M. (2018, May 30). Colleges are no match for American poverty. *The Atlantic.* https://www.theatlantic.com/education/archive/2018/05/college-poor-students/560972.

Cantor, M. R. (2019, Spring). Retention of long island millennials at a suburban community college: Are they college ready? *Journal for Leadership and Instruction, 18*(1), 36–41. https://files.eric.ed.gov/fulltext/EJ1222242.pdf.

College and University Food Bank Alliance. (n.d.). *About us.* Retrieved January 19, 2021, from https://cufba.org/about-us.

Georgia Northwestern Technical College. (2020). *GNTC food pantry numbers on the rise.* https://www.gntc.edu/112719-pantry.

Georgia Student Finance Commission. (2019). *Zell Miller scholarship program at public and private institutions.* https://gsfc.georgia.gov/search?search=zell&sm_site_name=gsfc.

Goldrick-Rab, S., Baker-Smith, C., Coca, V., Looker, E., & Williams, T. (2019). *College and university basic needs insecurity: A national #RealCollege survey report.* https://hope4college.com/wp-content/uploads/2019/04/HOPE_realcollege_National_report_digital.pdf.

Institute for Research on Poverty. (n.d.). *Training.* Retrieved January 19, 2021, from https://www.irp.wisc.edu/training.

Mercy College. (2018, September 7). *Student success series: Poverty simulation exercise* [Video]. (YouTube). https://www.youtube.com/watch?v=SwmsMK_tQA0.

San Juan College. (2015, January 7). *Bridges out of poverty at San Juan College* [Video]. YouTube. https://www.youtube.com/watch?v=hmSFdks-gTM.

Swipe Out Hunger. (n.d.). *About us.* Retrieved January 19, 2021, from https://www.swipehunger.org/aboutus.

U.S. Census Bureau. (2019, November 14). *Poverty: 2017 and 2018.* https://www.census.gov/library/publications/2019/acs/acsbr18-02.html.

Welfare Info. (2020). *Poverty rate rankings by state.* https://www.welfareinfo.org/poverty-rate/#by-state.

Part III

Engaging Students and Faculty in Learning

At the center of the community college mission is education, and at the center of education is the relationship between learning and teaching, between learners and teachers. Students and faculty share the responsibility for learning: Students must be prepared, willing, and open to new ideas; faculty, too, must embrace new ideas, new ways of teaching, and new approaches for motivating their students to succeed.

"Thinking Civically: Delta College Champions Community Engagement" demonstrates how several faculty members first engaged their colleagues and then students in adopting the Democracy Commitment. Focusing from the outset on building connectedness and community through social engagement and civic participation, the faculty fostered a sense of caring, involvement, and belonging that contributed in demonstrable ways to improving retention, completion, and also recruitment.

"Persistence and Completion: Solutions for the Classroom" shifts the focus from institutionally driven actions to improve the bottom line to discovering and addressing what students need and want in order to persist and complete. Using technology to understand individual students' needs and goals; crafting adaptive learning strategies; monitoring performance with data analytics; and providing useful and timely feedback, faculty can transform the classroom experience. Technology accompanied by engagement of faculty with course planning, selection, and registration resulted in marked improvement, not only in student persistence but also in satisfaction and success.

"Emulating Plan, Do, Study, Act (PDSA): A Model to Sustain Student Learning Outcomes Assessment" describes how one large college adopted and adapted Edward Deming's PDSA (Plan, Do, Study, Act) model for continuous quality improvement to address the challenge of developing, using, and improving a method for student learning outcomes assessment. The resulting PIMA (Plan, Implement, Measure, Act) Model created by a collaborative faculty effort promises to contribute to improved student learning.

Chapter Nine

Thinking Civically

Delta College Champions Community Engagement

Kimberly M. Klein

THE DEMOCRACY COMMITMENT

At Delta College, central to our daily mission are the equally important priorities of guiding our students to meet their educational goals and also instilling in them a sense of belonging and engagement. We've learned that students are often uncomfortable identifying what they care about outside of "I." We believe it is part of our job to help them engage with others and with their environment.

In an effort to move our students from a narrower "I" perspective to a more inclusive "we" perspective, we use a holistic approach. We strive to enhance their learning experiences by connecting them with the community of learners in their classrooms and also with the communities served by the college. With intentional, community-based activities, we demonstrate our commitment to "community" as central to our identity and begin to lay a foundation of the college's culture of engagement. Our hope is that our students will begin to see themselves as empowered members of a diverse group who, individually, have much in common.

When done effectively, this focus on a *culture of engagement* not only encourages everyone's recognition of shared values and areas of concern, but also develops a willingness to address those concerns. Raising awareness about the issues we care about collectively enhances our sense of belonging—and reinforces the shared certainty that belonging *matters*. This emotional attachment and shared commitment create a powerful force that transcends an academic experience. Through this gradual, but steady, process of involvement, students begin to place themselves more centrally within the larger community, understanding that their roles include responsibility, not only to themselves, but also to the greater good.

This change in teaching viewpoint came about in part after my colleague Professor Lisa Lawrason and I became involved in the Democracy Commitment, a national initiative designed to engage students in civic learning. Following our attendance at a national conference, we returned to campus full of passion and ideas. Our charge was to put this passion into motion, so we began to consider how to put this concept of civic learning into action at Delta College.

We knew that timing is vital. We were fortunate to have early momentum on our side, as we also were part of a larger, robust conversation regarding our general education requirements at Delta College. As we shared our ideas as part of this larger conversation, together, the faculty and administration then identified a "Think Civically" general education requirement. In doing so, the campus community purposefully extended a graduation stipulation across multiple disciplines on campus.

The Think Civically requirement is described in this way: "Demonstrate an understanding of diverse societies, ranging from local to global, in order to engage effectively in civic life" (Delta College, 2018/2019). This notion of engaging in civic life demands a deeper level of participation, ultimately challenging students to "care." By adopting the Civic Engagement graduation requirement, we set our institution on a course of accountability to bridge the gap between an isolated outlook and a broader global vision of society. We recognized that often our students' limited viewpoint is not enough, and that our mission must include a goal to challenge students from being passive members to being active contributors to society.

As we developed and strengthened our Think Civically component, what became obvious was that we needed to create more opportunities for action and, therefore, a campus *culture of action*. Through a variety of hands-on experiences, the faculty and staff collectively carried out our commitment to this value. One current American Politics student expressed this well in an evaluation response:

> Overall, this project and this class were some of the most applicable experiences in education that I've ever had. In the future, I'll be able to communicate and make plans from scratch with those I've never really worked with before.

Our expectation now is that students learn to dynamically shape their community through involvement. The logical extension of this work is that students are also shaping their classroom experience as we empower them with the knowledge, skills, and passion to do so. As Ronan (2011) stated,

> Civic learning actually engages all aspects of the human person—the head, through thinking, judging, deliberation, and advocacy, as well as through friendship with those co-involved in the public work; and the hands through voting, acts of service, and collaborative political action. (p. 5)

This level of action creates a buy-in response to an overall sense of belonging; in other words, students have significant stake in the outcome.

HOW DOES CIVIC ENGAGEMENT FIT INTO COMMUNITY COLLEGES?

> The main lesson that I learned through this class is that coming together as a team is just as important as being passionate and working towards a goal. Human resources are the best kind of resource you can have when working toward a positive change in your community, or on an even larger scale, such as trying to change the way our country functions. —Student comment from the Learning Community class evaluation

The philosophy of community colleges in the United States has changed since its inception when the term *people's colleges* was at the forefront and answered the populist agenda demanding access to social mobility (Trainor, 2015). From the inception, community colleges were viewed as innovators. The early comprehensive vision of junior colleges of William Rainey Harper and other boosters failed to come to fruition as the stark reality was that they were unable to compete with universities' name recognition and funding resources; hence, collectively they pivoted toward the expansion of opportunities, moving from being transfer institutions to an added role as vocational trainers. This transition gave rise to practical offerings deemed to meet job-market demands. Simultaneously, community colleges made a concerted effort to be committed and connected to the community. In doing so, their student bodies grew in diversity as they attracted students of color, nontraditional students, and returning veterans.

From the early days, a consistent tenet of community colleges was the expectation of adapting to the demands of society (O'Banion, 2019). The present-day community college is expected to bridge the gap that exists with a diverse body of students to provide a pathway leading to a successful completion of educational goals. This pathway is marked by multiple intersections specifically related to retention and completion. As such, these waypoints demand serious and ongoing discussions as we press to support students to stay on the path toward completion.

Focusing on Student Success and Completion

One of the mainstays along this pathway is Achieving the Dream (AtD), a national reform network dedicated to community college student success and completion. Supported by member colleges and foundation dollars, AtD examines best practices from a holistic and innovative perspective. Through data collection and collaboration, the AtD network helps colleges strategize best practices in order to impact results. As part of this work, an essential framework was developed that includes institutions building capacity in specific areas. One of the areas is student and faculty engagement and communication (Achieving the Dream, 2016). Keying in on this element, we, as community college faculty, must ask ourselves how we can impact student outcomes. It is clear that successful outcomes must include students remaining on the natural pathway that ultimately leads them through course completion, credit attainment, and eventual credential or transfer, thus successful journeys. There are, however, other intersections to consider that may influence the results.

We know that low-income, first-generation students and students of color are less likely to attend or finish university (Jensen & Jetten, 2015). The varying demographic realities on a national scale reflect just over 12 million community college students, of which 61% are not credit-seeking. Part-time students make up 73% of the student population, with women making up 56%, and the average age is 28. Additionally, 36% are first generation, 17% are single parents, 12% are students with disabilities, and 7% are non-U.S. citizens (AACC, 2018). As educators, we know that all students demand a level of guidance in their educational journeys. No single area of the college or the educational experience can possibly provide it all. But if we examine our role in their journeys, an important question becomes central: What can we, as faculty, do to enrich their educational experiences? One logical area is by building connections, and more specifically, by building "social capital."

Developing Social Capital

Social capital involves a sense of belonging. Robert Putnam (2000), in his bestselling book, *Bowling Alone*, expanded on the concept of the value of social networks. Putnam delves into the notion of social contacts and the effect these relationships have on the productivity of individuals and groups. Logically, a lack of social contacts will result in the opposite: a lack of productivity, both of individuals and groups. Research has suggested that students' backgrounds prior to entering higher education and the social capital linked to their backgrounds directly impacts their abilities to succeed in higher education. Simply put, those students who enter college as members of a vulnerable group—representative, for example, of the demographics listed above—have a lower chance of success because of a lack of social capital (Jensen & Jetten, 2015).

Community college students represent these demographics at a much higher rate. As members of lower socioeconomic status groups, they are faced with additional challenges as a result of their backgrounds. These students have greater difficulty creating social capital, making them more likely to face failure in the higher education environment.

HOW CAN CIVIC ENGAGEMENT PROMOTE COLLEGE COMPLETION?

[Social capital is] a societal resource that links citizens to each other and enables them to pursue their common objectives more effectively.—Stolle (as cited in Padgett, 2011, p. 31)

A failure in the higher education environment manifests itself in student retention and completion rates. Delta College reports a 4-year average fall-to-winter semester return rate of 76.27% and a 4-year average fall-to-fall return rate of 51.04%. Our full-time, first-time-in-any-college (FTIAC) students who are degree-seeking reflect a 4-year average of fall-to-fall retention rate of 62.75%. Our FTIAC students' graduation rate, based on completion in 3 years or less, is 15%, and the transfer rate is 25%, with a combined graduation and transfer rate of 40% (Delta College Institutional Research, 2020).

The harsh reality existing in higher education indicates that in the past 25 years the rates of college completion in the United States have not reflected any significant, marked change. In fact, despite all the research done in this area, institutions are not transitioning in using this information to formulate best practices, resulting in changed rates of persistence. In addition, the 2-year success rates indicate that only 1 in 10 community college students earns a 4-year degree versus the university entrance rate of 6 in 10 who earn a bachelor's degree within a 6-year period (Tinto & Pusser, 2006; U.S. Department of Education, 2019). Rather than focusing all our attention on why students fail, maybe we should be asking why students stay.

Belonging, Community, and Civic Engagement

Tinto and Pusser (2006) outlined five reasons why students stay in college: commitment, expectations, support, feedback, and involvement. An outcome of having social capital is a sense of belonging and a willingness to become involved within your community. In the academic arena, we can do more to provide opportunities that create a sense of belonging for students. Specifically, in our classrooms, we can enhance our students' sense of community through civic engagement opportunities, focusing on relationship-building and community outreach.

Civic engagement opportunities and involvement, though, are two-pronged: they must encompass both academic and social aspects. Social researchers have concluded that the more students are involved academically and socially, the higher the chances are that they will persist and graduate. Of note, this involvement has even more significance when it occurs during the first year of college (Tinto & Pusser, 2006). Involvement in the academic and social spheres can manifest itself in numerous ways. Tinto (2002) referred to academic membership, which results in a feeling of confidence within the academic arena. As a result of confidence in the academic area, students are more likely to reach out socially. Thus, both areas have the potential to influence each other (Barnett, 2011). The college classroom becomes the opportune place to promote and develop an environment where students feel connected and where they can be actively involved in their own learning process (Tinto, 2002).

Tinto (1997) recognized the role that institutions play in supporting student integration: "Generally speaking, the greater students' involvement in the life of the college, especially its academic life, the greater their acquisition of knowledge and development of skills. This is particularly true of student contact with faculty" (p. 600). Tinto's (1997) study found that involvement in a collaborative or shared learning group encouraged students to interact with each other, thereby building a quasi–support network. Through these shared classroom and learning experiences, students were more likely to fully engage with the social aspect of their college.

Student Engagement Improves Learning

As an educational component, civic engagement is considered a high-impact, best practice. Along with increasing students' sense of civic responsibility, reports have suggested benefits also include higher academic performance, enhanced problem-solving skills, and improved critical thinking (Information Resources Management Association, 2019). However, to reap the full rewards, these skills must be reinforced in multiple academic and campus settings to develop fully. Critical thinking, for example, once developed through civic engagement activities, can be readily transferred across academic and social areas of the college, thus enhancing the learning pathway for students.

Earlier research has also identified the powerful role that student engagement plays in improving learning outcomes. Dewey noted that in every experience there lies a social aspect (as cited in McDermott, 1981). Accordingly, Dewey suggested that the social atmosphere may act as a catalyst that can carry a person over down times in the future (McDermott, 1981, p. 446).

Research has supported Dewey's belief, showing that participation in campus social groups and activities results in positive grade outcomes, school satisfaction, and persistence through the junior year (Porchea et al., 2010). Porchea et al. (2010) also compared the effect of students' prior academic preparation to other psychosocial factors. Their findings suggested that factors such as social support, self-esteem, and social intelligence have a significant impact on persistence. In addition, extracurricular involvement was one of the strongest predictors of transfer readiness. These findings highlight the potential for student success when students are presented with opportunities to build social capital. Delta's strategy: expand the social capital across campus.

DELTA COLLEGE SIGNS ON TO THE DEMOCRACY COMMITMENT

The Democracy Commitment (TDC) is a non-partisan national organization dedicated to advancing democracy in higher education, and to make democratic skills available to all individuals who desire a voice and a seat at the table of local, state, and national discourse and action. To such end TDC provides a platform for the development and expansion of community college programs, projects, and curricula aimed at engaging students in civic learning and democratic engagement. —The Democracy Commitment (2017)

In order to build social capital college-wide, Delta College needed a mechanism. The high-impact practice of creating a college culture of engagement provided such a mechanism. The Democracy Commitment initiative at Delta College, established to "raise awareness, educate, and empower the Delta College community to enact positive change through social engagement and citizenship," was a holistic approach promoting a culture of belonging (Delta College, 2015).

As Dewey explained, it is not enough just to "prepare" a student for life by the transference of concrete skills; rather, education involves the holistic approach of experiences that enable a deeper level of learning (McDermott, 1981, p. 446). A sense of involvement through community engagement can fulfill the human longing to belong. Empowering students to be active and involved with their college and outside communities creates an environment of relevancy for students as it builds social capital. Delta College offered its students a broad area to build relationships as, together, we work intentionally to create a college *of* the community.

Who We Are

Delta College has been a pillar of the Great Lakes Bay community in mid-Michigan for over 55 years. Located in the middle of three counties (Bay, Midland, and Saginaw), Delta reaches thousands of Michigan residents, and we take pride in our commitment to serve our communities. Early in the application of Delta's involvement with The Democracy Commitment, the core team decided to use a dual approach. With the goal of empowering students and impacting their success rates, this approach combined on-campus experiences with community outreach. As we embarked on efforts to create a campus-wide culture that expects and demands student engagement, we knew that it was vital that this work included faculty and staff from various disciplines and work groups across Delta.

We also believed it was imperative that we include a wrap-around approach that would ensure that, no matter what our Delta students were involved in, they would encounter activities demanding their attention. The culture on and off campus needed to model the "citizen's" role in protecting public values and promote courage to stand up to address concerns. By modeling this level of engagement in citizenship, we could actively build social capital. While we knew that civic education is a proven strategy for building social capital (Kahne et al., 2006), to do this at the level we envisioned, we needed to identify spaces where there was high student traffic, and then "confront" them with the issues central to citizenship in a democratic society. To do this, we created a Democracy Wall.

The Democracy Wall Could Change Your World

The mobile Democracy Wall, built by students in a cabinetry class, was moved to various locations on campus. Weekly questions were posted on the wall, and students could use the wall to respond to the questions and to each other. This use of intentional "confrontation" space caused an incremental change in thinking about community on Delta's campus, and got the ball rolling as students began to reflect on their individual identities and stances as they related to the prompt. From this point, we expanded these intentional spaces and opportunities by creating an atmosphere of empowerment that would teach students strategies to address specific civic and community issues and provide a platform where they could problem solve, reflect, and ultimately make a difference.

Change Your World Week emerged as a week-long on-campus event that raised awareness of issues important to students, prompted them to consider new aspects and perspectives, and provided ways that they could engage with the issues and vie for positive change. Efforts included voter registration and get-out-the-vote drives to teach students the importance of using their voices.

All of the week's opportunities created avenues of access for increasing their sense of belonging. Students begin to see that, in order to have a sense of belonging, access must come first.

Open Access to Education and Community Engagement

By providing open access to education, community colleges have long been known as "democracy's colleges," and community colleges' commitment to outreach built a framework of unity and connection with their surrounding communities. This commitment to local communities required a pledge, not only to listen to the needs of the area in providing educational programs and opportunities, but also to commit to working alongside our communities in addressing real-life problems. This commitment is ongoing and perpetual; it cannot be turned off in difficult or challenging times. This unwavering obligation to establish a public presence and earn the trust of our partners was a key component in community colleges' origin and history. This commitment also provides a space for our students to go beyond their individual "I" existence, recognize their place in the "we" of the community, and build social capital. As our students build relationships with their classmates, they also solidify their presence within, and their commitment to, their own communities. Through this work, students begin to understand their roles outside the classroom, as citizens as well as students.

COMMUNITY OUTREACH BEGINS

The Democracy Project didn't end in our classrooms or at the borders of the college. Our community outreach engagement initiative began 7 years ago with our implementation of Public Achievement, a civics program with stakeholders from our K–12 public school systems. The program involved college students coaching younger students through a process to identify community issues important to them. Once they identified the issues, students researched problems associated with the issues. Next, the real work began as the teams designed and implemented an action plan to address each issue. This program acted as a springboard that eventually moved the work in a unique direction: the work shifted from high school-aged students toward primarily fourth and fifth graders.

It's a Bike Race

In building an experience of community with our young partners, we wanted to plant the seed that college was a possibility for everyone. A small group of Delta faculty and staff took on the task of designing an event that would be fun and would expose the youngsters to the college environment. We did this with a bicycle.

A bicycle provided us with the focus for our event: the "Race to College." Knowing that this age group could be a tough group to reach, we knew we needed to challenge them and entice them to participate in fun events outside of their typical school day and school experiences. We used a bicycle to demonstrate the power of choice. Our goals were to have the kids understand that (1) their selections had meaning, (2) they could choose to live a healthier lifestyle, and (3) they could also choose their academic future. By hosting the event at Delta College, we also hoped to increase their comfort with the college environment. The youngsters would spend the day in a college setting, walking the halls, sitting in classrooms, and essentially putting themselves in "college."

As we designed the Race to College event, we wanted it to fall under the umbrella of the Democracy Commitment initiative, both to supply the resources we'd need and to build on the Democracy Project's momentum. We earmarked $4,500 to purchase bicycles in addition to securing partial funding for helmets as a result of our partnership with the Field Neurosciences Institute, making the initial investment approximately $6,000. We worked with the owner of a local bike shop and managed to parlay our partnership into 25 Fuji mountain bikes that Delta would own. The purchased helmets would be given to the youngsters to keep.

Involving the Local and Campus Communities

A key community partner in this endeavor was the Michigan State Police and its troopers, who partnered with Delta's police academy cadets. Our police cadets took the lead in the helmet-fitting piece of the event, while the state troopers—using watermelons—demonstrated the importance of wearing a helmet. We intentionally designed activities that would bring the young people and the law enforcement community together, hoping to change the viewpoint of each group about the other. Operating in a relaxed, inviting environment created an opportunity for both groups to get to know one another on a different level.

Included in our plan was tapping into our diverse student body who could shepherd the younger students throughout the day. Our Delta student body mirrors the strengths and struggles of the Great Lakes Bay Region. They can relate to these youngsters as they have faced similar issues in their lives. Our mission included a sense of trust that the relationships fostered during this day would provide hope and the belief that anything is possible. We felt confident that what would emerge was that these youngsters would walk away with the notion that attending college was a realistic goal. We aimed at the participants embracing an "I can do this" attitude. From start to finish, social capital would be a by-product of this event, not only from the standpoint of the student body at Delta, but also from that of the student body of our K–12 partners. All of us involved in this event combined to build a social network. This level of participation unmasked the positive impact that an individual can have by getting involved in his or her community. The understanding of being able to make a difference is a lifelong skill.

At its inception in 2015, the Race to College event involved Delta students enrolled in one American Politics class. As a part of their graduation requirement, those students were required to perform 15 hours of a civic engagement outreach. Faculty at Delta were at liberty to design their civic engagement project in whatever fashion they chose. The American Politics classes that were involved in the Race to College event used this project as their engagement option. These 60 to 75 Delta students set out on a course to introduce the fourth- and fifth-grade students to Delta College. The grade-school students were each given a Delta College identification badge with their picture and their expected college enrollment date. The ID badges contributed to the social capital component and also gave the college the ability to collect data and establish a database that we can use to track their future entry at Delta.

WHAT DO THE STUDENTS THINK?

In an effort to assess the impact of this initiative, Delta students were required to write a reflection paper outlining their involvement. Often students expressed a consistent apprehension prior to the start of the event, although on the day of the event students recorded that the apprehension quickly disappeared. In two instances, although the class was finished, students continued to visit the elementary students at their home school, on their time. One student reported the following experience:

> I called all three schools and set up a meeting with the fifth-grade teacher from Jessie Loomis. I arranged to meet with her class every Friday. I spoke with them about the importance of listening and the importance of mathematics. I arranged to check back with them to see if the class is improving, I promised to bring pizza if they show improvement. My intent is to be very active with the students and see what develops.

Another student shared this result: "Working with those kids my first semester in college really made me realize that I wanted to be a teacher." Others commented on the project as a whole:

> I came out of this project knowing how to better handle people with different outlooks than my own. That in itself is an invaluable life skill that I am glad I can work on in school rather than in the workplace.

The added incentive of helping people in the real world rather than just working for a grade was an awesome opportunity.

EFFECTS ON RETENTION AND COMPLETION

We tracked the enrollment patterns for the 2017 fall semester for two groups (1) the students from the POL105 Engagement Project classes and (2) the students from the POL103 classes without the engagement project. The students enrolled in the Engagement Project classes reflected a higher rate of retention fall to winter (89.2%) than the students in nonproject classes (84.4%). For additional comparison, the overall college's fall-to-winter retention rates are 77%; thus, both government classes reflected higher retention percentages. Examining a longer retention window of fall-to-fall retention rates, the students in the Engagement Project classes had a 63.9% retention rate; those in nonproject classes, a 52.4% retention rate. Delta College's overall fall-to-fall retention rate is 52.1%. While retention rates are affected by multiple factors, the increased retention rates demonstrate clear value for the program.

PROGRAM CHANGES AND INNOVATIONS

The program has been in existence for over 5 years, and each year we have made changes in the delivery. Our community partnerships, though, have remained the same since the program's inception. As educators, we are trained to continually explore ways to enhance our lessons, improve student learning, and continually innovate—and this event was no different. One of our program innovations, in fact, was driven by a personal holiday trip. Completely by happenstance, I visited Naperville, Illinois, and encountered the national "Safety Town" project. This chance visit provided insight as to how our empowerment activity could potentially have a broader, long-term impact on the community. Our Delta team embraced the idea, and we immediately began to expand our partnerships.

Safety Program

In 2018, Delta leaders of the project partnered with our engineering faculty and students and requested that they embark on building a stand-alone traffic light. The traffic light is portable and is a miniature version of a working light that is found at traffic intersections. Attached to this light is the cross/don't cross signal, all timed at the precise intervals to teach the students when to cross safely. As part of our new safety event, our extension activity included an outreach program where Delta students created lesson plans addressing safety issues, and our community visits expanded to include two additional elementary schools that were not part of the Race to College event. For the safety project, we added sessions with kindergarten and first-grade students, teaching them lessons on bus safety, animal safety, and pedestrian safety. The program for fourth- and fifth-grade students focused on gun safety, fire safety, stranger danger, and bike safety.

The issue of safety has a way of bringing people together, especially when focused on our most vulnerable: our children. Being involved with a project whose goal is to keep youngsters safe is not only valuable, it has a feel-good result for everyone.

Honors Learning Community

Since 2020, this effort was enhanced once again through a commitment by Delta College faculty and administration with the creation of an honors learning community. A civic engagement government class was paired with an English class with the goal of completing a feasibility study for a permanent program designed to keep children safe. In their English class, students collected qualitative data from Saginaw residents for the proposed Safety Town. In their government classes, they used this information to develop community presentations and apply for potential grant programs. The students and faculty then partnered with the Delta College Foundation staff to identify community groups and events for the community presentations.

The sudden shifts that resulted on campus because of the COVID-19 pandemic limited many of the final project presentations; however, we were able to host an event at the local YMCA and established a relationship with Covenant Hospital to cohost another event. Both of these relationships will provide a foundation for future classes.

WHAT THE STUDENTS SAID

When the Honors Learning Community concluded its work in spring 2020, the faculty asked the students to reflect on their experiences and on what they learned. These two comments summarize well the reflections we gathered:

> Overall, this was a very interesting class, that in the end, I was glad I took. It really enhanced my life in general. Considering that I am naturally a shy person, and I do not like doing new things, going outside the box. But this class showed me that I cannot get by in the real world with my current attitude, that I will need to change, and this class has, I believe, started that process. To trust more people, to believe that there are others out there that want to change the community like our class.

I learned a lot about how important it is to help others. Being in this class, we had a lot of resources and we wanted to make a difference. I think that everyone in our class put all their effort into this. It was awesome to see other people care about coming up with a solution. It was also nice to see just how many other safety towns there are in the United States. So many people saw the issue with child safety and wanted to correct it. I think that it will affect my future because I learned that I can make a difference.

WHAT HAPPENS NEXT?

As colleges continue to innovate and find better, more effective ways to guide students to completion, the role of faculty to engage students actively in their learning becomes more apparent. At Delta College, we are proud of the successes of the Democracy Project and its efforts to move students from an "I" mentality to a "we" mindset, instilling a sense of purpose that is bigger than themselves. We are especially proud of the reports we hear from students who are seeing value in their work and ways to apply these tools and skills to their everyday lives and to their futures.

As faculty working on the project, we are devoted to continuing our efforts to identify potential partnerships between Delta and our community members to bring a permanent Safety Town to fruition. In just its early stages, the Safety Town event has impacted 250 kindergarten through third-grade students along with 50 Delta students. In the 5 years that Delta has hosted the Race to College event, we have touched the lives of 1,070 elementary students along with 325 Delta College students. Our consistent partners in these projects, the Michigan State Police and Jack's Bicycle Shop, as well as the six area elementary schools, are continuing to make this event a valuable community connection for the college as well. Our recent collaboration with Covenant Health Care Systems and the Saginaw YMCA has further established our presence within the surrounding communities of Delta College.

The purpose of the Democracy Commitment at Delta College is to raise awareness, educate, and empower the Delta College community to enact positive change through social engagement and citizenship. We are building social capital within the Delta College student body and are watching the ripple effect as education involves the broader community, not only physically but also emotionally. The engagement activities are establishing a sense of caring, enhanced involvement, and a sense of belonging. They are also building a foundation of social action. Delta College is committed to staying the course as we continue to engage students in the classroom, socially on campus, and through community outreach. Along the way, we are engaging the heart, the mind, and the hands of everyone who comes in contact with this work.

REFERENCES

AACC. (2018, April). *Fast facts 2018*. https://www.aacc.nche.edu/wp-content/uploads/2018/04/2018-Fast-Facts.pdf.

Achieving the Dream. (2016). *2016 annual report student success is what counts*. https://www.achievingthedream.org/sites/default/files/basic_page/atd_2016_annualreport.pdf.

Barnett, E. A. (2011). *Validation experiences and persistence among community college students* [Higher Education study 10:1353/rhe.2010.0019]. Project Muse. http://www.muse.jhu.edu/journals.

Delta College. (2018/2019). *Delta*. http://catalog.delta.edu/content.php?catoid=6&navoid=637.

Delta College Democracy Commitment Committee. (2015, December 8). Presentation to the Board of Trustees.

Delta College Institutional Research. (2020, May 3). *Dashboard*. https://dashboard.delta.edu/SitePages/Home.aspx.

Democracy Commitment. (2017). *About TDC*. https://thedemocracycommitment.org/about-tdc.

Information Resources Management Association. (2019). *Civic engagement and politics: Concepts, methodologies, tools, and applications*. IGI Global.

Jensen, D. H., & Jetten, J. (2015). Bridging and bonding interactions in higher education: Social capital and students' academic and professional identity formation. *Frontiers in Psychology, 6*, 126.

Kahne, J., Chi, B., & Middaugh, E. (2006, January). Building social capital for civic and political engagement: The potential of high-school civics courses. *Canadian Journal of Education, 29*(2), 387–409.

McDermott, J. J. (1981). *The philosophy of John Dewey: Two volumes in one: 1. The structure of experience 2. The lived experience*. University of Chicago Press.

O'Banion, T. U. (2019, February). *The continuing evolution of the American community college*. League for Innovation. https://www.league.org/istream-other/continuing-evolution-American-community-college.

Padgett, R. D. (2011). *The effects of the first year of college on undergraduates' development of altruistic and socially responsible behavior* [Unpublished PhD dissertation]. University of Iowa. http://ir.uiowa.edu/cgi/viewcontent.cgi?article=2437&context=etd.

Porchea, S. F., Allen, J., Robbins, S., & Phelps, R. P. (2010). Predictors of long-term enrollment and degree outcomes for community college students: Integrating academic, psychosocial, socio-demographic, and situational factors. *The Journal of Higher Education, 81*(6), 750–778.

Putnam, R. D. (2000). *Bowling alone: The collapse and revival of American community*. Simon & Schuster.

Ronan, B. (2011). *The civic spectrum how students become engaged citizens*. Kettering Foundation. https://files.eric.ed.gov/fulltext/ED539344.pdf.

Tinto, V. (1997). Classrooms as communities: Exploring the educational character of student persistence. *Journal of Higher Education, 68*, 599–623. http://dx.doi.org/10.2307/2959965.

Tinto, V. (2002, April 15). *Taking student retention seriously: Rethinking the first-year experience*. American Association of Collegiate Registrars. http://advisortrainingmanual.pbworks.com/f/Tinto_TakingRetentionSeriously.pdf.

Tinto, V., & Pusser, B. (2006, June). *Moving from theory to action: Building a model of institutional action for student success* [Research report]. National Postsecondary Education Cooperative.

Trainor, S. (2015, October 20). How community colleges changed the whole idea of education in America. *Time*. https://time.com/4078143/community-college-history.

U.S. Department of Education, National Center for Education Statistics. (2019). Graduation rates. In *The condition of education 2019* [NCES 2019-144]. https://nces.ed.gov/fastfacts/display.asp?id=40.

Chapter Ten

Persistence and Completion

Solutions for the Classroom

Carmen Allen

STUDENT EXPECTATIONS FOR LEARNING

After 22 years of teaching at Lincoln Land Community College (Illinois), I never really understood why some of my students were failing, dropping a course, or simply disappearing. No one even asked why these losses were occurring. Over time, I became more and more concerned that I didn't know the causes, nor did I have remedies for the students I lost. I decided that it was time for me to be proactive and attempt to better understand the student experience. More recently, the impact of the coronavirus pandemic increased the urgency of my mission to help students reach academic goals. With the help of technologies and new methodologies, I was able to find answers to some of my questions.

The pandemic of 2020 will forever be remembered by higher education as a time when spring courses on our campuses were transformed into online delivery and when online courses became the only option for our summer courses. The pandemic forced higher education to reexamine technology use for every employee and every student. Even before the pandemic, universities and colleges were consistently challenged by declining enrollment, reduced financial resources, and an increased demand for accountability. The pandemic has only intensified those issues.

The good news is that the pandemic has required the use of technologies that can contribute greatly to campus-wide retention efforts. In classrooms across the globe, the digital divide between those "who have" and those "who have not" is narrowing. This means that opportunities to connect or bridge the gap between faculty and students are increasing. For the first time at my college, we waived online course fees and provided laptops for both students and faculty who needed them.

Students make critical decisions about their classes—and the institution they attend—based on positive or negative interactions with faculty and the technologies being used. Learning expectations are driven by the demands of this digital revolution. When faculty proactively implement meaningful, thoughtful, and systematic solutions with enhanced technology, colleges and universities will be more likely to survive and thrive.

HOW DO WE DEFINE STUDENT SUCCESS?

Persistence and retention metrics are used to measure student success from semester-to-semester or fall-to-spring to diagnose the "health" of a college or university. These indicators drive the implementation of campus-wide initiatives, such as mandatory orientation or mandatory advising, that attempt to increase the total number of graduates.

Students define *success* differently. For them, it is the achievement of an academic goal regardless of the college they attend. Motivation to learn begins the process and contributes to persistence. It is persistence, then, that they need to achieve the goal—even when life's challenges throw them off balance.

Tinto (2016) suggested that, because institutional and student perspectives may differ, they should be addressed differently. He stated:

> To promote greater degree completion, institutions have to adopt the student perspective and ask not only how they should act to retain their students but also how they should act so that more of their students want to persist to completion. The two questions, while necessarily linked, do not lead to the same sort of conversations about institutional action. The latter, rarely asked, requires institutions to understand how student experiences shape their motivation to persist and, in turn, what they can do to enhance that motivation. (p. 3)

Community colleges can benefit from reevaluating how they invest in retention. Compared to the cost of advertising, recruitment, and admissions, retaining students is much less expensive. With a stronger focus on the classroom experience where students spend most of their educational journey, student success is more likely: "For community college students, the classroom is the primary connecting point to everything the college offers, and their instructors are potentially the most important bridge to both support services and other relationships they will form at the college" (McClenney & Arnsparger, 2012, p. 48).

WHY DO STUDENTS DROP?

For community colleges, efforts to identify the reasons for student attrition—the opposite of retention—are challenging because of inconsistent relevant data. For community colleges, comprehensive retention rate data generally exclude part-time students, returning students, transfer students, and students who prematurely leave after the first or second enrollment year. Retention formulas may also include students who probably should not be included, such as students who enroll, drop their fall courses, then reenroll the following fall. Further, there is also no specific measurement for students who take a cafeteria selection of courses that may not apply toward a specific degree, or for students who are trapped in non-credit bearing remedial courses.

A significant body of research, however, seeks to explain reasons for student attrition. Generally, five categories impact a student's decision to drop out:

1. Personal reasons: Lost, stressed, undisciplined, unmotivated, insecure, uninformed.
2. Social reasons: Alienation, isolation, being subject to negative peer pressure, uninvolved in college activities, weak relationships with faculty members or advisors.
3. Academic: Underprepared, underchallenged, poor study habits, doesn't see value in assignments and courses, low academic performance, part-time course load, lack of educational career goals, feedback is too delayed.
4. Life issues: Insecurity about finances, job demands, time-management issues, home and family difficulties, personal problems, health problems.
5. Institutional issues: Getting the runaround, operational issues (such as billing and scheduling), negative attitudes in the classroom, low-quality advising, low-quality administration, poor or indifferent teaching, outdated instructional equipment or technology.

These five categories contain two common factors: the classroom and the instructional faculty. If we can improve communication in the classroom and break down barriers that may exist between students and faculty, we can address many of these components. A first step is understanding our students and their expectations for learning and their education.

Learning expectations evolve as fast as the technologies being used by today's college students. It is now reasonable to expect "tech savvy" students who send and receive information at lightning speeds to expect the same experience in their college classrooms. Frustrations arise and course completion is inhibited when technically oriented learners are enrolled in courses taught by instructors with a limited level of digital literacy. Faculty who consistently rely on traditional classroom methods should be concerned that negative experiences—which are quickly and easily being communicated to other students using technology—may affect future enrollment. Inefficient teaching practices that consume energy and time could be replaced productively with effective and engaging student activities. In today's learning environment, and with the pressing academic response to the coronavirus pandemic, faculty are expected to deliver course content that infuses technology tools into the classroom experience.

WHAT ARE SOLUTIONS FOR THE CLASSROOM?

Innovative and affordable solutions that increase persistence and completion in the classroom include using Student Success Profile (SSP) data, effective student engagement, and student performance monitoring.

Solution 1: Use Student Success Profile (SSP) Data

Having a clear understanding of a student's academic history, barriers to academic success, future goals, and other pertinent data provides a Student Success Profile (SSP) useful for promoting student goal attainment. The collection and protection of student data are common practices in higher education; however, using these data proactively to help retain students and ensure their success is far less common.

Providing faculty with access to SSP data accomplishes two important goals. First, it offers the opportunity for students to receive personalized help from an additional source, and it confirms a message from administration to faculty that students should be viewed not just as a group of names on a roster, but as individuals within a group. For students who have identified an academic pathway or who have established career goals, faculty can recommend future courses to take, refer students to formal academic advising, direct students to investigate student clubs and organizations, and suggest events that support their areas of interest. Additionally, faculty familiar with workforce programs can provide information about career options or direct students to career planning services.

Another contributor to persistence involves faculty who intentionally and actively assist students with course registration. Without consistent or effective academic advising, students who aren't well informed will be more likely to make poor, very costly, and time-wasting decisions that affect their future. SSP data can make it easier for faculty and counselors to provide appropriate academic advising.

However, the use of student education records maintained by higher education institutions is closely regulated. Before institutions consider making changes to their distribution of student records and develop an SSP data source, they must have a clear understanding of FERPA mandates to ensure compliance. FERPA mandates may include stipulations covering the process by which students are informed about the use of their individual data. Institutions that decide to restrict access to SSP data based on concerns about possible student bias should consider, instead, providing employees who use this data with professional development training or instruction that ensures fairness to all students.

To create an SSP, each institution will need to determine these unique specifications:

1. What SSP data (current and new) will specifically assist with student retention and success?
2. How should SSP data be collected (the input process)?
3. How will SSP data be maintained, stored, protected, and secured?
4. Who will have access to SSP data (outputs).
5. What current or new software and hardware can be used?

If the institution does not currently have a software solution that provides SSP data or if the existing system does not adequately assist with student success, it should compare in-house solutions with third-party vendor solutions. An in-house developed campus solution requires a team of dedicated Information Technology staff to manage system analysis, design, and implementation. Third-party vendors may be more expensive, but because system development is complete, implementation and testing typically can occur sooner. The system can also be supported and housed off-site which, in turn, relieves the burden on in-house staff.

Data analytics products that provide SSP data are currently being used at colleges and universities across the nation. At Lincoln Land, we use McGraw-Hill Education's Zogotech, an extremely useful tool for assisting students. At Odessa College in Texas, implementation of this software led to an in-class retention rate that increased from an average of 83% in 2010 to more than 94% in 2014 (McGraw-Hill, 2016). Other products include Qlik-View from Qlik for business intelligence; R open-source software for predictive modeling; Tableau from Tableau Software; Rapid Insight; and SAP HANA from SAP.

Solution 2: Effective Student Engagement

When community college students are encouraged to actively engage with fellow classmates and faculty, they are more likely to complete their coursework. As Matson and Clark (2020) explained:

> When first-year students arrive on campus, they leap into a flurry of activities designed to ease their college transition. And while these programs can help foster student engagement, universities that focus on large events during orientation are missing a more valuable tool: namely, meeting and building a relationship with a professor. (p. 1)

When Gallup asked more than 75,000 students to reflect on their campus experiences, they found that only 27% of college graduates strongly agreed that they had a professor who cared about them as a person. A more optimistic statistic revealed that 63% of college graduates strongly agreed that a professor made them excited about learning (Matson and Clark, 2020). These data emphasize the many opportunities to increase student interaction that would be positively received by students.

Engaging, vitalized classrooms can significantly contribute to retention improvements. In order to understand what these activities mean, and in order to make transformational changes, we must transform teaching methods that are familiar and embrace new, innovative practices.

While it is the goal of education to transfer knowledge and skills to students, one of the most widely implemented instructional techniques that seeks to accomplish this goal is also one that can be the least engaging—the traditional lecture. At many institutions, larger lecture-based classes accommodate greater numbers of students, often in cavernous rooms with multiple-level seating. Lectures strive to enhance key concepts, adding value and depth to required reading, but if most students were graded on their listening abilities, they would very likely fail. While faculty who teach in large lecture settings can increase levels of engagement by adding demonstrations, technical devices, or open discussions to the mix, especially in these settings, faculty need to seek effective innovations and alternatives to enhance the transfer of knowledge and skills to students.

Students are more likely to persist and to maximize their performance when they are actively involved in their learning experience (Karpicke & Blunt, 2011). For students whose only connection to the campus may be the classroom, faculty can provide several engaging activities. Regardless of the delivery method (online, hybrid, or face-to-face), technology implementation is critical for students completing homework, learning course material, and completing assignments any time and any place. For these solutions to work, faculty will need training and best practice models. The end goal will be to create and maintain classroom designs that are effective, high quality, and also comply with the Americans with Disabilities Act (ADA). Specific student engagement solutions include course deployment using learning management software, well-designed videos, repetitive learning opportunities, and enhanced communication.

Use Learning Management Software for All Classes Regardless of Delivery

This first recommended practice of effective student engagement has become a necessity because of the pandemic. While this may not be a preferred practice for some faculty, providing students with immediate access to courses using learning management software (LMS), such as Canvas, Blackboard, or Moodle, has several advantages. Teaching and learning can be transformed from a set classroom location and time (synchronous) to any computer location at any time (asynchronous). At the simplest course design level, the benefits of converting printed course materials to e-documentation provide immediate student access to course information and a significant cost savings to institutions.

Further expanding course design to include learning unit instructions (assignments or modules) with automatically updated grades provides students with structured access to course materials and an up-to-date grade status. The design method that takes the most time and provides the greatest value is a high-quality course that can be copied for multiple sections and can be delivered in class or online. In-class courses supported by online content have the great potential to shift classes formerly infused with standard lectures to those with customized student assistance, enhanced learning activities, and groupwork.

Embed Videos Within an LMS

The second practice of effective student engagement requires the creation of well-designed videos embedded within the LMS. These videos are most effective when they provide value that extends beyond standard course materials. Video links from third-party sources can be extremely educational. Faculty can also create course specific videos that can be used to motivate, inform, or demonstrate complex concepts that need step-by-step simplification.

For those new to video creation, recording an in-class lecture—perhaps one with limited student interaction—is a starting point. One recorded lecture eliminates the time and effort required to present multiple in-class lectures. To provide a lecture outline, slide software such as PowerPoint, Google slides, Prezi, or Keynote can provide an enhanced presentation. The use of a completed video expands viewing options in-class or as homework. Requiring students to view a video before an in-class session (a.k.a. "flipping the classroom") allows for the opportunity to confirm student knowledge in class through a short quiz, a discussion or an applied learning activity. Even without a campus production crew, most mobile phones have video recording capabilities that can be easily uploaded to YouTube for sharing. Students will benefit as they can view a video multiple times, and they can use fast forwarding and back tracking.

Advanced video production can further enhance student engagement by providing computer screen shots, voice narration, and mouse click movement. For complex topics or for computer demonstrations, students would benefit from the use of computer screen capture videos. These can be recorded using software (e.g., Zoom recorded screen sharing, Screencast, or Camtasia), uploaded to YouTube, and shared using a video web link.

Another important component: It is a legal requirement that videos used for instruction apply closed captioning. Captioning can be extremely helpful for all students—not just for those who need special assistance. It is also critical for online courses to accommodate the needs of students with disabilities. Anderson (2020) indicated that "from a legal standpoint, the technology should always be usable for every student, and accommodations are required by law, unless it's an undue burden" (p. 16).

Require Repetitive Learning With Interactive Software

The third essential practice of effective student engagement is repetitive learning administered through interactive computer software. Repetition allows for a customized learning experience specific to learning progression and mastery of content. Through computerized simulation exercises, immediate feedback, and immediate grade results, this learning experience also known as personalization or adaptive learning, is unique, highly focused, and tailored to each student. This software can track large amounts of performance data and analytics that generate customized learning pathways for large numbers of students.

Interactive software is available for a wide range of academic specialty areas, and it often exceeds what many higher education institutions can afford to spend on development. Fortunately, several publishing companies provide a wide range of software products as an enhanced alternative to printed texts. For example, Pearson PLC offers Mylab for over 70 academic areas; Cengage Learning Inc. offers SAM and Aplia for over 11 academic areas; McGraw-Hill Education offers ALEKS; and Wiley offers WileyPlus. These publishers are eager to share their products with interested faculty and may provide faculty training. To ensure affordability for students, faculty should seek ways to negotiate and leverage pricing for learning material components such as print texts, e-texts, online content, and access codes for specialized software.

Enhance Communication Methods

The fourth effective student engagement practice uses technology that allows for essential communication between students and faculty. One-way communication that provides instructions or announcements to a group can be shared with campus email, phone calls and LMS-based announcements, assignments, and messaging. These traditional technologies are less likely to be immediately received by today's student than another more frequently used mode of communication—mobile phone texting. Even if unanswered, today's student is far more likely to check a text. It is a current technology that is efficient, easy to use, accessible, and extremely familiar to users.

For example, the texting app called REMIND has been a game changer in my classrooms. This tool, more than any other type of technology I've used with students, provides an immediate form of communication from any location. Students who reply are much more engaged, appreciative, and feel more empowered to express a wide range of concerns. REMIND is widely used in K–12 education to keep parents and students informed about homework. It can also be used effectively in higher education and is FERPA compliant. With REMIND, phone numbers remain private, setup is easy, and the application is phone and PC friendly.

Better yet, students can communicate with their instructor by way of individual screenshots, videos, and emoticons that are more likely to receive an immediate response. Faculty can send group or individual text messages in creative ways that include providing encouragement, acknowledging excellent performance, reminding students about deadline dates, notifying them of class meeting time adjustments, or alerting them to registration activities. Other group texting apps to consider include Facebook messaging, What's App, WeChat, and TextAim.

Solution 3: Student Performance Monitoring

Faculty who closely monitor the progression and completion of course activities will be better able to support students when they falter and to encourage students when they succeed. Course performance information that is easily accessible, pertinent, and that can contribute to successful intervention remedies can contribute greatly to student retention.

The Student Success Profile (SSP) may help faculty initially predict barriers to learning, but students who are derailed while courses are in progress are equally vulnerable. Instructors can intervene by identifying students who are struggling to participate, communicating with them about potential causes, and directing them to campus support service areas. Assuming that students know where to get help is not guaranteed, and even more importantly, students often need encouragement to take action. "Early alert" retention tools are currently being used by many institutions for intervention, but the tool name is inaccurate because warnings about poor student performance can occur at any time during the semester—early, in the middle, or later.

Data collected from student surveys can generate valuable feedback to instructors that provides personal information, identifies potential barriers to learning, and serves as a helpful resource. Conducting surveys also sends a nonverbal message that student opinions are valued. Survey data can help faculty make informed decisions about the need to contact support services for at-risk students. Free survey tools such as Microsoft forms, Google forms, or Survey Monkey are extremely effective.

LMS grades provide another effective way to monitor retention through leading indicators and to monitor success through grade evaluation. Leading indicators, which faculty can evaluate to predict future student success or failure, include last LMS log-in date, last date work was submitted, and grade results. Faculty can keep students informed about their retention status by adding a "red flag" field or an "instructor's feedback" field to the LMS grade sheet. Because students frequently check the LMS for their grades, using these fields allows for self-monitoring and makes them aware that their instructor is also monitoring.

ARE THESE TECHNIQUES SUCCESSFUL?

For five consecutive semesters I taught the same four courses in the areas of computer applications, computer programming, and systems analysis. From fall 2014 to fall 2016, I added retention tools to these course designs to test their effectiveness. Using our college's Blackboard LMS, I incorporated the following tools: a first-week survey that collected student data regarding academic goals and barriers to learning; interactive videos to introduce assignments and explain challenging concepts; frequent encouragement comments to the students; grade performance tracking measures; assignment activity feedback; and enhanced communication using text messaging.

The most noticeable retention improvement is shown below (see figure 10.1) for my Introduction to Programming (online) course. The two graph lines represent student starters and completers for each semester. For fall 2014, the gap between lines is wide (79% retention) and in spring 2016 the gap is very narrow (94% retention).

Retention rates for all four classes (see figure 10.2), covering the five semesters, indicate that except for one class, notable retention rate increases occurred from spring 2015 to spring 2016. During this 1-year period, I had gradually increased the number of retention tools I used in all classes. For the fall semester of 2016, retention rates for all classes were above 85%, which matched closely with the retention rates for all classes at Lincoln Land.

Success rate data for completers who earned a grade of A, B, or C are shown for all four classes covering five semesters (see figure 10.3), indicating that success rates at the end of fall 2014 varied greatly (60%–100%)

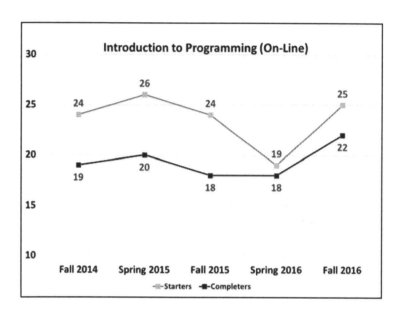

Figure 10.1.   Retention Enrollment Totals for Introduction to Programming (On-line). *Author created (C. Allen)*

when compared to those at the end of fall 2016 (78%–92%). While it is more challenging to draw clear conclusions from these data, at the very least, these percentage rates assist with future success rate forecasting. Another notable, but unclear, result is that the success rate in one course is flat over time, whereas success rates vary significantly for the other courses.

A comparison of the data from the Computer Applications (face-to-face) class with all online courses reveals notable findings. For this course, instruction was conducted through individual tutoring versus formal lectures; however, both the face-to-face and online sections of the course used exactly the same retention tools: early surveys, LMS content, interactive videos, and simulation software. Retention rates for this face-to-face section increased by 11.4%—a much higher increase than the other three online courses. Student success rates for this face-to-face section also increased by 24.2%—a much higher increase than the other three online courses. These retention rate increases suggest that the increased use of retention tools may have had a greater impact for the students taking the face-to-face courses than for those taking the online courses.

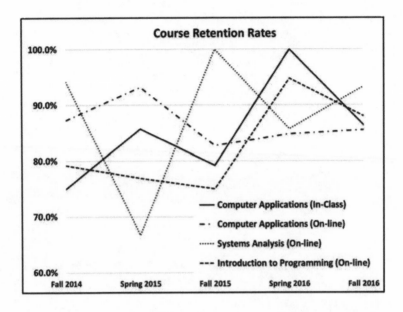

Figure 10.2.   Course Retention Rates for All Classes. *Author created (C. Allen)*

HOW CAN THESE TECHNIQUES BE USED CAMPUS-WIDE?

Compared to campus-wide retention initiatives that can be mandated by administration (such as student orientation or advising), implementing technologies in the classroom requires acceptance of and participation by faculty. Faculty who are passionate about innovation and creating change and who are dedicated to their students' success and course completion are vital. To encourage use of these new tools, the faculty need to feel empowered to forge forward individually with new solutions and ideas.

Within our computer science department at Lincoln Land Community College, we have had the opportunity to share classroom initiatives with our colleagues, with encouraging results. Institutional support for classroom initiatives must be available and flexible. An educational culture, for example, that encourages academic freedom with limited administrative input would benefit from a structure of collaborative faculty groups. When like-minded faculty can work toward a common goal, support each other, and share best practices, the results can be extremely influential and spread quickly across an institution.

Faculty also need ongoing professional development in the areas of retention, technology, and the integration of the two. Training should include explicit instruction in methods of promoting success, addressing implicit

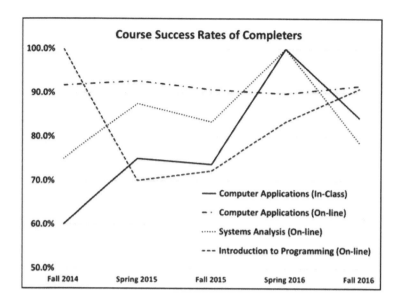

Figure 10.3. Course Success Rates for Students Who Completed With Grades of A, B, or C. *Author created (C. Allen)*

bias, building trust, and fostering interpersonal and intercultural relationships in the classroom. Contributions from highly engaged and respected professors, instructional support and innovation centers, and faculty mentors are all efficient ways that higher education can encourage faculty to use technology for increased classroom engagement.

On a large scale, classroom technology initiatives could create a cultural shift in teaching methodology that will require careful planning and guidance. Through intentional collaborative efforts between administration, faculty, and staff, community colleges have exciting opportunities for being proactive and innovative as they guide students toward completion.

Today's college students have grown up in an "information age" of rapid innovation and technological development, and they expect their education to be at the cutting edge of this innovation. Not only are these students comfortable with new approaches, but they also become competent in using them, are quick to adopt them, and prefer them to other methods of learning and communication. Thus, if they wish to remain relevant, to thrive, and to fulfill their missions, today's educational institutions need to move quickly to implement innovations in the classroom that contribute to technologically enhanced education.

REFERENCES

Anderson, G. (2020). *Accessibility suffers during pandemic.* https://www.insidehighered.com/news/2020/04/06/remote-learning-shift-leaves-students-disabilities-behind.

Karpicke, J., & Blunt, J. (2011). Retrieval practice produces more learning than elaborative studying with concept mapping. *Science, 331*(6018), 772–775.

Matson, T., & Clark, J. (2020). *Improve student outcomes by building caring faculty relationships.* Gallup. https://www.gallup.com/education/286514/improve-student-outcomes-building-caring-faculty-relationships.aspx.

McClenney, K., & Arnsparger, A. (2012). *Students speak: Are we listening?* Center for Community College Student Engagement.

McGraw-Hill Education. (2016, June 9). McGraw-Hill Education announces exclusive agreement with Austin-based data analytics provider ZogoTech aimed at increasing retention in higher education. *PR Newswire.* https://www.prnewswire.com/news-releases/mcgraw-hill-education-announces-exclusive-agreement-with-austin-based-data-analytics-provider-zogo-tech-aimed-at-increasing-retention-in-higher-education-300282324.html.

Tinto, V. (2016, September 26). From retention to persistence. *Inside Higher Ed.* https://www.insidehighered.com/views/2016/09/26/how-improve-student-persistence-and-completion-essay.

Chapter Eleven

Emulating Plan, Do, Study, Act (PDSA)

A Model to Sustain Student Learning Outcomes Assessment

Bruce Moses

ASSESSING STUDENT LEARNING IS A CHALLENGE FOR COMMUNITY COLLEGES

Over the last decade, the transparent and intentional focus on student learning outcomes has driven accountability at the community college level across the country. In spite of the fact that Pima Community College (PCC) in Arizona, like many community colleges, has made significant strides in assessing student learning outcomes, the college continues to face several noteworthy challenges in realizing a sustainable approach of assessment that is goal driven, evidence-based, and improvement oriented.

Since 1991, PCC has been cited by the Higher Learning Commission (HLC), its regional accreditor, six times to submit follow-up monitoring reports on the assessment of student learning outcomes. In 2013, a lack of systems and processes for assessing student learning was a major factor in PCC being placed on probation with the HLC. For various reasons, PCC continued to struggle to make the paradigm shift that is required to assess learning outcomes on a consistent basis.

Pima is not alone in this challenge. HLC's accreditation criterion 4B.2 stated, "The institution demonstrates a commitment to educational achievement and improvement through ongoing assessment of student learning" (Higher Learning Commission, 2019). A representative of the HLC suggested that more community colleges are out of compliance with this criterion and required to submit monitoring reports than any other issue (L.G.

Johnson, personal communication, April 6, 2018). In fact, satisfying accreditation requirements was the number 1 factor influencing community colleges' decisions to assess learning outcomes, followed by strategic planning (Nunley et al., 2011).

Several organizations, such as the American Association of Community Colleges (AACC) and their Voluntary Framework of Accountability and National Institute for Learning Outcomes Assessment (NILOA), have published papers to better understand the state of student learning outcomes assessment in community colleges. Despite the emerging efforts to assess student learning at community colleges, very few studies have provided direct, empirical results of student learning comparable across community colleges (Liu & Roohr, 2013, p. 1).

In the past, PCC's board of governors, executive leaders, academic administrators, and faculty viewed assessment as an optional activity rather than a fundamental aspect of faculty teaching responsibilities and an opportunity to collect data to improve teaching and learning for student success. For PCC and community colleges across the nation, demonstrating a consistent effort to assess student learning is a concern that affects everyone in the institution, and we are all facing this challenge together. Regardless of the requirements of the regional accreditors, the main reason for all community colleges to complete rigorous assessment activities is to inform improvement of teaching and learning.

The root of the problem for PCC lay in the fact that the faculty had not participated in a sustainable and successful model of assessment dating back more than 15 years. For many of them, implementing a model that endures obstacles such as changes in administration, adjunct faculty turnover, colleague resistance, inconsistent practices, and lack of resources complicated the situation. Also, as faculty everywhere can attest, assessment of student learning is fundamentally a complex undertaking by nature. While the goal is to assess at the course, program, and general education level consistently, many times no definitive approach exists.

PIMA'S CHALLENGES ASSESSING STUDENT LEARNING

Through a survey administered in fall 2015, the director of Pima's Office of Academic Quality Improvement identified some contributing causes of Pima's struggles with assessment. Among the most significant were (1) no comprehensive system of assessment, (2) learning outcomes that were not measurable, (3) very few professional development opportunities exposing faculty to best practices, (4) lack of collaboration, (5) different levels of understanding of what assessment entails, and (6) ineffective tools for collecting, analyzing, delineating, and reporting assessment results. Each one of these struggles posed significant challenges; together, they described an institution in crisis. In addition, some faculty voiced concerns about the challenges in writing solid measurable learning outcomes, the lack of guidance on what learning outcomes to assess, meaningless data from the homegrown interface, the heavy workload that ever-changing assessment presented, and confusing assessment terminology.

During the academic year 2015–2016, Pima's assessment processes were unpredictable, poorly controlled, and reactionary. Initially, an in-house data-collection interface system was created to save assessment results, and these results had to be input into the system, sorted, and disseminated to academic departments through a single point of contact at the college. The results were presented through a cluttered and difficult-to-use Excel spreadsheet. Program and general education learning outcomes were not collected on a college-wide level, and if these data were being collected, they were only collected at the individual department level. Documents to report results were not aligned across disciplines, and continuous quality improvements were not centrally tracked.

All of these challenges added up to what seemed like a Herculean task.

WHERE IT ALL BEGAN FOR PIMA

Using his experiences with the continuous improvement model, the associate provost believed that emulating the cyclical steps of Plan Do Study Act (PDSA) might provide the practical approach to guide, evaluate, and improve the effectiveness of assessment efforts that Pima needed. While the advantages of using a continuous improvement model are many, utilizing such a model to facilitate the process of student learning outcomes assessment can be challenging. To enhance PCC's success of achieving a sustainable outcome, Pima elected to emulate the highly popular iterative Plan Do Study Act four-step model to guide and evaluate its incremental continuous quality improvement (CQI) changes.

Continuous quality improvement of assessment provides a common shared language and understanding of assessment acumen, documented evidence of sustainable efforts to assess student learning outcomes over a longitudinal timeframe, and an infrastructure that supports good assessment practices, processes, data-management tools, and dissemination mechanisms. Research also suggests that systems and processes of colleges and universities in assessing learning outcomes are more readily available; however, there are very few studies linked directly to community colleges. According to Deming (1993), "An organization cannot sustain high-quality performance without effective leadership" (p. 53). Such leadership involves setting a vision, giving workers necessary resources (including education), and empowering them within their areas of expertise.

While the PDSA model has been highly successful in a variety of environments, Pima believed that emulating the cyclical steps could provide a practical approach to guide, evaluate, and improve the effectiveness of assessment efforts. Pima's assessment workgroup agreed and got to work.

PIMA'S RESPONSE AND INTERVENTION

PCC responded by taking on the challenge of the lack of a sustainable model by adopting Deming's Plan Do Study Act model for continuous quality improvement, a logical approach of incremental steps to assessment. According to Downey (2000), "The Deming wheel is the most famous model in CQI" (p. 8). The interrelationship of continuous planning, doing, checking, acting, and repeating that process over again serves as the basis for most applications of CQI. The PDSA model provides the repetitive quality improvement adjustments needed in the community college environment to safeguard the process.

We implemented the Plan, Implement, Measure, and Act (PIMA) model (see figure 11.1) as a standardized solution for assessment. Through the process, we wanted to evaluate current assessment of student learning outcome processes, data collection, results analysis, and outcomes reporting intended to improve the teaching strategies, curriculum design, and teaching effectiveness. The PIMA model is a solution to the challenge we encountered for years in implementing a sustainable approach to assessing student learning outcomes.

IMPLEMENTING THE PIMA MODEL

In February 2016, the Office of Academic Quality Improvement adopted the PIMA model of continuous quality improvement to inform efforts in implementing a sustainable structure of assessment. The focus of the model is to establish and maintain cycles of continuous improvement that regularly produce results that are meaningful and meet the needs of key stakeholders. We believed that academic units at PCC needed to go through a series of changes in assessment efforts to realize the paradigm shift the organization aspired to.

The office director began the process by bringing together "the willing," a critical mass of diverse and dedicated PCC faculty and staff who were fully invested in this paradigm shift to lead the implementation of the PIMA model and formed the Student Learning Assessment Workgroup (SLAW). Starting spring 2017, the workgroup met biweekly and over time has consisted of her staff, faculty from several departments (chemistry, science,

Figure 11.1. The Four Phases of the PIMA Model. *Author created (B. Moses)*

machine tool technology, nursing, writing, literature, honors, mathematics), deans, department heads, program directors, and curriculum coordinators, to ensure that the history of assessment and current practices are represented.

The Plan Stage

In May 2016, during the *Plan* cycle of the model, the workgroup evaluated current assessment activities using a faculty survey and campus meetings. Results of the survey were implemented into the annual assessment plan for academic year 2016–2017. The workgroup identified several opportunities for improvement, including processes for developing faculty expertise in assessment, evaluating appropriateness of all course and program learning outcomes, enhancing or replacing the current data management system, analyzing assessment results to improve student learning, documenting plans for continuous improvement, and identifying a single point of contact in each discipline to be accountable to the process.

The Implementation Stage

That fall, during the *Implementation* phase, subgroups of the workgroup divided up the opportunities for improvement and developed strategies that were vetted by the entire workgroup before implementation. Most of the work was completed during scheduled meetings via Google Docs and email feedback. A few areas of concern required additional time or resources before they could be addressed—for example, piloting a project to assess college-wide general education learning outcomes and developing capstone courses for some certificate and degree programs. At the end of 2016, the workgroup had completed two of the four phases of the PIMA model. Implementation actions for the Plan phase (which describes the work you plan to do) and the Implementation phase (which describes how you will implement your plan) were nearly complete.

THE MEASURE STAGE

At the start of 2017, the workgroup met monthly through the end of the semester. At that point, the group reviewed results and comments collected over the last academic year. These actions kicked off the *Measure* phase of the process, which allowed the workgroup to summarize and analyze data collected during and after implementation. Also, the group looked back and analyzed how successful the plan had been. After analysis, the workgroup began to identify numerous continuous improvement opportunities that emerged from the assessment data; the feedback from faculty, deans, department heads, discipline coordinators, administrators; and their own observations.

The Act Stage

Identifying these opportunities naturally transitioned the workgroup into the *Act* phase of the model. From these opportunities, the workgroup prioritized their work, by improving faculty engagement in student learning assessment; consulting and providing guidance to faculty peers; adopting promising methodologies, processes, and practices of assessment; and scaling up the use of the eLumen assessment management system. Additionally, we needed to create a pilot approach for assessing student mastery of general education outcomes, analyzing that data, identifying appropriate curricular changes, and reassessing for improvement. The Act phase has three possible actions:

The workgroup can (1) act to standardize, (2) act to adjust for continuous improvement, or (3) act to abandon what they implemented.

PIMA HAS EMBRACED ASSESSMENT

Collective Efforts: The Workgroup and Assessment Academy

The first action taken from the Plan phase, forming the workgroup, has been a vital resource to developing a robust and sustainable infrastructure for assessment. When it appeared that the group was becoming stagnant, the co-chairs decided to reassess the size of the group: Was the 18-member group too large to be productive? They decided, however, that the diverse nature of this group captured and factored in viewpoints that may not be realized with fewer members.

Another action that contributed to Pima's success was participating in the Higher Learning Commission Assessment Academy. The academy was a wonderful catalyst, contributing much guidance, insight, and support from the college's mentor and scholar. PCC's assessment academy team consists of eight members, a subset of the workgroup. This team brought a plethora of knowledge from the weekend-long assessment workshops. sharing the knowledge, learned activities, processes, expertise, and ideas that were garnered from these gatherings. After the Academy sessions, the workgroup then decided which practices to implement college wide.

Redefining Learning Outcomes

The review of general education, program, and course learning outcomes proved to be a value-added process evolving out of the implementation phase of the PIMA model. In fall 2017, faculty began to evaluate course and program outcomes to ensure they were clear, measurable, and capable of being assessed. All the members of the workgroup assisted in this process by situating themselves at each of the five campuses and being available to assist any faculty who needed support in evaluating their outcomes. Over 90% of the college's general education, program, and course learning outcomes were reviewed and approved for quality and measurability. This process is now ongoing and embedded into program review and course review, which occurs on a four-year cycle. In addition, when curricular modifications are now submitted, course and program outcomes are reviewed to ensure they are appropriate and relevant for transfer or industry standards.

The Role of the Discipline Coordinators

During the Measure phase, the workgroup learned that one opportunity for improvement would be to provide follow-up training for new and experienced discipline coordinators. Some coordinators had the perception that they were solely responsible for completing assessment evaluations, when in fact, faculty in their discipline needed to provide input as well. This communication gap negatively impacted the overall results of some disciplines' assessment efforts. Moving forward, Pima has identified these next steps: (1) ensure all faculty enter their data into eLumen, (2) arrange for departmental meetings to discuss the assessment results, and (3) file the report that reflects the discussion.

An intervention deriving from the Act phase of the model was standardizing a single point of contact in each discipline to be accountable to the assessment process. At PCC, every 3 years an election is held to elect a discipline coordinator. As of fall 2017, the discipline coordinator is the point of contact to ensure assessments and evaluations are completed. Although the participation of faculty entering their data—the rate of 88% has been outstanding—the percentage of evaluation and continuous improvement plans submitted has not been impressive. Thus, discipline coordinators and faculty participated in training sessions focused on analyzing aggregated data with special attention to the type of data (graphs and tables) that resonates best.

Adopting a College-Wide Assessment Management System

The institution's selection and implementation of eLumen, a nationally recognized assessment management system, is one of the most meaningful acts resulting from the PIMA model. eLumen allows for embedded reporting structures for discipline coordinators to analyze and report aggregated results. Pima's results have been significant: Both disciplines and programs used results that led to (1) modifying courses to enhance student learning, (2) meeting the target threshold of success, or (3) closing the loop on previously implemented strategies to improve student achievement.

Revitalizing General Education Assessment

General education assessment also saw impressive improvements. As of fall 2018, only 5% of disciplines had contributed to general education assessment. In spring 2019, the workgroup responded by hosting Assessment Into Action (AIA) Day, where 60 faculty analyzed aggregated data of two outcomes: (1) communication and (2) quantitative and scientific literacy and analysis. PCC's general education committee adopted the Association of American Colleges and Universities (AACU) VALUE rubrics for evaluating and discussing student learning achievement. Participating faculty agreed that insufficient mapping of courses to general education outcomes made it impossible for the college to draw meaningful, generalizable, and college-wide conclusions. Faculty also requested disaggregated data so they could perform more in-depth analysis.

In response to these requests, the workgroup developed a plan to increase faculty participation in assessing general education. The group trained department heads and discipline coordinators to map courses to general education outcomes.

Involving Adjunct Faculty in Assessment

As with many community colleges, the turnover of adjunct faculty can impact consistency of assessment efforts. PCC seeks to offset this turnover and maintain engagement and participation in assessment through a new faculty orientation on assessment that explains assessment practices, how faculty should enter data into eLumen, and how they can analyze their assessment results for improvement. This orientation is also available as a video with step-by-step procedures.

THE OUTCOMES OF PIMA MODEL

The PIMA model necessitates a team approach to addressing complex issues. Those guiding the process reported how uplifting and reaffirming it was to witness this faculty-led transformation taking place in the college's assessment of student learning.

During discussions at our planning meetings, the steps seemed to flow seamlessly into each other. We were confident that the PIMA model would be an improvement over past practice and encourage dialogue to improve pedagogy, curriculum, and student success strategies.

Since the implementation of the PIMA model, the college has made significant advancements in sustaining good practices in assessment. The use of the PIMA model has yielded significant results to date: First, the percentage of faculty reporting their course learning outcomes data increased from 3.8% to 83.8% from spring 2018 to spring 2020 (see figure 11.2), and the percentage of disciplines using the assessment results to effect change reached 67% in the same period (see figure 11.3). The percentage of programs assessing program learning outcomes increased from 4% in 2018 to 50.3% in 2020 (see figure 11.4), and the percentage of programs using these assessment results to improve their programs reached 15.8% (see figure 11.5). Finally, the percentage of disciplines assessing GELO increased from 5% in fall 2018 to 45.6% in spring 2020.

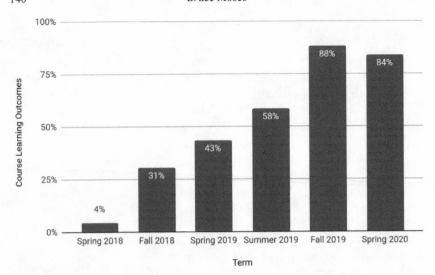

Figure 11.2.   Percentage of Course Sections Assessed Each Term. *Author created (B. Moses)*

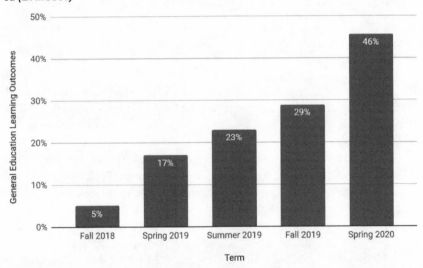

Figure 11.3.   Percentage of Disciplines Assessing General Education Through Course Mapping. *Author created (B. Moses)*

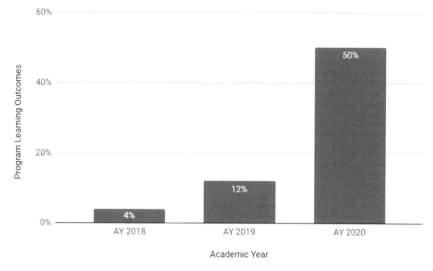

Figure 11.4.   Percentage of Programs Assessing Outcomes by Academic Year. *Author created (B. Moses)*

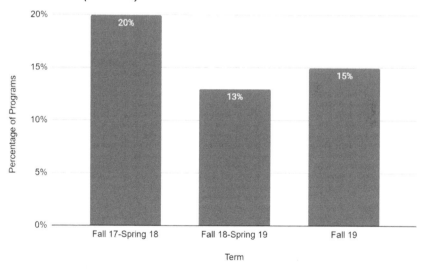

Figure 11.5.   Percentage of Programs Using Results for Improvement. *Author created (B. Moses)*

In academic year 2018–2019, Pima's assessment processes were defined and proactive. Departments were tailoring their processes to align with the college's standards. While some faculty were still using the home-grown interface to collect results, many departments were now using eLumen to collect program, course, and general education outcomes data. Data and results were immediately accessible from faculty and academic administration desktops in a variety of formats: line graphs, data tables, and pie charts that were sortable with the click of a button. The documents to report results were submitted in two formats: Word documents that admittedly were still problematic, and eLumen reports that were systematic, functional, and consistent. Because of these recognized limitations, the College mandated eLumen as the sole assessment management system at the end of fall 2018.

CONCLUSION

As of fall 2019, Pima's assessment processes were revitalized, measured, and controlled. All data for student learning outcomes are now collected through eLumen. Results are immediately available in a variety of easy-to-understand—and use—formats. Reporting documents are all aligned, systematic, functional, and consistent.

So, what's next? As we move forward, we will shift our focus to continuous process improvement of the system, working with faculty to improve consistency in our data reporting language and increase the submission percentage of documented quality improvement plans.

Several conclusions are evident from this effort. The workgroup wanted a collaborative faculty-led continuous improvement approach that would deliver a seamless, replicable, and sustainable process for faculty to engage in assessment. For years, the use of the business-like principles of the PDSA cycle has been scrutinized—and often rejected—by the academic world. Nevertheless, Pima's workgroup experiences validate applying the PDSA structure to organize and implement sustainable initiatives in assessment. The workgroup iterated these four phases of the PIMA PDSA model and persisted through systematic levels of maturity in assessment. Collectively, these phases emulate the cycle for learning and improvement originally developed and taught by Deming.

The PIMA model outlined in this essay required 4 years and a team of dedicated faculty and staff to reach its current level of success. Without the perseverance of a tremendous group of colleagues, this initiative would have ceased after the Plan phase. Community colleges can take away some meaningful lessons learned from this innovation by PCC. The first is key: If you do not have a resilient team and the ability to move at a deliberate and meaningful pace, you should not try this model.

The workgroup's foundational approach to decision-making continues to rest on the belief that acts of change must be based on data-driven evidence. These data and analyses will determine what actions should be taken and whether previous solutions implemented were effective. The PIMA model allowed for the workgroup to be empowered by data and results for decision making throughout the Plan and Act phases.

In addition, we created dependency and naturally supportive relationships that have "normalized" assessment by (1) building the capacity for planning and action through the PIMA model, (2) empowering and rewarding faculty who emulate continuous quality improvement principles, (3) educating the faculty through professional development and achieving widespread support, (4) linking cross-functional areas and reducing silos, and (5) emphasizing the use of results in both planning and decision-making.

REFERENCES

Deming, W. E. (1993). *The new economics: For industry, government, education.* Massachusetts Institute of Technology, Center for Advanced Engineering Study.

Downey, T. E. (2000, April 10). *The application of continuous quality improvement models and methods to higher education: Can we learn from business?* Technological Education and National Development (TEND) Conference, Abu Dhabi, United Arab Emirates.

Higher Learning Commission. (2019, February). *Criteria for accreditation.* http://www.hlcommission.org/Policies/criteria-and- core-components.html.

Liu, O. L., & Roohr, K. C. (2013). Investigating ten-year trends of learning outcomes at community colleges. *ETS Research Report Series, 2013*(2), i45.

Nunley, C., Bers, T., & Manning, T. (2011, July). *Learning outcomes assessment in community colleges.* National Institute for Learning Outcomes Assessment.

Part IV

Responding to Changing Needs

This series of essays is framed with an acknowledgment of the importance of *grit*—for both students and institutions.

"Innovation in Challenging Times: Community College Responses to the COVID-19 Pandemic" characterizes and reports on the shape of innovations both in student support services and in academic affairs in six different colleges.

In another variation on the same theme, "Student Success During CO-VID-19: A Case Study From Eastern Iowa Community Colleges," relies on interviews with a cross-section of individuals from one college community to document the impact of the pandemic on students and their success facing the challenges of teaching and learning.

From a different angle, "Creating Institutions of Excellence" argues for the importance of a culture informed by unrelenting commitment to improvement that is driven by meaningful data. The personal leadership narrative acknowledges the centrality of a college's most important resource—its people—to its success.

The final essay, "The Beliefs Agenda: An Extraordinary New Paradigm for College Completion," argues that the time has come for community colleges to step beyond a focus and action plan based on the statistics of persistence, retention, and completion. It is time to understand the power of beliefs—the beliefs students have about themselves and the beliefs of the college (teachers, counselors, staff, and administrators) about teaching, learning, and equipping students to be successful in making a life as well as a living.

Chapter Twelve

Innovation in Challenging Times

*Community College Responses to the
COVID-19 Pandemic*

Brenda Sipe

A NEED FOR IMMEDIATE RESPONSE

A few short weeks before March 2020, community colleges were operating normally, oblivious to the events that would leave them racing to get courses, student services, operations, and communications moved from their brick-and-mortar locations to new online spaces at lightning speed. Indeed, the COVID-19 pandemic brought unique and unprecedented challenges to community colleges and their leaders. But community colleges have a history of being positioned at the forefront of innovation, and many are, once again, leading the way with their ability to develop large-scale innovative solutions to a myriad of problems, finding opportunities in the midst of challenge.

Because community colleges offer a lower-cost educational alternative while also providing students with accessibility, convenience, and high job placement rates, they were called a *catalytic innovation* more than a decade before the COVID-19 crisis occurred. Christensen et al. (2006) used the term and explained that catalytic innovation creates systemic social change through scaling and repetition; meets needs that are either underserved or overserved; offers products or services that are less costly than existing alternatives; and generates resources in new ways. This description fits the history, mission, and identity of community colleges. As an innovation themselves, innovation can be said to be in the DNA of community colleges (O'Banion et al., 2011).

The business world regards innovation as essential to growth and survival of organizations (Sydow & Alfred, 2013). Institutions and businesses that practice innovation build knowledge about new markets and resources, develop a reputation for solving the most difficult problems (Kanter, 1999), and create competitive advantage (Khazanchi et al., 2007; Crossan & Apaydin, 2010). Numerous sources have argued that companies and organizations that do not innovate will not long survive (Tierney et al., 1999; Jung et al., 2003; Hogan & Coote, 2014; Kao, 2017). Our nation's leaders also consistently believe in the value of innovation to save our country and economy from disaster, and over history, this has in fact occurred on numerous occasions (O'Banion et al., 2011).

In education, innovation is a way of creating new practices that improve student learning and outcomes; drive organizational effectiveness; and encourage development of new educational products. These innovations can be small-scale, incremental, or large-scale. Innovation, though, in every form, is particularly needed during challenging times. Not only is innovation needed, but also, as Drucker (2002) stated, unexpected wide-ranging occurrences and overnight changes (such as the COVID-19 crisis) actually make available fertile ground for innovation.

While there is a large body of research on innovation and some research on innovation and crisis intervention at community colleges, it is too early, as yet, for research on how innovation has occurred at community colleges during the COVID-19 pandemic. We continue to hear daily stories of challenges and successes, of institutions stepping up to find a solution to a seemingly insurmountable problem.

HOW DID COMMUNITY COLLEGES INNOVATE DURING COVID-19?

We used our network of community college professionals to capture some of the innovative practices being used across the country. We asked our colleagues about innovation on their campus. How does a community college make use of an existing culture of innovation during a crisis? How are some community colleges leading the way in solving some of the difficult issues facing higher education during the COVID-19 pandemic?

This study focuses on six community colleges in several states that used innovative practices in specific ways to solve problems during the COVID-19 pandemic. The study took place approximately 1 month into the COVID-19 pandemic quarantine, during mid-April 2020.

A basic qualitative research design, which makes meaning of experiences, is appropriate for understanding how community colleges used innovation to cope with and thrive during the COVID-19 crisis. During informal interviews, community college leaders from the DCCL network were asked about their institutions: How innovative their college was before the pandemic; how communication within their college has changed; what innovative initiatives the institution has adopted; and how the crisis has fostered innovation.

Informal telephone interviews were held with leaders in a variety of roles at each of six community colleges in four states during mid-April 2020. Participants included the following:

- Talia Koronkiewicz (Cohort 4), vice president for student affairs, McHenry County College, Illinois
- Aimee Belanger-Haas (Cohort 8), dean of business and applied technologies, Clark State Community College, Ohio
- Peter Lacey (Cohort 9), vice president of student services, St. Clair County Community College, Michigan
- Sedgwick Harris (Cohort 6), vice president for student affairs and enrollment, Northampton Community College, Pennsylvania
- Pamela Lau (Cohort 3), executive vice president and president elect, Parkland College, Illinois
- Jon Mandrell (Cohort 3), vice president for academics and student services, Sauk Valley Community College, Illinois

Their responses provided the insights that follow.

WHAT IS INNOVATION?

The word *innovation* relates to an activity that creates focused change in an organization through hard and purposeful work (Drucker, 2002). Innovation has traditionally focused on using current technology in new markets, or on developing new technology, but now also encompasses finding innovative ways to create value for the user and the organization (Carlgren, 2013). According to Kao (2017), innovation is "the ability of individuals, companies, and entire nations to continuously create their desired future" (p. 19). There has been disagreement among researchers about whether change needs to be successful in order to be called innovation.

Several related terms provide insight into our discussions with the community college leaders.

- *Invention*, according to the *Oslo Manual*, is "the first occurrence of a new product or idea," while "innovation is the first attempt to carry it out in practice" (Fagerberg, 2005, p. 4).

- *Process innovation* involves developing or improving customer service, organizational efficiency, or administrative operations (Khazanchi et al., 2007).
- *Incremental innovation* is shorter term or project focused, while organization-wide, long-range innovation is more disruptive, or far-reaching (Sydow & Alfred, 2013).
- *Disruptive innovation* is innovation that ensures the future success and viability of the organization, but is harder to achieve (Sydow & Alfred, 2013).

The COVID-19 pandemic required organization-wide, disruptive innovation to address the wide-ranging changes we were facing. For our discussion, because these new practices have not yet been assessed for their long-term effectiveness, innovation is the implementation of any new ideas, whether or not the ideas prove to be successful.

COMMUNITY COLLEGES AND INNOVATION

Historically, community colleges have responded to opportunities and challenges with innovative ideas and practices. These include stackable credentials, structured pathways, student services, accelerated remediation, and new learning models, to name a few (Bosley, 2016). Some of the resulting innovations have been small-scale or incremental, such as the development of new courses or programs, but some have been systemic and large-scale. Valencia College, for example, redesigned the college's shared governance structure in response to an organizational challenge (Bosley, 2016).

To flesh out a definition of *innovation* appropriate to community colleges, in 2011, O'Banion and colleagues conducted a research study with national leaders in innovation. The researchers started by developing 10 definitions of *innovation* based on a review of literature; then, in a workshop with the innovative leaders, they narrowed the list to six that best reflect the community college mission. These six were presented to their research participants and the following two definitions were developed and adopted: (1) "the development or adoption of new or existing ideas for the purpose of improving policies, programs, practices, or personnel" and (2) "the creation of new opportunities that are transformative."

In expanding their research, O'Banion et al. (2011) acknowledged that, because it can be difficult to sustain a culture of innovation at community colleges and, thus, be prepared to face challenges, they then studied the characteristics of innovation and innovators. They found that innovative institutions had similar characteristics: (1) key leaders who support and encourage innovation; (2) risk-taking that is encouraged and innovation that is rewarded; (3) successful innovation that supports college goals; and (4) successful innovators work in teams.

Earlier research supported the collaborative, risk-taking environment essential to innovation. A study by Murray and Kishur (2008) indicated that when community college presidents collaborate with others during a crisis, particularly their leadership teams, they are more satisfied with the outcome. Leaders who tolerate failure support collaboration instead of encouraging employees to compete with one another (Farson & Keyes, 2002). According to Michael Dell, CEO of Dell Computers, innovation is about taking risks and learning from failure (Farson & Keyes, 2002).

WERE THESE COLLEGES INNOVATIVE BEFORE COVID-19?

To begin our conversations, we asked our study participants to define *innovation*. Their responses covered many of the same features we noted in our definitions:

- a continuous process improvement, always looking for new opportunities to do something better;
- new technologies and new explorations that can influence lives;
- trying to be more responsive to students and not let obstacles in our way;
- doing something different in order to address an issue or find a solution to an ongoing problem; and
- any initiative or focus that is centered without the fear of failure and have the willingness to take risks to support students.

The leaders all agreed that their institutions were innovative in response to the pandemic, but what about the environment before COVID-19? All participants agreed their college possessed a culture of innovation prior to the COVID-19 crisis. One participant stated, "He [our president] is very student-focused, and really leads with an innovative and entrepreneurial spirit, and that allows us to think outside box." Another said,

> Our president is very in tune with innovation and seeking to push the boundaries and push our people to do different and better [things]. Status quo is not acceptable, and our team responds to that. That innovation mindset has greatly helped our leadership team to make sure we continued to operate [during the pandemic].

These responses also support the findings of O'Banion and colleagues' (2011) study regarding the importance of a top leader who supports innovation at community colleges.

WHAT TYPES OF INNOVATIONS OCCURRED
DURING COVID-19?

During COVID-19, community colleges needed to swiftly change many of their processes as well as how they taught students and how they did business. Large-scale innovation was needed. The interviewed leaders all described similar experiences of working quickly to make sure the needs of students and faculty were met, all the while in a fluctuating environment.

Student Support Innovations

McHenry County College (Illinois)

One of the areas needing attention was student support. How would students be kept engaged during the move to online learning? McHenry County College (MCC) created and launched the Navigator program to support students during COVID-19. This idea was completely new and immediately had the support of the president. Implementation came together fast because of a spirt of support and caring throughout the campus.

The navigator is a person who was a point of contact for students during the transition to online-only format for both instruction and student support services. The majority of classes scheduled for the spring 2020 semester had a student navigator enrolled in the course to provide additional support to students. The navigator, who is enrolled in the online course, is responsible for connecting students to support services and community resources; monitoring student performance to proactively refer students to academic support; assisting in support and coaching students to adapt to online learning; supporting students who may need guidance with the Canvas learning platform; and directing all content questions to the faculty.

More than 90 employees from a variety of roles across MCC's campus agreed to take on this role in 880 online courses. Employees were trained and supported by a student navigator leadership team. For some employees, such as displaced cafeteria workers, this became their full-time job and provided the ability to keep their employment. Others who already had full-time jobs volunteered to serve as student .navigators in addition.

Northampton Community College (Pennsylvania)

Northampton Community College (NCC) knew that students might consider dropping out of school in response to COVID-19 restrictions and the move to online classes. NCC used their academic advisors, called success navigators, to communicate with students via Google Voice. After this system was functional, they extended the application to faculty use as well. The college then began a call campaign. Callers talked with students about their transition, and, for any who indicated they might withdraw, asked them to wait 2 weeks and give the new format a try before they dropped out.

The college also conducted a survey of students to identify critical needs as the pandemic affected many jobs and access to other resources. The college also purchased Chromebooks, initially 200, using funds reallocated from another source, and initiated a loan program for students without a laptop. Additionally, as they learned more about student needs, the president initiated a support fund using donations from the college community, employees, and friends of the college to help students in need. The survey had identified students struggling to pay gas or electric bills, or to meet other basic needs; the college was able to connect with these students and pay bills for them or issue gift cards to meet immediate needs.

Parkland College (Illinois)

One of Parkland College's first responses to the pandemic was to set up a call center. Initiated by the president and the leadership team, the project was quickly embraced by the college community. The call center is staffed by volunteer employees from across the college using Microsoft Teams on their home computers. The project's challenge was that every campus phone needed to be connected to a unified system so the first person to hear it ring could answer. A book of FAQs was quickly developed to provide volunteers with basic information on topics including financial aid, technology, academics, and accessible or open facilities. Lau reported:

> This was a massive operation because ordinarily the phone operator will send you along and someone will take care of it. There are people managing those teams, call center teams were trained, and the FAQs needed to be updated regularly at first. Sometimes you get one of those bigger phone calls, and then he [the president] picks up if it's a bigger issue. So, we are kind of triaging. . . . It's been a collaboration across the college, and staff members think, "While I am sitting home, I can do something." It is coordinated communication and collaboration.

St. Clair County Community College (Michigan)

One student service innovation that St. Clair County Community College adopted quickly following the pandemic quarantine was online advising. Advising appointments were quickly changed from an old booking system (SARS), which was already obsolete and under discussion for replacement, to MS Bookings. Within the first week of the crisis, leaders realized that the old system would not be able to accommodate new needs. The decision was quick: A vice president and director worked together to set up MS Bookings, and they moved the college's system to virtual face-to-face advising. Lacey reported, "We won't go back to restrictive live face-to-face appointments.

We are doing things in a very different way, on weekends and evenings—at the convenience of students. The flexibility is awesome."

Academic Innovations

Clark State Community College (Ohio)

At Clark State Community College innovations were needed so courses typically taught face-to-face in studios that require extensive technology or equipment could be taught online. For example, prior to the pandemic, theater students were putting on a play, with students designing sets in a Stagecraft course. The instructor quickly modified course outcomes so students could access materials and instruction and build smaller versions of stage models at home. A diesel instructor worked with his adjunct faculty to live stream a demonstration of engine repair, using web cam technology inside a vehicle. These recorded demos provide additional advantages of being available for students to review multiple times at their own convenience. A CNC instructor obtained permission to record demos on a CNC mill and lathe at an employment site. These demos, too, can be viewed on demand.

Program Development Innovations

Sauk Valley Community College, now dubbed internally as "Cyber Sauk," developed training and workforce programs to serve its community in new ways. They converted existing services on the credit and non-credit side to new levels when the pandemic struck. For example, they helped an eighth-grade student whose day camps were cancelled by providing entrance into Sauk's online instruction, and they are actively engaging with workforce opportunities:

> The minute we hear about layoffs, we reach out to those industries and ask how we can come to town—virtually—and help, how they can start a new chapter in life based on hardships. Maybe it's a virtual workshop or to come back to school, or to [engage in] workforce training. We're consulting with these individuals about opportunities.

HOW DID COMMUNICATION OCCUR?

Several of the innovations mentioned by our participants relied on new approaches to communications with students. Communication with all faculty, staff, students, and the community understandably changed in numerous ways because of the pandemic. In addition to much greater reliance on software and technology, participants mentioned streamlining and eliminating old cumbersome ways of communicating during the crisis. Creative and innovative technology were used by various employees across the campuses. Faculty found ways to contact students regularly, not simply for course work but to check in on their well-being. Other participants mentioned how the crisis had built on the strengths of departments and of individual employees who were already working well before the pandemic. Some mentioned the preexisting strengths of their communications team to reach campus stakeholders quickly and effectively.

Lau (Parkland College) noted,

> Any book on crisis management will tell you [that] your messages need to be clear and consistent. What I felt really good about is how we've crafted our messages together [as a leadership team], so we are getting feedback from faculty and staff thanking us for the clear direction. We are keeping everyone together, making everyone feel they are wanted and cared for. We are making sure that kind of communication gets done.

There is agreement among leaders that "communication has increased tremendously . . . mostly by email. We offer people more opportunities to collaborate with faculty, staff, and administration. . . . Really it's a heightened level of communication, more hours in the day," stated Harris (Northampton Community College). "Effective communication has been vitally important," stated Koronkiewicz (McHenry County College), but "we're still figuring it out."

UNTESTED INNOVATIONS

During the pandemic, innovations were needed so quickly that they were not able to be prototyped and tested as they would be under normal circumstances, and solutions were scaled up quite rapidly. "In a dream world, we would have had a pilot and weeks of training," stated Koronkiewicz (McHenry County College);

> We couldn't get stuck in that mindset of needing to be able have measurable results. How do we do something immediately that connects our students [was our overriding concern]. We continually say, "what do the data say and what's the best practice?" This was not the time for that.

Harris (Northampton Community College) said, "It didn't get tested. We made alterations and modifications as we ran into challenges. Stop, pivot, move in this other direction. There's no set plan. Nobody has a blueprint, but students had immediate need."

For Parkland College's Call Center, Lau said,

The testing was when we launched it, so it was interesting. The first week, it was shelter-in-place, then 10 days later it became stay-at-home. During shelter-in-place, the 5 [call center] people sat 6 feet part. So that first week was actually testing, because we had the technology but needed to make it effective after we learned what type of questions we got. Improve it as you go along [was our perspective]. People are eager to help but they were not seasoned. We were willing to try it out with the amount of information we had, but there was trial and error with a lot of guidance. Several of us listened in on the questions so the ones manning the calls would know how to approach these questions. Then those that were in charge of the specific areas crafted the answers and put those into the FAQs. So, we changed it to be uniformly broad enough messaging, and then gave it to people. We trusted that the information was going to be right.

Koronkiewicz (McHenry County College) noted:

We did a couple things in the past year that helped this transition move smoothly. We had been trying to break down silos, so now orientation is an all-campus event, where we have 100 employees—faculty and staff—and opportunities for cross training in different student services areas. All that cross training and expanding our orientation made this easier because they [employees] already had the mindset.

WHAT'S THE IMPACT OF THESE INNOVATIONS?

The community colleges where these innovations have taken place are already noting significant impacts of the new initiatives. Plans are also underway for tracking data and systematically assessing new initiatives.

"We are just working on that now," said Koronkiewicz (McHenry County College) regarding the Student Navigator program. "We think it will be data collected by students and faculty in class [focusing on] the variables that impact persistence and retention. It will be very hard to pinpoint the Navigator as the reason for success." McHenry is identifying the specific kind of data they will need, and how and what information they will be capturing. One approach they're considering is student and faculty surveys.

When the pandemic forced Northampton Community College to look at their annual retention data earlier in the year, they learned that student withdrawals were down during spring semester 2020, compared to the same time in 2019. Because of the timing of their data collection, they were unable to identify clear causes, but felt that the campus' extra interventions and focus on student support may have prompted at least a portion of the decrease. At St. Clair County Community College, the early registration numbers for fall 2020 registration showed significant increases over previous years. As the summer progresses, these colleges will be collecting data to attempt to determine if any of the pandemic innovations contributed to the successes.

From an academic standpoint, students will be tracked to see how well they do in the next sequence to make sure they learned what they needed during spring 2020. Lacey (St. Clair County Community College) said, "We are blessed with an awesome set of dashboards and we're using data to inform all these decisions. It's looking at exact data." Mandrell (Sauk Valley Community College) stated:

> Yes, it's really important we capture the data, everything including grades. If a student leaves, we have implemented a process where they state why they left. What we know historically is that online learning leads to lower success rates, so we are going to see how our new tutoring services [are affecting] whether we implement these services long term or for future pandemics.

WILL INNOVATION BE SUSTAINED?

According to our participants, many of these innovations will be sustained in one form or another for the short-term, as long as online courses are the mainstay of community colleges' offerings. Even after some courses return to face-to-face, and the effects of the pandemic are behind us, it is likely these innovations and ways of teaching will remain, especially if they are proven to be effective, or more effective than previous approaches.

Many of these student services were available pre-pandemic, but they are now being taken to new levels. At St. Clair County Community College, advising will remain more accessible and flexible to fit a variety of student schedules. Lau (Parkland College) agreed:

> We are learning there are things we will keep doing. It made us think: what would be the next thing we would want to do? So now we are calling and asking which set of students may benefit from our calls? Which students have more needs? It's coordination and collaboration. It's not a measure of success, but it shows a progress toward understanding our direction.

Mandrell (Sauk Valley Community College) said,

> We've also incorporated new ways of communicating with students at registration. We hear at graduation "the hardest part of college is coming in the front door." Now we don't have a door. So, we are reaching a population now without a door. Students who physically struggle. We can now reach them too.

CONCLUSION

Community colleges have needed innovative approaches to cope with the COVID-19 pandemic and to continue their mission of serving students. The innovations have, in some cases, replaced processes that were either already failing or that could not function in their normal fashion once the colleges moved to quarantine status. Because of the nature of the pandemic crisis, most of the innovations have been large-scale, even disruptive—since the crisis itself was disruptive—and were scaled up rapidly. All the innovations were subject to testing and ongoing improvements, and some have shown promising early outcomes. Many new ideas and initiatives will likely occur as a result of these initial innovations.

All participants reported their colleges had a willingness and ability to innovate. They innovated more easily during a crisis because they had institutional support for innovation and previously practiced innovative thinking. Their statements support O'Banion et al. (2011), who found that innovation is most successful when the college president is innovative and there is institutional support for risk taking and innovation.

The experience of these participants also confirms that successful innovation occurred collaboratively as part of a team, as shown in earlier crisis management research (Murray & Kishur, 2008). Other colleges and agencies are also collaborating with each other to find solutions to new problems. Mandrell (Sauk Valley Community College) said:

> Never before have I seen institutions coming together. So, on a daily basis, community college instructors, staff, and administration are coming together to approach things from a more systemic view. For the CARES act money, many colleges are uniting to decide how the money will be dispersed. A lot of institutions are working together as one, and stakes are high.

Harris (Northampton Community College) stated, "We've collaborated with agencies in a way we never would have before [the pandemic]."

The pandemic also fostered gratitude for existing resources among the participants. They consistently mentioned the importance of having a good infrastructure, staff, and resources prior to the pandemic, and indicated a renewed appreciation for them. At Northampton Community College, it was the college's endowment that provided needed resources; at Clark State Community College, it was an earlier decision to require instructors to have a Blackboard course shell; at St. Clair County Community College, extensive data dashboards; at McHenry County College, a student service mindset; and at Parkland College, a robust communications team. In every story, there was appreciation for the support and contributions of all college employees. Based on their solid foundations, college-wide support, and resource structure, these colleges were able to innovate more easily during a crisis.

Lau (Parkland College) shared words of advice for leaders facing a crisis:

> Every cloud has a silver lining, and never let a crisis go to waste. A lot of good stuff will be gained from this, but one of the best is that crisis management is actually working with people. It is not only how we manage people, but the

quality of the people we have working at the college is crucial to how we manage. You help your people flourish in your community when push comes to shove, and when there's a big crisis it's how we value the individuals in the college community.

As the crisis eventually fades from our everyday consciousness, many of the lessons learned from the early days of the COVID-19 pandemic will remain with us, and so will the innovations. Some innovations will be transformed into even better processes or products by those who continually try to find better ways of educating students and improving outcomes. As these community college leaders have demonstrated, commitment to the community college mission involves personal commitment to making things better, even in the face of the biggest crisis of our time. The changes they have made solved immediate problems and will surely have a positive impact on the future of these colleges and their students.

REFERENCES

Bosley, A. (2016). Collaboration design. *Leadership: Journal for Post-Secondary Leaders, 22*(1), 22–25.

Carlgren, L. (2013). *Design thinking as an enabler of innovation: Exploring the concept and its relation to building innovation capabilities* [Unpublished doctoral dissertation]. Chalmers University of Technology.

Christensen, C. M., Baumann, H., Ruggles, R., & Sadtler, T. M. (2006). Disruptive innovation for social change. *Harvard Business Review, 84*(12), 94–101.

Crossan, M. M., & Apaydin M. (2010). A multi-dimensional framework of organizational innovation: A systematic review of the literature. *Journal of Management Studies, 47*(6), 1154–1191.

Drucker, P. F. (2002). The discipline of innovation. *Harvard Business Review, 80*(8), 95–104.

Fagerberg, J. (2005). Innovation: A guide to the literature. In J. Fagerberg, D. C. Mowery, & R. R. Nelson (Eds.), *The Oxford handbook of innovation* (pp. 11–26). Oxford University Press.

Farson, R., & Keyes, R. (2002). The failure-tolerant leader. *Harvard Business Review, 80*(8), 64–71.

Hogan, S. J., & Coote, L. V. (2014). Organizational culture, innovation, and performance: A test of Schein's model. *Journal of Business Research, 67*, 1609–1621.

Jung, D. I., Chow, C., & Wu, A. (2003). The role of transformational leadership in enhancing organizational innovation: Hypotheses and some preliminary findings. *The Leadership Quarterly, 14*(4–5), 525–544.

Kanter, R. M. (1999). From spare change to real change: The social sector as beta site for business innovation. *Harvard Business Review, 77*(3), 122–132.

Kao, J. (2017). *Community colleges in the age of innovation*. The League for Innovation in the Community College.

Khazanchi, S., Lewis, M. W., & Boyer, K. K. (2007). Innovation-supportive culture: The impact of organizational values on process innovation. *Journal of Operations Management, 25*(4), 871–884.

Murray, J. P., & Kishur, J. M. (2008). Crisis management in the community college. *Community College Journal of Research and Practice, 32*, 480–495.

O'Banion, T., Weidner, L., & Wilson, C. (2011). Creating a culture of innovation in the community college. *Community College Journal of Research and Practice, 35*(6): 470–483.

Sydow, D., & Alfred, R. (2013). *Re-visioning community colleges: Positioning for innovation.* Rowman & Littlefield.

Tierney, P., Farmer, S. M., & Graen, G. B. (1999). An examination of leadership and employee creativity: The relevance of traits and relationships. *Personnel Psychology, 52*(3), 591–620.

Chapter Thirteen

Student Success During COVID-19

A Case Study From Eastern Iowa Community Colleges

Naomi DeWinter

VOICES FROM THE PANDEMIC

In early March 2020, higher education in eastern Iowa faced challenges it had never faced before. But, then, so did education at all levels and in all states across the United States. As the global pandemic reached Iowa, leaders in all sectors—government, corporate, and education—made the decision to quarantine and isolate.

Eastern Iowa Community Colleges (EICC), which serves over 7,000 students on the banks of the Mississippi River at Muscatine, Clinton, and Scott community colleges, faced a difficult decision about its spring semester. Then, on March 13, 2020, each college moved all of its courses and student services to online.

The classes and services took different forms, as instructors, staff, and students discovered varying levels of comfort and access to technology. The colleges finished out the spring semester fully online, and it seemed, with each week, increased understanding and capabilities of serving students remotely.

As president of Muscatine Community College and vice chancellor of student development for EICC, I talked with several students and faculty during this transition. I wanted to hear about the transition from them. How did they adapt? What challenges did they face?

The following stories come from a cross-section of the student body and the faculty. The voices include a speech instructor, an instructor in the non-credit English Language Learning program, a biology instructor, the Student Senate president and member of the League of United Latin American Citizens (LULAC), an F-1 international student, and the Phi Theta Kappa vice president.

Their stories are stories of hope, creativity, flexibility, and persistence. When we talked, I asked about the challenges that instructors faced in keeping students engaged and the ways they relied on and incorporated technology. I asked students how they stayed motivated and connected to the college, about what they missed most about being on campus, and about how the college helped and supported them.

While others have written about the design of online services when students choose to take online courses (e.g., Dadgar et al., 2013; Gaines, 2014), I write about a significantly unique challenge. Students who chose to take face-to-face classes were suddenly forced to complete the semester online. Even students who were previously online faced many new challenges: public access to technology was shut down; young children were at home, as K–12 schools and child-care centers closed; and family members were also now working from home.

HOW IT STARTED

In the beginning, the college put significant effort into switching classes from face-to-face to online, putting many student services in a secondary role because of the timing of the emergency. It was preregistration, prior to payment deadlines, and prior to graduation. All hands were on deck to assist students in converting to an online course experience. With the unknown length of campus disruption, there was some belief, including my own, that full student services could return to campus before too long. New student registration was delayed by a couple of weeks. Decisions to cancel graduation or develop a virtual graduation were put on hold, as information changed rapidly about the pandemic and the effects on our communities. As president, I maintained regular contact with the Public Health Department, receiving health and safety guidance and keeping track of the number of new cases every day.

While remote student services were prepared, the focus was first on giving students access to information about college and community services (Ludwig-Hardman & Dunlap, 2003). Food pantries were relocated to allow for drive-up service; emergency funds were established through our foundations; and college and community hot spots were added. A new webpage was built that collected all relevant information for remote student services in one place. As the weeks went by and advisors, other student services professionals, and students became more comfortable with the new remote reality, the college began to focus more on creating and maintaining student relationships and serving individual developmental needs (Ohrablo, 2016).

After a student survey revealed that our students needed access to mental health counseling, online counseling and support groups were quickly added. A partnership for existing online tutoring was expanded. Small group check-in sessions began with TRIO students; one-on-one Zoom advising appointments began; and student engagement events were held, some with higher attendance than when offered on campus. Just as faculty did in their transition to online teaching, Student Services professionals used various technology tools including Microsoft Teams, Zoom, and Google Voice when interacting with students and with each other. In a survey conducted a few years earlier at University of West Florida (Gaines, 2014), students indicated a strong preference for face-to-face advising sessions. Advisors shared that preference; however, that option was eliminated as we responded to the pandemic and was replaced by technology tools, which professionals and students alike adopted and became increasingly comfortable with as time passed.

According to Tinto's (1993) model of student retention, two systems influence our students' institutional experience: a social system and an academic system. After the campuses closed on March 13, the college essentially eliminated the social system—informal peer group interactions were nonexistent and formal interactions occurred very occasionally. All extracurricular activities were cancelled. Tinto (1993) added that both systems are interdependent, that is, when they work together in harmony, they can reinforce each other to benefit the student (p. 119). In this case, we were limited to one system—the academic system—for an indefinite time period.

WHAT IMPACT DID THIS HAVE ON STUDENT SUCCESS?

Deana Dawson—Phi Theta Kappa Vice President

Deana Dawson had been a student at Muscatine Community College (MCC) since 2017. Last May, when she completed her associate of arts degree, she was determined to stand up from her wheelchair while receiving her diploma. As she did so, the audience erupted in cheers.

Deana had already decided to enroll in online courses this spring semester. Because it's more difficult for her to navigate the snowy roads with her wheelchair, she did not feel some of the same effects of the change to online classes in mid-March. Before the pandemic, however, she had been coming to campus regularly for tutoring, doing homework, meeting with her advisor and checking in with some of the trusted staff members. Deana commented, "I seem to be able to get more done when I'm on campus. When I'm at home, I see that the dishes need to get done, the laundry needs to get done, and I get distracted." During her college career, Deana acquired some strong student success skills. She printed all materials for a week's worth of classes in the

MCC library so that she wouldn't have to rely on technology while she was studying and could work ahead: "That's how MCC has helped me to become prepared: I learned to stay ahead in my classes, and I don't fall behind."

Deana is an extrovert who, since she had not left her apartment since March 11th, found the increased isolation difficult. Every morning, staff assisted with her daily routine, but for the rest of the time, she was online. "Facebook is my friend; email is my friend; chat rooms are my friends," Deana told me. "Before this all happened, I knew nothing about Zoom. It frightened me. I was dragging my feet. Now I'm on it all the time!" As vice president of Phi Theta Kappa (PTK), a national community college student honors' association, Deana had stayed in touch with other MCC PTK members through Canvas, our campus' learning management system (LMS). Deana attended a virtual leadership conference and met several other PTK students from other Iowa community colleges with whom she now stays in touch. She also contacted the president of the PTK Honor Society by email after that virtual conference to express how valuable the experience was. The next morning, a response from the president was in her inbox. "I'm making more connections now than I was in person. There are no limits to the internet! I, frankly, don't like limits," Deana shared with me.

One of Deana's wonderful traits is that she remains positive under any circumstance. "I always ask myself, are we going to stay positive?" she told me. While I was asking Deana if she needed any help from the college, she was quick to offer her assistance to our other MCC students, thinking of how she might help others:

> If I can help a student set themselves up for success, that's how I want to spend my free time. They might be inspired by my story. Pandemic or not, emergency or not, we have to help others. When we come back together, we will be much more close-knit. Everything we see is going to be like new.

Deana will graduate with additional credentials in administrative office support in May of 2020 and is expected to keep on track with her academic journey.

Daniel Salazar—Student Senate President, LULAC Member

Daniel Salazar is a second-year student at Muscatine Community College. He is the president of Student Senate and member of LULAC Council. Daniel commented:

> This has definitely not been easy. For me, I like to be there (on campus) and work with people. For the first week, I had lost my motivation. It was difficult to have no classes to go to at a specific time. It took me a second to get back on

board. Thankfully, I was able to pick myself up and see how I was doing. It wasn't good enough to wake up at 3pm and miss the day.

Daniel lives with his parents and younger brother, a freshman at Muscatine High School: "It's been difficult to separate my roles—when I'm home, I can usually play or relax; but now I'm studying from my room all the time. When is the time to play?" Daniel is currently unemployed:

> I am a waiter at a local restaurant, but I haven't worked for many weeks. I haven't filed for unemployment because I think there are others who need it more. I can rely on my family to help me through.

Regarding the switch to online classes, Daniel told me:

> I survived with trial and error. I break things up in smaller chunks now. On Mondays, I focus on my Monday classes. Same for the rest of the week. I also started using audiobooks. I used to make fun of people who listened to, not read their books. Now I enjoy listening to podcasts and audiobooks. I can fidget and still pay attention to the content! All of my instructors have employed different methods: One instructor posts videos of lectures that I listen to; one has us read ahead and provides an outline in separate modules by author. When the class gets together, it's to discuss what we learned and read on our own about that author. For my computer class, it's more about putting my own time in to do the work. Class is offered by Zoom, if students want to have more formal time with the instructor. Finally, another instructor sends out weekly announcements of what's coming up for the week to help us try to stay organized.

We discussed that there are instructors who go more in-depth with class discussions and some who are more straightforward. Just as there are differences between instructors when you take in-person classes, there are differences after going online with content and style of teaching. The faculty members' personalities show up in the way they've set up their online classes, too.

Daniel has also continued to serve his community. His mother works in public health as a school resource navigator, and she is his inspiration for his own spirit of service. The Iowa state-wide director of the League of United Latin American Citizens gave him a list of people—Latinos from across Iowa—to call to see if they needed to be connected to services. The director also asked Daniel to show others how to set up a video for Zoom: "I had access to the technology, but I had never used Zoom myself. I thought I better update myself, so that I can help other people!" Daniel added:

> I'm saddened that all of the clubs had to stop doing things. We are going to have to work together to change how we do things. We can't do this on our own. I see Student Senate leadership as more of a support system for the other

clubs, not doing our own events but maybe acting as a point-person for others. The LULAC Collegiate Council worked with Jennifer Zamora, the Latino Outreach Coordinator at the Iowa State University Extension and Outreach, offering a drive-by ceremony for the MHS "Salir Adelante" students who are graduating.

Fiona Juniku—International Student

When Fiona first arrived in the United States, she received a scholarship to attend a private high school in Arizona. Her academic performance was strong, and she got accepted into several colleges. However, she realized that cost would be a huge factor that might prevent her from attending a U.S. college. She returned home to Gjakova, Kosovo, for the summer to decide what to do from there. By coincidence, a neighbor, Bujeta Vokshi, started telling her about Muscatine Community College, her own alma mater. Bujeta told her about the option to live on campus and reassured Fiona that Muscatine is a small, friendly city. Fiona came to Muscatine in 2018 and enrolled at MCC.

Fiona's mom is a teacher and her dad is a phone technician. Her hometown in Kosovo is much more densely populated than Muscatine, and they have not yet had an opportunity to visit her here. Fiona had planned to return to her home for the first time in summer 2020; however, travel restrictions due to the pandemic put an end to those plans. Fiona was also living in on-campus apartments, which were shut down in early March. Her first concerns were about housing: "Should I just go back home and possibly drop out of college? I didn't want to do that, but it was a very stressful situation for a while." The college, working with the city, found temporary housing for students who had no alternatives. Fiona's plan became to graduate in December 2020 and return home to Kosovo at that time. She wanted to transfer to a university to study business management but was not sure of scholarships that could help her with the costs:

> When I first moved to Muscatine, I knew no one. People were friendly, but I found them to be reserved. The students stayed within their own circle of friends. Since then, I've made a lot of friends and connections, through my classes, through Young Democrats, and [through] my job as a tutor in the Success Center.

Fiona added:

> My favorite teacher is John DaBeet. I feel like he was not just a good teacher but also easy-going. If I had trouble with a subject, he would explain it in a very hands-on way that made it easy to understand. I feel that switching to online courses has actually made things easier for me. I hadn't taken any online courses previously. Now I can go at my own pace, I can work ahead, if

the subject comes easily to me and I can focus on the subjects that take a little more time. How the online courses are set up reflect the personalities of my instructors and the subject area, e.g., in science class, students are in touch more often with their instructor. My instructors offered me one-on-one Zoom sessions, if I had questions.

Zach Campbell—Speech/Communication Instructor at Muscatine Community College

In March 2020, Zach was teaching three classes: one was a high school section for local high school students; one was an 8-week hybrid class that had just begun at the time of the shift to online; and one was a 16-week on-campus section. An 8-week professional communication course for agriculture students was set to end on April 2nd and, thus, was not overly affected by the campus closure. For the course that just started, Zach set aside the first 45 minutes of class to respond to student questions. He stated, "Students had a lot of questions and just wanted to dialogue. I didn't have all of the answers but did my best to calm their fears and let them know we can do this together."

Zach admitted he normally sent a tremendous amount of communication to his students. Students received at least three communications about the same topic: one email from Zach, one email from EICC, and another email that is posted into student announcements in LMS. Students have told him it's annoying to receive so many messages, but they were also thankful. Zach left nothing to chance.

Zach continued to teach synchronously, using Zoom during the regularly scheduled class times, but found that only half of his students regularly attended, due to work hours changing, limited Wi-Fi, and/or increasing responsibilities to take care of parents or siblings. He gave the students two options for their public speaking assignments: (1) give their presentations live to the class during the regularly scheduled class times or (2) record their presentation and share it with him privately. The students' preferences were, for the most part, split between the two options.

Zach was also very conscious about maintaining equity and access for his students: "When students have self-identified as having struggles, we rack our brains together to find a good solution for them. I want to make sure that every student is connecting with me somehow." He added:

> When we are in the classroom with students, it can be easy to forget that not every student has equal access to resources when off campus. Unless a student comes to us and discloses their needs, shortcomings, problems, etc., we just simply don't know. It is easy to (innocently) assume everything is okay even when we know from community statistical data that it may not be. Now that we are working remotely/online, it quickly put into perspective how many

students are actually "not okay" and don't have some of the resources available to them and just how much they rely on the services offered at our campus locations.

Rachel Riley Smock—English Language Acquisition (ELA) Instructor

Normally, one finds a bustling group of students practicing their English skills in the McAvoy Center at Muscatine Community College outside Rachel Riley Smock's classroom. About a dozen countries are represented by the students in the class, from China and the Ivory Coast, to Brazil and Congo. After mid-March, all English language learners, like the rest of campus, moved to an online format.

On Monday and Wednesday mornings, during their regularly scheduled class times, Rachel held her English language classes using Zoom. They discussed what happened to their families in their home countries and shared in their worry about their loved ones. Some students have asked her about her oldest son, who was working on a cruise ship in the Gulf when the pandemic first appeared. They understood her worries when she was unable to connect with him because they were feeling similarly about their families. Rachel began each class by checking in with her students, finding out how their families were doing around the world. "It helps them to feel not isolated," Riley Smock commented. "A few students who weren't able to attend our regular face-to-face sessions have even popped back up. It's been a fantastic tool!" The students expressed a shared gratitude at the services available to them through MCC, such as the food pantry and emergency funds.

In addition to the classroom time, students had access to "Burlington English," an interactive online teaching tool. They were already using this tool even before the pandemic shift to online, so this was not something new to students. This tool helped them practice their English skills on their own in a fun manner. For Rachel, communication among her colleagues was equally important; all of the ELA instructors met weekly via Zoom to share successes and challenges and to support each other.

About 2 months prior to our interview, students started introducing Rachel to "What's App," a communication application. By using the app, students can share documents, send photos, and easily stay in touch. Rachel also installed the app on her phone and began to use it with her students. Rachel started forwarding all the information she received about college and community support to her students through the app: "A day does not go by without people from four or five countries conversing with each other on this app." They maintained lots of social connection, despite social distancing. Rachel remained positive about this online experience:

This experience has made me look at teaching again in a new light. Yes, some of it is the technical side, but another side is the social side. Look at the community we are able to provide to our students!

Zach Spersted—Biology Instructor

As a faculty member in the Biology department, Zach Spersted faced additional challenges when the pandemic moved classes to the online format. His lab-based courses required online alternatives, and his highly interactive class sessions felt constrained by the online format. He remained positive and innovative throughout the process:

> The spring transition went pretty well. We were just starting into sections that we could do outside by enjoying nature or going to a park (while maintaining social distancing). We also used a lot of paper labs instead of wet labs. I treated my online classes similarly to my face-to-face classes. I pre-recorded the lectures and utilized my slides to explain concepts. That way, students could see and hear the topics explained. Students were able to watch the lectures whenever they wanted, and importantly, watch certain parts again that they didn't fully understand the first time. I held optional Zoom sessions for students, and these worked terrifically. We would work together to find different analogies to explain concepts, as the same analogy did not always resonate with every student.
>
> I held the Zoom sessions from my kitchen table. I would try to find something in my kitchen that I could use to explain a concept, so that students could see the transfer of knowledge from a classroom to the real world. Recently, I was explaining how a plant cell differs from an animal cell. I found a black plastic take-out container in my kitchen—something that most students could identify with—and used it to explain the geometric shape of a plant cell and activity within the cell.

Zach also discussed the things he missed most by not being with his students:

> When I'm recording a lecture at 11 pm in my kitchen, I have to generate my own energy and enthusiasm. In the classroom, it is easy to have a lot of energy and enthusiasm because I love talking about science with people and seeing them get excited about science. Using Zoom, I can gauge students' understanding much better.

Zach indicated that in the future, he would consider making the Zoom sessions a mandatory part of his online classes, as they are a great way to check in on students and make sure they are not being left behind:

> I explain to my students that falling behind in learning is like suffering from credit card debt. If you let it go on too long, you are overwhelmed by the

amount you owe, or the amount you are behind. I want to help them keep on pace and on track with the content.

Another thing he missed is the chance for students to interact with each other: "Many times, students in my classes help me come up with different analogies and they teach each other important concepts. In the online format this spring, we did not have that."

For Zach's online summer courses, he stated he would use equipment and chemicals on campus to record some labs. He believed that by students using worksheets and observing him performing the labs, they would be able to learn what is most critical in his lab courses. He was comfortable with the fully online format:

> It's not critical to their learning for them to actually perform the labs them-selves. It is critical that they observe, infer, and make analogies from what they see. I will not tell them the answers, but I will probe them for the answers.

LESSONS WE'VE LEARNED

The spring of 2020 was like no other spring semester I have encountered in my professional career. Information and our understanding of the Coronavirus was coming at such a fast pace that we were struggling to make long-term decisions. A decision made one week was no longer relevant the next because of changing conditions. While I continued to take notes from our many meetings, unless I could share them within 24 hours, I didn't share them at all, as we had moved well beyond those topics. As the pandemic quarantine wore on, we became better at offering remote student services and students became better at participating and getting the information, even if not during the synchronous sessions. For example, we began offering online mental health support groups twice a week. Attendance at the live events was often fewer than six participants. After a few days, however, we could see that hundreds had viewed the recorded sessions. This motivated us to continue.

Access to Technology

Access to educational technology has been a critical issue for our institutions, especially in our more rural settings. We learned early about the difficulties many of our students face in accessing technology. One of our college and career counselors who serves students in two rural schools observed that staying connected with students became nearly impossible for one of their sites. One of the schools is located in a town that includes a meat-packing plant that had an early Coronavirus outbreak. Not only did many of these students not have at-home technology access, but all of the individuals who tested positive were Latino, providing another painful example of the dispar-ities in the effects of the pandemic.

EICC almost immediately offered students a laptop rental program for both credit and non-credit students, and we worked with others to develop public Wi-Fi hotspots as we became aware of gaps in access to technology. To address technology access issues, we decided that, for the fall 2020 se-mester, we will offer full-time students a laptop or an equivalent discount to their tuition discount. We want to ensure that more, if not most, students are not left behind because of lack of equipment. All classes will include an online component through the LMS and faculty are encouraged to use Zoom as needed or as desired. By building these capabilities into all classes, we will be prepared if we have to suddenly turn our courses and services online again.

Rethinking How to Teach

Many faculty have told me that this crisis has changed the way they looked at teaching. "It has to be more individualized," a colleague told me. Even with small class sizes and our strong focus on teaching and learning, EICC has average retention and persistence rates, comparable to many other commu-nity colleges. We lose some students because they do not see themselves as part of our community; we lose others because they don't connect with the academic support services they need. All of us, in both academic and student services roles, have to hold ourselves accountable for staying on course with this individualized, student-centered manner of working with students that we saw reflected in the interviews collected here.

Grit

I continue to be amazed by our students' grit and compassion for each other and for us. We know that our students juggle multiple roles, but many take these roles so naturally that they are hidden from us when we see them on campus. When they were working from home, those multiple roles and chal-lenges became more evident. They had family members who struggled with health concerns. One of our students was related to the first Muscatine County Coronavirus-related death. Hundreds lost their jobs. Others saw their hours increase as they worked in essential services, such as health care and grocery stores. Despite this, in conversations with their advisors, many stu-dents asked their advisors about themselves, wondering and caring about how they were coping. In my interviews with students, I was repeatedly asked about my family's health and my work life and received offers of assistance from the students. Our students continue to amaze me with their determination, strength, and humanity.

Genuineness

Another thing I realized through these conversations is that everyone—faculty and Student Services professionals—has their own approach to working online, just as they have different ways of approaching their work in "normal" circumstance. Certainly, some adapt to technology more quickly than others, but I saw every individual striving to find and employ a unique and genuine way in which to connect with our students. The varying efforts and approaches were illustrated in the different ways each used available technology, structured appointments and meetings, and arranged student check-ins.

I could not be more proud of the faculty and staff at EICC as they stepped up to the pandemic, looked it in the face, didn't back down, and continued to serve our students. This experience has made us a stronger institution and made us more flexible, resilient, and open to change. I know that we will continue to find and use new tools to connect and engage with our students, no matter what the "new normal" looks like.

REFERENCES

Dadger, M., Nodine, T., Bracco, K. R., & Venezia, A. (2013). *Integrating student supports and academics.* West Ed.

Gaines, T. (2014). Technology and academic advising: Student usage and preferences. *NACADA Journal, 34*(1), 43–49.

Ludwig-Hardman, S., & Dunlap, J. (2003). Learner support services for online students: Scaffolding for success. *International Review of Research in Open and Distance Learning, 4*(1), 1–15.

Ohrablo, S. (2016). *Advising online students: Replicating best practices of face-to-face advising.* https://nacada.ksu.edu/Resources/Clearinghouse/View-Articles/Advising-Online-Students-Replicating-Best-Practices-of-Face-to-Face-Advising.aspx.

Tinto, V. (1993). *Leaving college: Rethinking the causes and cures of student attrition* (2nd ed.). University of Chicago Press.

Chapter Fourteen

Creating Institutions of Excellence

Lori Sundberg

A CULTURE OF EXCELLENCE

When you arrive on the main campus of Kirkwood Community College (Iowa), you will be struck immediately by the overall beautiful appearance of the campus, its modern buildings, and well-manicured grounds that convey instantly to visitors the level of attention that goes into their care. Venture into its buildings, and that belief will be reinforced at every turn.

One of the outstanding features that Kirkwood delivers to its students and communities is a state-of-the-art 72-room boutique hotel that provides a learning space for our culinary and hospitality management students—the only one of its kind in North America and one of just three four-diamond hotels in the state of Iowa. Adjacent to the Hotel at Kirkwood, you will find an equestrian and livestock facility that supports not only Kirkwood's agricultural programs but also the state of Iowa's equestrian needs.

Among other unique features of our campus, visitors will find a vineyard and winery. The college's Katz Simulation Lab provides a learning space for nursing, respiratory health, EMS, and other health programs that rivals the health facilities and technology of many universities. Kirkwood possesses the only cadaver lab housed at a community college in the state of Iowa. The Horticulture program provides the greens for the salads served at the Hotel at Kirkwood, and the beef and pork for the hotel restaurant come largely from Kirkwood livestock. The varied ways Kirkwood distinguishes itself as a community college are many, but in short, I believe what sets Kirkwood apart from other community colleges is its drive for a culture of excellence. That culture is the lifeblood that flows through its campuses.

Community colleges, and higher education in general, are facing one of the most, if not *the* most, disruptive times in its history. As the number of high school graduates continues to decrease and competition becomes more fierce, institutions must distinguish themselves on certain key characteristics that spell out in no uncertain terms what students and families can expect from a college education. Many institutions are attempting to distinguish themselves on the platform of excellence.

Strategic plans from several community colleges stress institutional priorities of excellence in teaching and learning, or excellence in student outcomes and assessment, or even excellence in athletics. However, what I've come to know from being a leader at Kirkwood Community College and at my former institution, Carl Sandburg College (Illinois), is that true excellence is achieved by creating a *culture of excellence* that undergirds and permeates the entire fabric of an organization and becomes the lifeblood of how it thinks, plans, and behaves.

Excellence cannot exist in just a particular area, rather it must become the identity for the entire institution. Without it, an institution cannot achieve the broad, sweeping, and integrative culture of excellence that is necessary, in Jim Collins's (2001) words, "to break through that which is average and achieve excellence." I believe that institutions with embedded and enduring cultures of excellence are created by understanding the key components of organizational culture; possessing an unwavering and unrelenting commitment to data and continuous process improvement; believing their employees are fundamental and key to their success; and lastly, holding precious the importance and value of intellectual curiosity and always considering new ways of doing things. Without any one of these important components, developing a culture of excellence is next to impossible.

ENVIRONMENT AND COMPETITION

The fact that we've been facing for years is that the number of high school graduates is declining. That decline has prompted an urgency among all institutions of higher education that perhaps we haven't seen before. Overall enrollment for higher education is down 2.9 million since its last peak in fall of 2011 (Marcus, 2019). Because of this decline, a recent study of 500 leaders at colleges and universities identified increased competition as the number 1 challenge (VOA Student Union, 2019). At the same time, the Department of Education reported that, in 2018, the country had the fewest number of institutions in its history (VOA Student Union, 2019). In a fairly recent interview, the online publication *The EvoLLLution* shared,

> Like their university counterparts, community colleges are facing an uncertain future: lower enrollments, changing student demographics, and increased competition from universities looking to grow their share of workforce development programming and are prompting community college leaders to look to

the future of their institutions and develop strategic responses to the challenges of tomorrow. (Roark, 2018)

These are disruptive times, unlike any we have faced in the recent history of community colleges. The increased spotlight on student outcomes in community colleges has led institutions to understand that, in order to remain competitive and survive, they must differentiate themselves from their competitors. The success rates of the institution's students are publicly available, allowing parents and students alike to research and compare institutions based on their persistence, retention, and completion data.

At the same time, institutions set priorities and goals with a defined commitment to excellence in teaching and learning, or to excellence in student assessment and outcomes. However, while those are worthwhile and important goals for all of us in community colleges, I would argue that creating an institutional culture of excellence is more fundamental to the overall success of those initiatives.

For example, excellence in teaching and learning does not happen in a vacuum and will be difficult to integrate without the appropriate use of data and without efficient processes that allow for timely and important feedback. At both of the institutions where I've served as president, a teaching and learning center is strictly dedicated to providing supports to faculty in the classroom. Furthermore, these supports are based upon solid research. Instead of creating a pocket of excellence that likely will be unsustainable on its own, both institutions created an underlying foundation of excellence that is embedded and infused in the organization and serves as the guiding light for all that it does.

THE IMPORTANCE OF CULTURE

Many of us have heard Peter Drucker's quotation, "Culture eats strategy for breakfast," meaning that the influence of culture and its impact will readily overshadow any organizational strategies that are put in place, particularly if they are in conflict with the culture. The best definition of culture is from Edgar Schein (1990), the preeminent expert on organizational culture. He states that culture "will be the cognitive in that the perceptions, language, and thought processes that a group comes to share will be the ultimate causal determinant of feelings, attitudes, espoused values, and overt behavior" (p. 110).

Culture is, in short, that difficult-to-define or difficult-to-put-your-finger-on "thing" in an organization, but what most people describe as being a "you know it when you see it" phenomenon. I describe it as fundamentally the way an organization sees itself. This is clearly evident at Kirkwood. It is evident in the way the custodians and the roads and grounds personnel keep the appearance of the college, but it's also evident in the values that Kirkwood has embraced to support student success. Additionally, it's apparent when you talk with faculty and staff and see the level of pride that they take in what they do.

Being the best is what Kirkwood does. And Kirkwood does it, not for the recognition, but because that is who and what Kirkwood stands for: Excellence in all that it does. For a college to develop a culture of excellence, the need to understand these basic principles is paramount. Schein (1990) also stated, "It is desirable to distinguish three fundamental levels at which culture manifests itself: (a) observable artifacts, (b) values, and (c) basic underlying assumptions" (p. 111).

How does a college then develop these artifacts, values, and assumptions? Fundamentally, this is the role of leadership, but it can't be created or perpetuated solely by leadership. The nature of organizational culture is such that it must be a shared vision between leadership and the greater college community that holds dear the aspiration for nothing short of excellence in all that it does. My observation is that the faculty and staff at Kirkwood drive excellence as much as the leadership does. Once there is a shared understanding, then as Schein (1990) described, the culture develops through those shared assumptions. Those assumptions then become embedded in the institution's vision, mission, and values, as well as manifesting in the artifacts an organization shares with its campus community. The vision of Kirkwood is: "to be the community college leader in regional, national, and global education" (Kirkwood, 2021, p. 4).

The culture, then, becomes that one thing that serves as the guiding light for the way the organization thinks, plans, and behaves going forward. It provides the foundation on which everything else is built and permeates the entire fabric of an organization.

While considering culture is important, it's just as important to understand how it works. We can find guidance from Schein (1990) again: "Culture perpetuates and reproduces itself through the socialization of new members of the group" (p. 111). In short, culture is a learned and shared experience that is interchanged between leaders and employees but also among and between employees. It is a dynamic process that grows over time as the internal consistency grows.

UNRELENTING COMMITMENT TO DATA AND PROCESS IMPROVEMENT

The next important component of creating an institutional culture of excellence is an unrelenting and unwavering commitment to data and process improvement. As the saying goes, what gets measured, gets accomplished.

Institutions that focus on excellence also keep a laser focus on their data. It is an incomplete notion to think that the data tell the whole story of an institution because they do not, but what they do for an institution is direct it to where it needs to dig deeper to understand its outcomes.

So much of what we have done in our institutions has come from instinctual thinking or what we rationalize will work or what feels like common sense, and yet, how often have we tested our data to discover that in fact we were not correct in our assumptions? A good example is the use of first-year-experience courses. At Carl Sandburg College, we implemented a first-year-experience course for those students who were attending for the first time in higher education. It seemed like an excellent way to help those students newest to higher education and provide them with all of the academic skills that we thought most important.

We hypothesized we would find that those who completed the class successfully would have higher retention rates and higher GPAs. However, at the end of the first year, the data showed no improvement in either semester retention or GPA. We found no measurable differences at all. So what were we missing? We could have just decided that it didn't work and moved on to another new idea, but we would have missed some valuable understandings of the data.

Obviously, the data were in conflict with our assumptions, but a deeper dive was needed to determine why the course was not working. Was the course in alignment with what students needed? And there is exactly where we found our answer. In listening to students, we found they had a greater need for time-management skills. Our course had been heavy on all things academically focused, but students first needed to learn how to manage their time. We reworked the content of the course to better develop time-management skills.

Another key distinction came from faculty. They believed they needed to act more as coaches rather than instructors. They believed this course was different and their role should be to become a student champion. As a result, the course became more relational and more focused on the student and his or her needs to succeed. Once the course was redesigned, it began to generate the results that everyone thought it would.

Today, students who complete the first-year-experience course have term completion rates ranging from 84% to 86%. The critical lesson, then, is how an institution uses its data to make accurate and solid data-informed decisions. The hard numbers provide the "where" to look, but it's incumbent on the institution to dig deeper and discover the "why" of the numbers. That is where the richness and beauty of data-driven decision-making manifests.

An unwavering commitment to process improvement is crucial as well. An institution can't be a place of excellence with processes implemented from 20 years ago, 10 years ago, or even 5 years ago. There has to be a relentless quest to improve the way we conduct business on behalf of our students and the academic side of the institution. The adage that we do things a certain way because this is the way we've always done them will lead to a certain death of excellence. The question must be: If we were starting a new college today, how would we support the institution with the most up-to-date, technologically efficient, and streamlined processes that we could find? Often, just by coming together to map out processes, we can immediately see where one or more steps can be removed thereby improving and reducing as well as seeing where a process needs to be fundamentally overhauled.

This is where institutional effectiveness (IE) earns its keep. This is when we bring the key people from the institution together to see where processes cross departments and get hung up at various stages. Carl Sandburg College used process mapping for all HR processes, hiring, interviewing, negotiations, payroll taxes, data assurance, disposal of assets, and several accounting processes. At Kirkwood, hiring processes have been mapped by classification, as well as student billing processes.

There is no end to the refining and restructuring of processes at a community college. At Kirkwood, we rely on Dr. Connie Thurman to lead institutional effectiveness; she also led IE at Carl Sandburg College. Her background is in lean processes, and she possesses a black belt in six-sigma. When I say there has to be an unrelenting commitment to process improvement, I'm serious. It is worth the time and cost of getting the right people trained in process improvement.

At Kirkwood, we now use process mapping for new initiatives as well. Our Innovation Fund was a new initiative, and the IE team used process mapping to develop the procedures for it. It is not the glamourous side to what we do, and we frequently like to push this to the back burner, but this work is what fundamentally supports the entire institution and allows us to deliver an education to our students that is second to none. Less time is taken up with executing routine processes, allowing more time and resources to be focused on our mission of educating and supporting students.

EMPLOYEES ARE THE KEY

What I have learned over the years is that, without a doubt, employees are the key to an institution's success. I've seen organizational structures that should have been prohibitive to the effectiveness of an organization because of added layers or the convoluted reporting process for specific departments. For example, there are varieties of departments to where functions such as marketing, institutional research, library services, tutoring, institutional effectiveness, public safety, and so on can report. In some cases, the reporting relationship is a hindrance, yet if the right people are serving in roles across the institution, by virtue of their talents, dedication, and commitment, the organization thrives despite its organizational clumsiness.

On the other hand, I've seen very direct and succinctly structured organizations where reporting relationships and departments were aligned, and channels of communication and decision making *appeared* to be clear. And yet, with the wrong people within their respective roles, the processes are stymied, and the institution is stuck at every turn. When communication is fractured and incomplete, not allowing for good decision making, then morale suffers and ultimately goals cannot be attained.

The key is to ensure that the institution has the right people in the right jobs. I believe understanding "job fit" is essential and investing in professional development, a *must*. I am a proponent of Jim Collins and his belief that you must have the right people in the right jobs. Collins (2001) stated when talking about organizations that go from good to great,

> In fact, leaders of companies that go from good to great start not with "where" but with "who." They start by getting the right people on the bus, the wrong people off the bus, and the right people in the right seats. And they stick with that discipline—first the people, then the direction—no matter how dire the circumstances.

I've seen people in the wrong jobs struggle and fail and lose their confidence. On the other hand, I've seen people in the right job light up, gain confidence, and propel themselves on to even greater heights than I could have foreseen. The classic case is of the brilliant faculty member who is beloved by all of his or her students who goes on to become a dean. All of the skills that made the person a fantastic faculty member are not the same skills that will make a good dean. The paperwork and administrative duties can be mind-numbing and completely frustrating for some faculty. They don't always flourish in the dean role, and they can become miserable.

On the other hand, I had a faculty member at Sandburg who was so beloved in the classroom that I was told I should not encourage her to become a dean because of the loss it would be to our faculty ranks. However, I could also see that she would be an outstanding dean. Therefore, I encouraged her to become a dean, and she loves the work. I'm confident that if she ever desires to become a college president, she would make a great one. On the staff side, I've had very detailed, organized employees who prefer being individual contributors apply to work in positions in student life. The fit was completely off. Student life employees are the definition of what it means to be flexible. When working with students, student life staff must manage changing dynamics and work as a team. The detail, process staff are needed elsewhere.

In summary, "job fit" is essential for organizations committed to organizational excellence. It should be the basis for how we consider who and to what position we promote people. However, we can't stop there. We have to provide employees with the professional development necessary to achieve their potential. This cannot be emphasized enough: employees are key to the overall success of the organization.

INTELLECTUAL CURIOSITY

The last component for institutional excellence comes from encouraging an institution to maintain its curiosity and to realize that excellence cannot be sustained by staying the same. As society changes, institutions need to question how they must change to meet those changes in society and still maintain their commitment to excellence. The goal is not to create excellence for some period of time, but to carry it forward indefinitely. The institution must be willing to try new approaches, new products, and new ways of delivering education to ensure the institution stays on the cutting edge—some could say the bleeding edge—of excellence.

A strong tie to staying with what has been, and not being open to what could be, has to be viewed as a deficit. Some will argue that it is better to stay with the tried-and-true rather than take a chance on that which is uncertain. But isn't that how all great things have been discovered—by an individual or organization who was willing to challenge the status quo and offer up new ways of considering an accepted practice or approach? The institution has to be encouraged to indulge in this curiosity with a no-judgment mindset if initiatives fail. Initiatives will fail and that has to be expected and welcomed.

At Kirkwood, we just recently developed an Innovation Fund that supports new initiatives employees believe can help the institution innovate and better support our students. While Kirkwood has always been innovative—it has held a board seat on the 19-member League for Innovation in the Community College since 1987—formalizing a defined process had yet to happen at Kirkwood. Innovation ideas sprang up from all directions, and the institution funded what it could. We decided that formalizing the process and allowing for greater input could possibly help us even more in our quest to continue our innovative spirit.

We launched the initiative in 2020 with a FY 2021 implementation plan. In the first year, we received 23 proposals for over $900,000. We were genuinely appreciative of the level of curiosity and innovative ideas that existed within our institution, and we were astonished at the number of applications in the first year of this program. Each project has to complete an outcome assessment tool, and we know that some of the projects will not be successful, and that will be okay. From a leadership perspective, I think it's safe to say that all of us have learned some of our greatest and hardest lessons through failure. What we also know is that each failure leads us a little closer to that which is going to be a success.

WHAT CAN A CULTURE OF EXCELLENCE MEAN FOR COMMUNITY COLLEGES?

Institutions with cultures of excellence don't just happen. They have to be cultivated and there has to be a clear understanding of the complexities of institutional culture and how to foster and work within it. It takes time for an institution to develop the assumptions, norms, and behaviors that will lead it to excellence. Employees play a significant role in developing that culture and having the right employees in the right positions across the organization is essential to their success and ultimately the institution's success. There also has to be an unrelenting focus on the institution's data in order to understand the insights that the data can provide. It is only through digging into and questioning the data that the institution will be able to tease out the implications and meanings that are not so visible from only the numbers.

An unwavering commitment to process improvement is the least glamorous part of creating an institution of excellence, but it is essential. It is, perhaps, the most important aspect to supporting the overall operation of the college. And lastly, creating and maintaining an institutional curiosity that allows employees to explore and consider new ways of doing things really provides the final piece to developing a culture of excellence. If any of these components is missing, I believe an institution can have an adequate culture and can, perhaps, be top performing for a while. However, to build an enduring culture of excellence for today's community colleges, we must recognize and embrace all of the components.

There are no shortcuts, but once an institution arrives at excellence, it seldom wants to go in another direction. Kirkwood can never go back to being an average institution. That is simply not how the college identifies, thinks, or behaves, and it's definitely not how it approaches the way it provides the student experience. The beauty of developing this culture is that it takes on its own momentum, and as Collins (2001) stated, "In building a great company or social sector enterprise, there is no single defining action, no grand program, no one killer innovation, no solitary lucky break, no miracle moment. Rather, the process resembles relentlessly pushing a giant, heavy flywheel, turn upon turn, building momentum until a point of breakthrough, and beyond." Once an institution's flywheel has been set in motion, it can continue to sustain an institution's momentum for excellence.

REFERENCES

Collins, J. (2001, October). *Good to great.* Fast Company. https://www.jimcollins.com/article_topics/articles/good-to-great.html#articletop.

Kirkwood Community College. (2021). Kirkwood Community College: Strategic plan, FY2021–2023. https://www.kirkwood.edu/_files/pdf/institutional-effectiveness/kirkwood-strategic-plan-fy2021-2023.pdf.

Marcus, J. (2019, October 19). Radical survival strategies for struggling colleges. *New York Times.* https://www.nytimes.com/2019/10/10/education/learning/colleges-survival-strategies.html.

Roark, I. (2018, October 5). The evolving world of community colleges: Market position, competition and the future. *The EvoLLLution.* https://evolllution.com/revenue-streams/workforce_development/the-evolving-world-of-community-colleges-market-position-competition-and-the-future.

Schein, E. H. (1990, February). Organizational culture. *American Psychologist, 45*(2), 109–119. http://erlanbakiev.weebly.com/uploads/1/0/8/3/10833829/schein_1990_organizational_culture.pdf.

VOA Student Union. (2019, December 3). *US college leaders see too much competition ahead.* https://www.voanews.com/student-union/us-college-leaders-see-too-much-competition-ahead.

Chapter Fifteen

The Beliefs Agenda

An Extraordinary New Paradigm for College Completion

Lee Ann Nutt

BELIEFS ARE POWERFUL

Community colleges attract some of the grittiest students of any sector of American higher education. These students succeed while raising children (often as single parents), working multiple jobs, and coping with food and housing insecurities. Despite these complex challenges, they maintain high grade point averages, rarely miss a class, and submit assignments by the stated deadline. However, community colleges also attract two other general categories of students: (1) those who secretly wonder if they are "college material," and (2) those who are unprepared to cope with adversity and being challenged. Students in these categories likely struggle to finish an assignment, a course, and a semester.

Beliefs students hold about college, about what it takes to be successful, and about themselves are what differentiates the students described above. Beliefs are powerful catalysts. They drive actions and motivate outcomes. Constructive, productive, healthy beliefs compel people to take actions that result in amazing accomplishments. Beliefs are also powerful inhibitors. Destructive, harmful, unhealthy beliefs can be paralytic, preventing someone from accomplishing anything, or propelling them to engage in behaviors leading to failure.

Beliefs are indeed powerful, and they are also underestimated and undervalued in the national effort to improve college completion rates, commonly referred to as the Completion Agenda. For almost a decade, research-based foundations, professional associations, and community colleges have invested millions of dollars and thousands of hours focused on those things over which colleges have the most control—policies, processes, practices, programs, and pathways. However, the Completion Agenda does not adequately address the most important component: people. It is an incomplete agenda.

Although the Completion Agenda has fallen short of its goals of drastically improving college completion rates, the efforts have been tremendously valuable. Community colleges, which have a legal obligation and moral responsibility to be the best institutions they can be, are better as a result. However, they must also acknowledge two fundamental realities: (1) perfect policies, practices, programs, and pathways are impossible to attain and sustain, and (2) if a student does not believe they belong, believes they are incapable of learning, or doesn't believe in being challenged or accepting academic supports, it won't matter how good the college is at what it does.

It is time to shift the community college culture from the Completion Agenda to the Beliefs Agenda. The mission of the Beliefs Agenda is to equip more students not only to finish college, but also to have the capacity to overcome adversity, cope with challenges, and finish what they start. At the core, the Beliefs Agenda acknowledges that what students believe determines why some finish strong despite the obstacles they face, and why some students cannot finish anything, including an assignment.

Community colleges must no longer overlook, ignore, or underestimate beliefs students hold. Beliefs are fundamental to the ultimate outcomes of student success initiatives. The wrong beliefs, even in the right environment, will prevent full achievement of desired results. The right beliefs about college, about what it takes to be successful, and about themselves will propel students to complete college and succeed in life.

WHY ARE BELIEFS IMPORTANT?

Two key facts support shifting the culture from the Completion Agenda to the Beliefs Agenda: (1) student completion rates for community college have improved only slightly despite intense effort and investment over the past decade, and (2) indications of students' inability to function effectively in a higher education environment are growing.

Data reported by National Student Clearinghouse Research Center (NSCRC) in its *Signature 18 Report, Completing College 2019 National Report* (Shapiro et al., 2019) indicated 2.3 million people entered postsecondary education for the first time in the fall 2013 across all institution types (public 4-year, public 2-year, private nonprofit 4-year, and private for-profit 4 year). Six years later, 59.7% (1.4 million students) completed at some institution in the United States (not necessarily where they started). This figure is the highest overall combined completion rate ever achieved. The lowest combined completion rate since 2006 was 52.9%. While this combined rate is movement in the right direction, the fact that 40% of students do not complete a degree in 6 years means there is more room for improvement (Shapiro et al., 2019).

While overall completion rates have slowly improved when all institution types are combined, students starting at community colleges consistently have the lowest completion rates of students who start at other types of American higher education institutions. Only private, for-profit, 4-year institutions have had a lower completion rate than community colleges. The completion rate for the fall 2013 cohort of starters in this type of institution surpassed community colleges. According to the same NSCRC report, the 6-year completion rate for the 2013 cohort of entering students was 40.8%, which is also the highest completion rate ever achieved (Shapiro et al., 2019). However, the completion trend line has been basically flat since 2006. Community college completion increases should be significantly higher given the immense effort to improve completion rates for the past decade.

In addition to having the lowest completion rate, 43.2% of the fall 2013 cohort of students starting at a community college are no longer enrolled in any institution. This percentage has been trending slightly downward, which can be interpreted as a good sign. Only private, for-profit, 4-year institutions have a higher percentage of students in this category at 46.2%. However, the percentage of students no longer enrolled at public and private 4-year institutions is much smaller, 21.9% and 15.9% respectively (Shapiro et al., 2019).

Further evidence of the need for the Beliefs Agenda are the increasing mental and emotional health issues of students. Research indicates that anxiety, depression, and crippling disengagement are prevalent among students. These issues manifest as a decline in emotional readiness for college, fear of failure, the need for constant reassurance, lack of ownership for learning, and many other detrimental behaviors.

According to the fall 2017 American College Health Association (ACHA) *National College Health Assessment* (ACHA, 2018), 60.9% of college students felt "overwhelming anxiety" within the last 12 months, 67.3% felt very sad, 51.7% felt things were hopeless, and 39.3% felt so depressed "it was difficult to function." Additionally, 86.5% felt overwhelmed by all they had to do (ACHA, 2018). Similarly, Peter Gray (2015), a research professor at Boston College, shared in "Declining Student Resilience: A Serious Problem for Colleges" that students are afraid to fail, they do not take risks, and they need to be certain about things. For many of them, failure is catastrophic and unacceptable.

WHAT ARE THE COMPONENTS OF THE BELIEFS AGENDA?

The Beliefs Agenda provides a new model for improving completion rates and empowering students to function effectively in higher education. To institute the Beliefs Agenda, community colleges must engage in difficult work. They must (1) establish a set of desirable beliefs students need to hold; (2) identify beliefs students actually hold; and (3) utilize Strategic Experience Management to influence the development of desirable beliefs and outcomes.

Establishing a Set of Desirable Beliefs

Three strategies can be used to establish a set of desirable beliefs: (1) draw on our own experiences as educators, (2) apply existing research about student beliefs, and (3) conduct new research to validate theories about student beliefs. To draw on our own experiences at the local level, we need to ensure that the process of establishing desirable beliefs is cross-functional and meaningful. Gathering input from a variety of perspectives (including students) ensures a comprehensive approach, engages people in creative collaboration, and will help institutionalize and deepen faculty and staff commitment to the effort.

At the national level, establishing a set of desirable student beliefs should also become part of the student success narrative. Doing so will help shift existing deficit narrative tendencies to a more positive asset-based narrative. Higher education graduate programs, professional associations, and policymakers can incorporate the development of desirable student beliefs into their own contexts and agendas as well.

Existing research about student efficacy and agency, often referred to as non-cognitive factors, abounds. Markle and O'Banion (2014) summarized findings of five meta-analytic studies conducted since 2004 on non-cognitive factors. They state that these studies have conclusively demonstrated three important points about non-cognitive, affective factors: (1) non-cognitive factors are stronger predictors of retention than high school grade point average and test scores (which are measures of cognitive abilities), (2) they predict student success, and (3) their predictive ability is significant.

While existing research on non-cognitive factors is prevalent, more research is needed on student beliefs. This is a key opportunity for community college researchers, leaders, and policy makers to contribute to the literature. We need to research and validate the set of desirable beliefs that contribute most to student success.

Identifying Beliefs Students Actually Hold

Every single student shows up with preexisting beliefs based on their prior experiences. However, it is highly probable that students are not conscious of their beliefs or their belief bias, which is easily, subconsciously, and unintentionally confirmed. Formal and informal mechanisms can be used to identify what students currently believe.

Formal means, such as the Ebberly Center Survey of Student Learning Beliefs and Behaviors, can be used to gather information on student beliefs on a large scale. Developing additional formal means of collecting and identifying student beliefs is an opportunity in higher education.

Informal means can be used to identify beliefs on an individual level. This kind of research can be intensely personal. Intentionally building trusting relationships with students, taking time to get to know them, and just asking them what they believe are examples of informal ways of identifying beliefs.

Utilize Strategic Experience Management

Strategic Experience Management (SEM) is the intentional creation and alignment of experiences with desirable student beliefs. College faculty and staff are always creating experiences for students. The absence of intentional alignment to a set of desired beliefs can lead to the unintentional perpetuation of debilitating beliefs. Faculty and staff are likely unaware this is happening. Therefore, SEM requires a culture of accountability and commitment as every person in the college plays a role in experience creation.

How Does the Beliefs Agenda Work?

The Beliefs Agenda requires colleges to expand the completion narrative to include student beliefs. As such, a set of desirable beliefs students need to hold should be developed for each of the following three categories: (1) beliefs about college, (2) beliefs about what it takes to be successful, and (3) beliefs about themselves. Classifying a set of desirable beliefs is essential; however, so is identifying and acknowledging beliefs students actually hold. It is likely the two sets of beliefs do not align. Finally, to make a real difference, the Beliefs Agenda must go beyond identifying desired and actual beliefs. The essence of the Beliefs Agenda is the process of *intentionally managing* the student experience so the desired beliefs are formed.

Establish a Set of Desirable Beliefs About College

Beliefs students hold about an individual institution will be unique for each college, depending on location, type, size, mission, demographics, and a litany of other possible variables. For instance, a local community college may want students to form beliefs around each of the following: (1) afford-ability, (2) caring and competent faculty and staff, (3) programs leading to good paying jobs, (4) courses transferring to 4-year universities, (5) diversity of the student body, (6) equitable opportunities for everyone, and (7) prepar-ing students for life after college.

Establish a Set of Desirable Beliefs About What It Takes to Be Successful in College

GRIT—an acronym for Growth, Resilience, Instinct, and Tenacity—pro-vides an excellent framework to develop a set of desirable beliefs about what it takes to be successful in college. *GRIT* is defined as "your capacity to dig deep, to do whatever it takes—especially struggle, sacrifice, even suffer—to achieve your most worthy goals" (Stoltz, 2014). Stolz defines the compo-nents of GRIT include:

- Growth: "your propensity to seek and consider new ideas, additional alter-natives, different approaches, and fresh perspectives";
- Resilience: "your capacity to respond constructively to and ideally make good use of all kinds of adversity";
- Instinct: "your gut level capacity to pursue the right goals in the best and smartest ways"; and
- Tenacity: "the degree to which you persist, commit to, stick with, and relentlessly work at whatever you choose to achieve" (p. 20).

Community colleges should consider a wide range of desirable beliefs about what it takes to be successful in college, using GRIT as a framework. A key part of the Beliefs Agenda solution is further research, development, and institutionalization of these concepts framed around significant quantities of high-quality GRIT. The list was identified through a review of the literature on adversity, grit, and mindset, as well as personal and professional experi-ences. While the list below is not comprehensive, it provides a sampling of beliefs about what it takes to succeed in college.

Growth: mindsets that seek fresh ideas, perspectives, and information.

- Looking at a problem from a different perspective can help illuminate a solution.
- Seeking help is a sign of strength.
- Using academic support resources makes a difference.
- Understand that constructive feedback is useful.
- Know it is okay to stop doing something that is not working and begin trying a different approach.

Resilience: responding constructively to and being strengthened by adversity.

- Pursuing a worthy goal takes time and effort.
- Acknowledge that challenges are normal.
- Know that challenges can be overcome.
- See that setbacks are precursors to progress.
- Accept that failure is a friend to be embraced, not an enemy to be avoided.

Instinct: reassessing, rerouting, and readjusting pursuits and approaches.

- Pursuing my goals should be done in a way that has a positive impact on myself and others.
- Spending purposeful, quality time on learning is more important than quantity of time on task.
- Adjust the approach if it is clear that improvement is not occurring.
- Understand that purposeful practice leads to better outcomes.

Tenacity: sticking to and relentlessly pursuing a chosen worthy goal.

- Accept that hard work matters more than talent.
- Having a passion for a worthy goal affects success more than intelligence.
- Struggling, sacrificing, and sometimes suffering are necessary to achieve goals.
- Trying a new approach when things get hard, reevaluating the goal, and asking for help will help me remain committed.

Establish Desirable Beliefs About Themselves

Beliefs students hold about themselves are the most powerful and have the greatest potential to affect desired results. Much historical research and evidence exists confirming the direct and predictive relationship between self-efficacy beliefs and student academic performance. According to Bandura's (1986) social cognitive theory, how people behave can often be better predicted by the beliefs they hold about their capabilities than by what they are actually capable of accomplishing.

Students with high self-efficacy, or strong beliefs about self, are confident in their competence and expect they will perform well in school. They approach difficult tasks as challenges to be mastered, show greater interest and deeper engagement in activities, and set challenging goals and sustain efforts over time. They also bounce back from setbacks and failures that are attributed to insufficient effort or lack of skills that are attainable. If all students had high self-efficacy beliefs, the Completion Agenda would be irrelevant.

Community colleges should consider a wide range of desirable beliefs framed around GRIT, including the samples listed below. As above, this list was identified through a review of the literature on adversity, grit, and mindset as well as personal and professional experiences.

Growth: mindsets that seek fresh ideas, perspectives, and information.

- I can learn.
- Intelligence can be developed.
- Struggling to understand something means learning is occurring.

Resilience: responding constructively to, and being strengthened by, adversity.

- Learning is a process, and sometimes it is difficult.
- Past experiences and current circumstances do not dictate my future potential.
- I create my own destiny.
- I am not entitled to anything, but I can achieve success when I put forth the effort.

Instinct: reassessing, rerouting, and readjusting pursuits and approaches.

- I belong in college.
- I am responsible for my own learning.
- Others want me to be successful.
- Using academic support resources is a sign of strength.
- I am worthy of success.

Tenacity: sticking to and relentless pursuing a chosen worthy goal.

- With hard work and effort, my potential is unknown and unlimited.
- When I cannot give my best effort, I can still give it all I can.
- Having to deal with imperfect people and less-than-ideal situations is a fact of life.

Identify Beliefs Students Actually Hold

In addition to establishing desirable beliefs, it is necessary to know what our students actually believe. By knowing this, we can do more to help them succeed beyond putting them on a pathway or imposing a mandatory policy on them.

Formal measures can be used to gather data about student beliefs. A survey could be given or colleges could create their own means for gathering this data. It is recommended these measures be given to students (and the results shared) early in their experience at the college—such as in a student success course or in orientation. Advisors can also work with the results.

Helping students discover their beliefs is essential for the student and the institution as increased self-awareness alone can be transformative. This awareness can help students choose better behaviors and achieve better outcomes. Likewise, knowing what students believe can inform and influence institutional policy and process as well as personal interactions.

STRATEGIC EXPERIENCE MANAGEMENT

Past and present experiences drive beliefs students hold. Experiences will either perpetuate currently held beliefs (good and bad) or lead to the adoption of new beliefs (good and bad). Therefore, colleges must be thoughtful and intentional about creating experiences to foster desirable student beliefs. Colleges must also bravely eliminate experiences that detract from their desired outcomes.

Unintentional experiences occur all the time. Employees can be busy, overworked, and simply have bad days in the office (or classroom) as they interact with students. However, experiences create beliefs people hold and some detract from successful accomplishment of desired student and college results. Being very intentional about creating the right experiences to form the right beliefs and actions requires structure, which Strategic Experience Management can provide.

Colleges must address three main categories of experiences: (1) connections, (2) classrooms, and (3) care. Experiences in each of these categories drive what students believe about college, about what it takes to be successful in college, and about themselves.

Connections encompass all the ways that students interface with the college. For example, connections include social media, communications, outreach efforts, application and registration processes, financial aid policies, onboarding and orientation, and student life involvement opportunities. Colleges must evaluate their connection experiences to make certain they perpetuate the desired beliefs we need students to hold and to avoid affirming debilitating beliefs.

Classroom experiences encompass teaching, learning, course delivery modes, programs, and curriculum. What happens in the classroom is powerful. An empowering interpersonal teacher-student relationship is known to make an incredible impact on positive self-efficacy beliefs.

Care. The student experience extends beyond the classroom. Academic and support services should also be included in the effort to develop healthy student beliefs. These services fall into the "care" category. How well we care for students can drive beliefs about what it takes to be successful in college. Library, tutoring services, counseling, disability services, registration, advising—all can identify how these services foster desirable student beliefs.

BECOMING EXTRAORDINARY COMMUNITY COLLEGES

Excellent community colleges, according to Josh Wyner (2014), author of *What Excellent Community Colleges Do: Preparing All Students for Success*, achieve progress on four Aspen Prize critical outcomes:

1. Completion: Students earn associate degrees and other credentials while in community college, and bachelor's degrees if they transfer.
2. Equity: Colleges ensure equitable outcomes for minority and low-income students, and others often underserved.
3. Learning: Colleges set expectations for what students should learn, measure learning, and use that information to improve.
4. Labor market: Graduates get well-paying jobs.

These stated outcomes are very important and should be baseline for all community colleges. However, community colleges can be more than excellent. They can be extraordinary.

Extraordinary community colleges embody the ideals of excellent institutions as just described, but that is not all. Extraordinary community colleges purposefully help students develop beliefs that will empower them to deal successfully with daily challenges, fear less, achieve more, and overcome major adversity. Extraordinary community colleges transform talent into achievement, convert potential into capacity, and increase human capitalization. They include student beliefs in the narrative and activity associated with college completion. They strive for extraordinary results and hold the following beliefs:

- All students can succeed if they hold desirable beliefs about college, about what it takes to be successful, and about themselves.
- Finishing a degree or certificate is important, but equipping students for life after college matters more.
- Colleges have a responsibility to provide the best experiences possible for student learning and personal development. However, student success matters more than institutional success.
- The college experience should be more than transactional. The college experience should be transformational.

In addition to the above institutional beliefs, beliefs faculty and staff hold about students, about learning, and about themselves is also critical to achieving better completion results. The short list below is a starting point for more research and discussion:

- Talent is prevalent among students, but it is not sufficient without high-quality GRIT.
- High-quality GRIT enables students to compensate for adversity, disadvantage, and perceived shortcomings.
- High-quality GRIT enables students to compensate for lack of adversity, advantage, and perceived virtues.
- Learning is a process, challenges are normal, and transformation takes time.
- Everyone plays a significant role in creating experiences for students that lead to beliefs that drive actions for desired results.

How truly amazing it would be if everyone in a college held these beliefs and acted on these beliefs. It is highly probable that many people working in community colleges today already hold beliefs aligned to student success and development of GRIT. To intentionally state, nurture, and align these beliefs on a collective scale, however, would be such a huge difference maker and could produce extraordinary results.

What are extraordinary results? Changed beliefs. Imagine students who showed up not believing they belonged in college finishing strong and accomplishing great things in life. Imagine students who believed they were entitled to a degree, who did not take personal responsibility, and did not know how to work through adversity—who now accept accountability, work hard, and know how to overcome challenges and adversity. Imagine students who succeed and learn how to improve the quality of their GRIT.

What are extraordinary results? Finishers. Students will be equipped to do more than just progress down a pathway. They will develop agency and hope. Imagine a nation of students who want to finish and choose to finish because the choice is ultimately theirs to make. They choose what to finish, if they finish, and how they finish. And they finish everything.

Through the Beliefs Agenda, community colleges can help students discover what they believe about college, what it takes to be successful in college, and how they can develop their best selves. Beyond discovery, application of the Beliefs Agenda can equip students to develop desirable beliefs needed to function effectively in higher education and achieve their desired results. Community colleges must create meaningful, intentional, thoughtful experiences that lead to the development of healthy, constructive beliefs about working hard, being resilient, overcoming challenges and thriving through adversity. Why? College is hard. Life is harder.

MOVING THE BELIEFS AGENDA FORWARD . . . WITH GRIT

Access to higher education defines the American community college. That completion rates are now one of the biggest challenges facing community colleges is likely an unintended consequence of expanded access. For the past decade, the Completion Agenda united the nation's community colleges as they collectively endeavored to fix the quitting problem. Because of these efforts, community colleges are better. Some have even become exceptional. Despite major improvements in community colleges, there have only been minor improvements in completion rates.

It is time to reflect, reroute, and adjust the collective approach from the Completion Agenda to the Beliefs Agenda. The college completion rate is still a valid measure of student success for the Beliefs Agenda, Likewise, key performance indicators such as persistence from one semester to the next and overall success in a course are also valid measures. Colleges should continue to track these. Retention, persistence, and degree completion should increase as a measure of the higher aims of the Beliefs Agenda. These will be indicators that measure effectiveness of experiences created for students, but they will no longer be the ultimate goal.

The ultimate goal is for students to acquire the beliefs and abilities to finish well, deal with normal challenges of daily living, and use their adversity to fuel their achievement. As such, access and completion do not have to continue to move in opposite directions. Colleges can change the inverse relationship between access and completion through the Beliefs Agenda, which has the potential to change higher education in tremendous ways. To realize its full potential, brave leaders, governing boards, teachers, and staff themselves must be willing to exhibit significant quantities of high-quality GRIT.

They must demonstrate *growth* by seeking and considering new ideas, additional alternatives, different approaches, and fresh perspectives about student success and completion. They must be *resilient* by constructively responding to and adjusting their student completion and success efforts. They must improve their *instinct* and pursue the right goal, which is the lifelong success of students, not just increased college completion rates. They must continue to exhibit *tenacity* in their missional pursuit of transforming lives and turning adversity into achievement. To demonstrate the required GRIT starts with believing in the importance of the Beliefs Agenda and embracing the work as a calling. Additionally, community colleges must demonstrate compassion, commitment, and proficiency:

- Compassion means treating students as human beings first. It means providing access for all, being committed to diversity, equity, and inclusion. It means caring for students.

- Commitment means going "all in" for students. It means having an emotional commitment, attachment, identification, and involvement with students.
- Proficiency means being good at what we do, organizationally and personally.

Community college students' challenges and disadvantages are not deficits to ignore or wish away. Instead, they are foundational building blocks for human capitalization. They may even be the very force that enables students to complete college and excel in the marketplace and in life.

Knowing, nurturing, and fostering beliefs is the work of extraordinary student-ready colleges who commit to the Beliefs Agenda. This difficult work will have a dramatic impact on student completion rates and influence overall life success.

REFERENCES

American College Health Association. (2018). *American College Health Association: National college health assessment II: University of Southern California executive summary fall 2017.* American College Health Association.

Bandura, A. (1986). *Social foundations of thought and action.* Cambridge University Press.

Gray, P. (2015, September 22). Declining student resilience: A serious problem for colleges. *Psychology Today.* https://www.psychologytoday.com/us/blog/freedom-learn/201509/declining-student-resilience-serious-problem-colleges.

Markle, R., & O'Banion, T. (2014, November). Assessing affective factors to improve retention and completion. *Learning Abstracts, 17*(11). https://www.league.org/sites/default/files/private_data/imported/occasional_papers/2014_11_Learning%20Abstracts_Assessing AffectiveFactors.pdf.

Shapiro, D., Ryu, M., Huie, F., Liu, Q., and Zheng, Y. (2019, December). *Completing college 2019 national report* [Signature Report 18]. National Student Clearinghouse Research Center.

Stoltz, P. G. (2014). *GRIT: The new science of what it takes to persevere, flourish, succeed.* Climb Strong Press.

Wyner, J. W. (2014). *What excellent community colleges do: Preparing all students for success.* Harvard Education Press.

Afterword

Sandra J. Balkema

A VISION FOR APPLIED RESEARCH AND SOLUTIONS

From its initial conception, the DCCL program was designed to be relevant, practical, and applied. Over the 10 years of the program's existence, these concepts have remained at the center of the program's vision.

When the DCCL program welcomed its first students in 2010, we often joked that we were "putting the wheels on the bus as it traveled down the highway." While all of the major pieces were in place—curriculum, faculty, advisory board, and leadership team—many of the day-to-day processes needed to be fleshed out as we, and our new students, moved forward.

One of these pieces was taking the vision for DCCL research and dissertations and putting it into practice. Given the emphasis on relevance, DCCL learners were encouraged from the start to conduct research that would enhance and advance the effectiveness of their colleges.

COURSES AND FACULTY SUPPORTING THE PROCESS

The DCCL program structure—and its faculty—are key components of the research vision. DCCL is built with an integrated dissertation process: Instead of researching and writing the dissertation after all coursework is completed, DCCL students start thinking about their dissertations from the very first day, using their coursework, academic reading, and interactions with experts from the field as they explore research needs and opportunities.

Two other program features also had significant impact on DCCL dissertations and processes. First, as an EdD program, DCCL stresses practical, application-based work in courses and in dissertation research. Second, our faculty are working professionals—they are senior leaders in community colleges across the country. Their roles as leaders are vital, as they bring their expertise to our students. They aren't academics who "study" community colleges; they lead them. Through their readings and assignments, DCCL students learn from these experts, identifying significant research needs, applying appropriate data to institutional problems, and crafting innovative ways of viewing problems and solutions.

DCCL prepares future leaders through an "inquiry-based, problem-solving, action-oriented approach" (Ferris State University, n.d.). The program's focus was driven in part by a 2005 Lumina Foundation report (Bailey & Alfonso, 2005) that stressed the importance of data-driven decision-making in community college research and calling for institutions to create and maintain "a culture of evidence." The program also embraced Alicia C. Dowd's (2005) response to that report, which emphasized that the goal should be "a culture of inquiry, one in which data move out of the limelight, and practitioners move to center stage." In that article, Dowd (2005) identified three key practices that a culture of inquiry must include:

- Work to identify and address problems by purposefully analyzing data about student learning and progress.
- Engage in sustained professional development and dialogue about barriers to student achievement.
- Have the capacity for insightful questioning of evidence and informed interpretation of results. (p. 2)

A CULTURE OF EVIDENCE AND
PRACTITIONER-FOCUSED RESEARCH

Many educational researchers in the early 2000s stressed the importance and value of developing a "culture of evidence" in our institutions and valuing "practitioner" research, including the Achieving the Dream initiative, whose research publication series was titled "The Culture of Evidence Series." Estela Mara Bensimon (2007), in her presidential address at the Center for Urban Education, University of Southern California, was one of the first of these researchers who stressed moving research into the hands of practitioners:

> If, as scholars of higher education, we wish to produce knowledge to improve student success, we cannot ignore that practitioners play a significant role. More specifically, if our goal is to do scholarship that makes a difference in the lives of students whom higher education has been least successful in educating (e.g., racially marginalized groups and the poor), we have to expand the scholarship on student success and take into account the influence of practitioners— positively and negatively. (p. 445)

It is enlightening to compare the vision for practitioner-based research that dominated the landscape at this time with the 1977 policy statement from the Council of Graduate Schools that was still dominant in 2000: "The doctoral program is designed to prepare a student for a lifetime of intellectual inquiry that manifests itself in creative scholarship and research" (p. 1).

Bensimon and colleagues (2004), in fact, made an earlier argument for practitioner-based research and compared traditional and practitioner-as-researcher models:

> The traditional model of research production calls for a division of labor between the manufacturers of research findings (researcher) and the consumers of those findings (practitioner). In the traditional research model, the researcher defines the problem to be studied, selects the appropriate methods, collects data, interprets them, and reports the findings. . . . Consequently, the knowledge obtained through research tends to remain unnoticed and unused by those for whom it was intended. (pp. 105–106)

The DCCL program began, then, grounded on this practical, application-focused research at center stage. DCCL students were encouraged to study their own institutions, to identify critical issues, to develop solutions that would move their institution forward, but also to contribute to the collective knowledge about community college challenges, helping all to advance and improve.

In that same vein, Ferris's DCCL program was among the first in the nation to encourage and support the product dissertation. In developing their dissertation research plans, while many of our DCCL students embraced traditional data-driven research approaches for understanding institutional and academic issues, many others found creating solutions—such as training programs, manuals and guidebooks, or resource materials—an effective contribution. Both groups saw their research as a valuable method and significant avenue for "giving back" to their institutions—and their profession.

THIS BOOK IS EVIDENCE

The chapters collected in this volume were written by DCCL graduates, students, and faculty. The work described here is evidence of the "culture of evidence" that is central to the DCCL culture. Not only must effective leaders use data as the foundation for their decision-making, but they must also encourage and support the exploratory, ever-questioning mindset of a researcher. Whether they are responding to immediate, crisis-driven events—such as the COVID-19 pandemic's effects on education in spring 2020—or seeking to understand a long-standing deeply ingrained issue—such as racial injustice and ethnic disparities in education—effective leaders must rely on evidence. These chapters describe institutional initiatives, programs, and ideas that are all grounded in a belief that individuals can effect change and can make a difference. This belief is, in a way, a byproduct or "reward" of a strong culture of evidence; as Vanessa S. Morest (2019) wrote, "The reward for establishing a culture of evidence is reflective practice" (p. 26).

Ten years of DCCL dissertations reflect the beginnings of this reflective practice. Our completed dissertations number over 125, on topics extending from issues related to student success and effective teaching and learning, to organizational culture and leadership development. Research into student success programming is by far the largest group and strongest focus of DCCL dissertations, reflecting our students' commitment to developing, assessing, and improving institutional efforts to improve student lives through access to education. Product-based dissertations also comprise a significant percentage of our students' work, nearly 25%, including new advising models, FYE course experiences, programs to assess prior learning, and mid-level leadership-development training. Another powerful group of dissertations examines the career paths, experiences, and voices of community college leaders and community college students. These studies capture the voices of community college's past and future, providing a valuable historical record and vital leadership lessons.

Over the past 10 years, we have built a program that instills a culture of learning and contributes to scholarship for application. DCCL dissertation research—and the ongoing work of our graduates in their institutions—holds great promise for maximizing our impact on students, colleges, and communities across the nation. DCCL is committed to this same philosophy and is proud of the contributions our students' dissertations—and their ongoing research—have contributed to the conversation.

REFERENCES

Bailey, T., & Alfonso, M. (2005). *Paths to persistence: An analysis of research on program effectiveness at community colleges.* Lumina Foundation for Education.

Bensimon, E. M. (2007). The underestimated significance of practitioner knowledge in the scholarship on student success. *The Review of Higher Education, 30*(4), 441–469.

Bensimon, E. M., Polkinghorne, D. E., Bauman, G. L., & Pena, E. V. (2004, January). Doing research that makes a difference. *The Journal of Higher Education, 75*(1), 104–126.

Council of Graduate Schools in the United States. (1977). *The doctor of philosophy degree. A policy statement.* Cited in Barger, R. R., & Duncan. J. K. (1982, January–February). Cultivating creative endeavor in doctoral research. *The Journal of Higher Education, 53*(1), 1–31.

Dowd, A. C. (2005). *Data don't drive: Building a practitioner-driven culture of inquiry to assess community college performance.* Lumina Foundation for Education.

Ferris State University. (n.d.). *About DCCL.* Retrieved January 11, 2021, from https://www.ferris.edu/HTMLS/administration/academicaffairs/extendedinternational/ccleadership/AboutDCCL.htm.

Morest, V. S. (2009, Fall). Accountability, accreditation, and continuous improvement: Building a culture of evidence. *New Directions for Institutional Research, 143*, 17–27.

Appendix

DCCL graduates represent:
28 states
103 colleges

DCCL graduates reach over 1.6 million students

leadership development transition
adjunct faculty non-traditional
globalization STEM perceptions collaboration
advising Latinx URM leadership
persistence how-to barriers
student services placement
community college program
innovation completion
veterans FYE motivation
mentoring retention diversity
apprenticeships best practices accessibility

| Regional Impact | Institutional Impact | Student Impact | Impact on Research and Practice |

DCCL graduates serve CCs in many roles.

Presidents – 3%
Vice Presidents – 14%
Directors and Deans – 37%
Faculty – 24%
Coordinators, Advisers, Technologists – 22%

DCCL graduates' research provides data and solutions reaching all areas of higher education.

| The DCCL Program | DCCL Faculty |

Cohort Model → 3 Year Completion → Applied Focus

Created for leaders of mission-driven, 21st-century community colleges.

150 years of President experience
125 years of VP experience
90 years of Dean experience

DCCL courses are taught by experienced college leaders, teaching by example.

FERRIS STATE UNIVERSITY

DOCTORATE IN COMMUNITY
COLLEGE LEADERSHIP
CELEBRATING TEN YEARS

Author created (DCCL program/commissioned art)

About the Editors and Contributors

ABOUT THE EDITORS

Sandra J. Balkema, PhD, is the dissertation director for the DCCL program. In this role, she supports the graduate students throughout their dissertation journeys, from identifying research topics and approaches and selecting a dissertation chair and mentor, to defense and subsequent publishing of the final dissertation.

Roberta C. Teahen, PhD, is the director for the DCCL program and serves as a faculty member and dissertation advisor. Dr. Teahen has served in multiple faculty and leadership roles at a community college and at Ferris, where she was most recently associate provost. She is a long-time champion of community colleges and takes special pride in mentoring others and encouraging innovation and excellence in higher education.

ABOUT THE CONTRIBUTORS

Carmen Allen, EdD, is a professor at Lincoln Land Community College (Illinois) and an alumnus of cohort 5 of the DCCL program. With a focus on enhanced teaching and learning techniques, she uses early intervention tactics, evaluation of student data, and personalized communication approaches. These techniques have significantly improved her relationships with students and increased her student retention and completion rates.

Armando Burciaga, EdD, a graduate of DCCL cohort 7, is the director of TRIO Student Support Services at Red Rocks Community College (Colorado). He serves on numerous committees that include the reaccreditation of the college, institutional strategic planning committee, and enrollment management. As a first-generation student, Armando champions a welcoming and inclusive environment for students unfamiliar to higher education.

Michael A. Couch II, EdD, a graduate of DCCL cohort 7, currently serves as the director of financial aid outreach at Ivy Tech Community College (Indiana). He also is an adjunct professor at Indiana State University in the Educational Administration doctoral program. He engages in research, presentations, and critical conversations about college affordability, enrollment management, leadership assessments, leadership experiences of African American males, and minority male initiatives.

Naomi DeWinter, EdD, is a graduate of DCCL cohort 1, serves on the DCCL National Advisory Board, and is an adjunct faculty member. After working at a community college in Michigan for many years, Naomi and her family moved to serve a community college in Muscatine, Iowa, part of the Eastern Iowa Community Colleges. As president, she works to connect the college with the community, increase minority completion rates, and improve access to college through community partnerships.

Abdel-Moaty M. Fayek, EdD, graduate of DCCL cohort 6, is the dean of business, computer science, and applied technologies at De Anza Community College (California). He has served higher education in several roles, including interim vice president of workforce development and institutional advancement at Foothill College; and professor, chair, and graduate advisor at California State University, Chico. He is an experienced, visionary leader with a keen sense for strategy and forward thinking and a passion for STEM careers and the high-tech industry.

Cheryl M. Hagen, EdD, is a graduate of cohort 5, and currently serves as vice president and chief student affairs officer at Schoolcraft College in Livonia, Michigan. A tireless advocate for students, Dr. Hagen believes that a supportive campus climate makes for a safer campus and is continually looking for ways to improve the student experience from first contact through graduation.

Daniel Herbst, EdD, graduate of DCCL cohort 4, is the vice president of student affairs at Henry Ford College in Dearborn, Michigan. In this role, Dan collaborates with all student affairs departments and campus safety. He is a peer reviewer for the Higher Learning Commission and a former president of the National Council on Student Development.

Kris Hoffhines, EdD, a graduate of DCCL's Harper College cohort, is the associate dean of advising services at Harper College (Illinois). In addition to leading a large advising staff at the college, Dr. Hoffhines champions issues of social justice and equity for all students on her campus.

Tina L. Hummons, EdD, a graduate of DCCL cohort 6, currently serves as the registrar for Sinclair Community College (Ohio). She engages in research, presentations, and critical conversations about college affordability, enrollment management, leadership assessments, leadership, and scholastic experiences of African American male college students.

Saundra Kay King, ABD DCCL, cohort 7, is the senior executive director of academic affairs for the Technical College System of Georgia. In this system office role, she provides oversight to academic programs and policies for the 22 colleges in the technical system and advocates for the alignment of programs to workforce needs in Georgia. Through this alignment, direct pathways for students to succeed and achieve their personal goals are met.

Kimberly M. Klein, EdD, a graduate of DCCL cohort 1, is a professor of political science and cochair of the Democracy Commitment at Delta College (Michigan). Her passion is evident through her campus involvement in creating a civic culture as part of the college's intentional strategies held on and off campus to encourage students to become active creators of their environment.

Margaret "Peg" Lee, PhD, is an active member of the DCCL Program's National Advisory Board. Dr. Lee is president emeritus of Oakton Community College (Illinois) where she also served as a vice president and English faculty member. She is an avid traveler, spokesperson for peace and equity, and loving parent and grandparent.

Bruce Moses, EdD, a graduate of DCCL cohort 4, is the associate provost at Pima County Community College District (Arizona). He serves as the district's accreditation liaison officer and oversees academic quality and compliance. Bruce is a pace-setting leader who champions high-performance principles and continuous improvement districtwide.

Paige M. Niehaus, EdD, a graduate of DCCL cohort 5, is the vice chancellor of innovation and student success, Wayne County Community College District (Michigan). She serves as the chief institutional development and innovation officer of WCCCD, supporting the chancellor's institutional change priorities. Paige guides efforts focused on WCCCD being a student-centered institution.

Lee Ann Nutt, EdD, an adjunct faculty member in the DCCL program, is the president of Lone Star College–Tomball and is the primary author of *Complete the Agenda in Higher Education: Challenge Beliefs About Student Success*. Each day she strives to make a difference for others through her leadership and commitment to learning.

Brenda Sipe, EdD, a graduate of DCCL cohort 6, is director of continuing education at Northern Arizona University, NAU Online, and Innovative Educational Initiatives. She is implementing a plan for the development of the university's microcredential program, and also oversees workforce analysis. She will be developing innovative programs that match workforce needs and improve students' job skills.

Joianne L. Smith is the president of Oakton Community College. Her passion for student success and equity informs her leadership approach.

Lori Sundberg, DBA, an adjunct faculty member in the DCCL program, is currently the president of Kirkwood Community College (Iowa). Prior to coming to Kirkwood, Dr. Sundberg served as president for Carl Sandburg College (Illinois). She started her community college career in institutional research and remains very data driven to this day.

Ruth Williams, a student in DCCL cohort 9, serves as the assistant vice president for academic affairs and dean of curriculum and instruction at Oakton Community College. She has been a leader in strengthening a connection between student learning outcomes and student success.